Hurricane of Independence

The Untold Story

OF THE DEADLY STORM AT THE DECIDING MOMENT OF THE AMERICAN REVOLUTION

TONY WILLIAMS

SOURCEBOOKS, INC.®
NAPERVILLE, ILLINOIS

Published by Sourcebooks, Inc.

P.O. Box 4410, Naperville, Illinois 60567-4410

(630) 961-3900

Fax: (630) 961-2168

www.sourcebooks.com

Williams, Tony

  Hurricane of independence : the untold story of the deadly storm at the deciding moment of the American Revolution / Tony Williams.

     p. cm.

  Includes bibliographical references and index.

  1. Hurricanes--United States--History--18th century. I. Title.

QC945.W56 2008

973.3--dc22

2008015082

Printed and bound in the United States of America

LB 10 9 8 7 6 5 4 3 2 1

To
Lynne – my calm in the
stormy sea of life

ACKNOWLEDGMENTS

I accumulated a number of debts researching and writing my first book. The first round of thanks goes to the librarians who cheerfully aided me. I conducted much of my research and rewrote the manuscript at Colonial Williamsburg, first as a curious scholar and then as a Fellow at the Rockefeller Library. I owe a deep gratitude to the director, Jim Horn, and his staff. I also want to thank the librarians at the Swem Library at the College of William and Mary for all of their assistance. Patty Hinson at the Newport News Mariners' Museum pleasantly conversed with me over the telephone and immediately sent me a critically important article for my research.

Many dear friends have read the manuscript, offered incisive suggestions, lent encouragement, listened for hours to my musings, helped with my websites, set up talks, and wrote recommendations. Their friendship is one of the great joys in my life. Cliff and Melissa Allen, David Bobb, Louise Desilets, Dave Dilyard, Conor Dugan, Mark and Heike Elfendahl, Raymond and Nancy Fahrmeier, Anita and Burt Folsom, Jeff Giauque, Doug and Susan Gephardt, Alice Herring, Chuck Jones, Jeff and Jessica Lavoie, Steve Menaquale, Tom and Suzanne Neely, Peter Schramm, Chris and Cathy Swann, Mike and Tess Thome, Ben Trotter, the Williamsburg Knights of Columbus, and all my friends at the neighborhood coffeehouses around town where I did most of my writing. My dear mother, Fran Banta, has been my biggest fan in everything I have ever done. A special note of thanks goes to my friend, Bruce Khula, a dear friend, and his lovely wife, Sally.

My former history students at Hampton Roads Academy were brutally honest in telling me that another one of my other manuscripts about the American Revolution sounded a little boring, but that the book about the hurricane was one that I should definitely work on. I am glad that I followed their advice. My years at Village Academy were some of the most delightful of my life because of the fine students I encountered. In all, there are too many outstanding students to name any particular one. Because of them, I left teaching for a writing career with a heavy heart.

Dr. Sarah Skwire made perhaps the biggest sacrifice when she happily offered to take time away from a cocktail hour at a conference in Savannah, GA, to help me translate some French materials.

I want to thank Patty Brett, Sharon Lewis, and the ladies of the Xi Zeta Iota chapter of the Beta Sigma Phi sorority for allowing me to tell them the story of the Hurricane of Independence in my inaugural lecture about the book.

Thanks to Milt Thompson for helping this book come to fruition.

Special thanks go to Sourcebooks for taking a chance on an unpublished author and their interest in this book beginning when it was a short proposal. Ewurama Ewusi-Mensah cheerfully received the drafts and guided it to the editorial staff. Peter Lynch shared my vision and enthusiasm for this book and dramatically improved it with his skilled eye. Sara Kase cheerfully answered one thousand and one questions by phone and e-mail. Best of all was meeting owner Dominique Raccah and her "family" at the Sourcebooks 20th anniversary party in Chicago. The quality folks at Sourcebooks are as friendly, supportive, and responsive as an author could hope.

My deepest appreciation goes to my wife, Lynne, for supporting my transition from a teaching career to a writing career. She cheerfully watched our two small children and told me to steal away for short spells to write this book. For that reason and so many others, this book is dedicated to her. Without her support, I could not have written this book or achieved any of my dreams.

CONTENTS

AUTHOR TO READER

On September 2, 1775, an unnamed hurricane crashed into the Outer Banks of North Carolina and Norfolk, Virginia. Hundreds of people, mostly sailors, were killed when they were caught unawares by the deluge of the storm surge. The hurricane raced up the east coast, striking all the important colonial capitals. The tempest indiscriminately affected the lives of everyone in its path: Englishman and American, Tory and Patriot, wealthy planter and poor yeoman, statesman and common citizen, slave and free, general and militiaman, sailor and landlubber. The cast of characters in this book features well-known founders including George Washington, Thomas Jefferson, Patrick Henry, George Wythe, Peyton Randolph, Landon Carter, Benjamin Franklin, Charles Carroll, Alexander Hamilton, Abigail and John Adams, John Witherspoon, Henry Knox, and Benedict Arnold. But it also includes ordinary individuals such as sailors, escaped slaves, farmers, artisans, merchants, militiamen, women, and fishermen.

Although this book traces the path of a destructive force of nature, its importance ultimately is about the humans it affected. At the time, Americans in each of the capitals were engaged in a heroic struggle for independence. The War of Independence had started only months before when the patriots proved that they could hold their own against professional British soldiers. Meanwhile, in the halls of capitol buildings and taverns, statesmen and ordinary citizens debated in a free society about the ideals for which the citizen-soldiers of the Continental Army were fighting and dying. These principles soon were enshrined in the Declaration of Independence, which stated that Americans had the right to govern themselves only by their own consent.

They were written on the hearts of all who sacrificed for the cause of independence.

Thus, this powerful hurricane, which has come to be known as the Hurricane of Independence, struck at a dramatic moment in the founding of America. It is a perfect metaphor for the tempestuousness that wracked American society in September 1775, and for the preceding and subsequent decades as a "new order for the ages" was founded.

The relatively unknown Hurricane of Independence is shrouded in mystery. It wreaked havoc and destruction in the American colonies from Williamsburg to Boston, and eventually hit Newfoundland. Other forces may have come into play, which we will examine in this book.

An important part of the mystery includes why the hurricane struck. People of the eighteenth century had very little understanding of the nature of hurricanes and other natural disasters. Virtually everyone believed that the hand of Providence was responsible for such an event as this tempest. Americans believed in a wrathful God who punished their sins and a merciful God who protected them from their enemies.

George Washington spoke often of Providence and saw America as a favored nation under the protection of divine Providence. He later reminded Americans to offer humble thanks for God's "kind care and protection as the people of this country previous to their becoming a nation, for the signal and manifold mercies, and the favorable interpositions of his providence, which we experienced in the course and conclusion of the late war."[1]

But, with the Hurricane of Independence, the will of heaven may have been as inscrutable as Abraham Lincoln said in his Second Inaugural Address. Many Americans agreed with Washington's belief that God was on America's side. Yet, at the beginning of their mighty struggle for independence, with God supposedly favoring their cause, the destructive Hurricane of Independence struck American shores and rolled over its revolutionary capitals. As the patriots attempted to discern the will of God, they probably were confused about why God would punish them rather than send a storm against the British Isles or destroy a fleet of redcoats that were coming to rob Americans of their liberties. Could it be a divine signal that their cause was not quite as favored as they led themselves to believe? Did God really support revolutionaries fighting for their freedom? After all, Europeans argued for hundreds of years that God granted divine right to monarchs to justly rule their people according to the natural order of the universe.

There was, though, a theological belief that God still could be on the side of America even if they were suffering divine punishment. Most Americans believed that God punished all sinners, striking down the enemies of his chosen people, but also chastising the favored to keep them on the path of righteousness. As Rev. John Witherspoon, President of Princeton College, and a signer of the Declaration of Independence, preached, "that all the disorderly passions of men, whether exposing the innocent to private injury, or whether they are the arrows of divine judgment in public calamity, shall, in the end, be to the praise of God."[2] So, it may not only have been British tyranny that brought the hurricane to America, but Americans themselves: It was a heavenly reminder to live virtuous lives.

Many preachers (and others) argued that Americans were covenanted as God's Chosen People just like the ancient Jews. As Congregationalist preacher and classmate of Samuel Adams at Harvard, Samuel Langdon, later stated, "The signal interpositions of divine providence, in saving us from the vengeance of a powerful irritated nation from which we were unavoidably separated by their inadmissible claim of absolute parliamentary power over us...We cannot but acknowledge that God hath graciously patronized our cause and taken us under his special care, as he did his ancient covenant people."3

After all, the Hurricane of Independence killed both Americans and British, wreaking a great deal of havoc on both sides. So, it may not have been entirely clear whom God was favoring. Perhaps God was on the side of the Americans in their glorious cause for liberty and was punishing the British for their tyranny. Many Americans thought so. Reverend Abraham Keteltas painted a stark moral contrast of the British and Americans, stating that heaven blessed the American cause while the British were aligned with Satan. "It is the cause of justice...and the cause of heaven and against hell—of the kind parent of the universe, against the prince of darkness, and the destroyer of the human race."4

It was an aptly named hurricane.

The Hurricane of Independence struck America after nearly a decade of resistance to British taxes. It hit very soon after the time for argument had passed, after the opening salvos of armed conflict were fired. Less than one year later, the Americans would sign the Declaration of Independence, in which they stated their grievances and causes for separation. More importantly, they made Enlightenment arguments about the natural rights and equality of human beings and about the purposes of government. But, it would take eight long years of war after September 1775 to make independence a reality.

The hurricane struck the major revolutionary capitals, including New Bern, Williamsburg, Annapolis, Philadelphia, New York, and Boston. These capitals were not only the sites of educated representatives debating revolutionary issues with great erudition, but also of ordinary people who took literally to the streets to defend their liberty with their lives by confronting enemy officials and soldiers.

The capitals also were the sites of many of the most important battles in the early part of the Revolutionary War.

The story that follows is a narrative history of a deadly hurricane and some of the key Revolutionary-era events that were occurring in each of the American capitals that it crashed into. It is a portrait of the people, capitals, and moods of the American people at the critical time of the beginning of their War for Independence. They were deciding whether they would willingly enter into the "storm" of revolution, and they would have a real hurricane test their strength and resolve to endure, as well as their faith in the guiding hand of Providence.

I have modernized spelling and capitalization, not with an eye for strict grammatical accuracy, but rather for readability.

To encourage students and citizens to read the letters and diaries of the Founding Fathers and ordinary heroes themselves, I have tried where possible to refer to the most easily accessible published sources, which appear in the bibliography. Many of these fascinating volumes are inexpensive. I know that most readers will not go to a university library or archives to browse through musty volumes and obscure documents, but I hope they will use the bibliography to read through primary sources on their own. Knowledge and use of the principles that founded our country would aid in the free debate of our own tempestuous times.

THE STORM OF REVOLUTION

Under the cover of darkness on the cold evening of December 16, 1773, Samuel Adams and a large throng of irate Bostonians descended upon the waterfront where the *Dartmouth*, the *Eleanor*, and the *Beaver* lay gently bobbing in harbor waters. Many were Sons of Liberty, a revolutionary group who had fought British tyranny on the ground for the better part of a decade. They had torn down homes and customs houses of despised royal officials like Thomas Hutchinson, burned those same officials in effigy while the flames illuminated their incensed faces, and lobbed a generous amount of snowballs, rocks, and curses at the redcoats patrolling the streets.

The swollen crowd had just emerged from a democratic mass meeting where ordinary citizens deliberated about their rights and liberties. Less soberly, these free citizens went outdoors, yelling out war cries and slogans of liberty. Such a meeting would have been unheard of in nearly every part of the world, but they were subjects of England who had the traditional rights of Englishmen, and they were used to a century and a half of governing themselves by their own consent.

After backing down and repealing hated taxes several times because of violent and economic American resistance, the British ministry and Parliament stubbornly insisted on imposing its will to tax the colonists from the distant mother country. Americans were being taxed on tea and did not like the idea one bit. But something more important than paying a few pennies on imported tea was at stake. "What is it we are contending against? Is it against paying the duty of 3d. per pound on tea because it is burdensome? No, it is the right only…as Englishmen, we could not be deprived of this essential and valuable part of our Constitution," explained a Virginian named George Washington.[1] Members of the democratic mob in Boston that December night expressed the same sentiment, though louder and more animated than the calm Virginian.

As a biting wind whipped across the water, about fifty men dressed like Mohawk Indians and, wielding hatchets, boarded the *Dartmouth* and the other two ships as a crowd watched from Griffin's Wharf. They were there for one thing: to make "Boston Harbor a tea-pot tonight" with hundreds of crates of imported tea (342 crates, to be exact). They hoisted the crates on deck from the holds, broke them open, and summarily dumped their precious contents into Boston Harbor. The men were remarkably precise and restrained in completing their mission. Almost no other damage was done to the *Dartmouth* (except for a broken lock, which was quickly replaced) since the men were not simple vagrants vandalizing the ship for a cheap thrill. They were free men who were protesting the violation of their sacred rights and defending themselves against the loss of freedom that threatened to engulf them in slavery.

Samuel Adams, the leader of the Boston Tea Party, stated, "Our enemies must acknowledge that these people have acted upon pure and upright principle." Reviled Royal Governor Thomas Hutchinson may not have agreed with Adams's assessment, but he did correctly predict that, "an open and general revolt must be the consequence."[2]

The British response was swift and severe. Parliament imposed a series of harsh measures called the Coercive Acts, which attempted to force the liberty-loving men into submission. The laws closed Boston Harbor and essentially stripped away the right of Bostonians to govern themselves by their own consent. These laws would remain in effect until Bostonians made good on the £10,000 worth of tea they destroyed and learned a lesson in obedience and submission.[3]

Calling the acts "intolerable," the colonial response was just as swift. Word raced across the colonies to outraged Americans. Expressing their solidarity with the suffering people of Boston, they met in local democratic conventions and sent representatives to a colonial-wide Congress. The colonists corresponded with each other, keeping abreast of events as they happened and bolstering each other's courage. Resistance to a common tyrant helped forge and shape an American identity and spirit of common cause. That cause was liberty.

Yet, there was another prevalent view of the Intolerable Acts that they were a divine reminder to God's chosen people to be virtuous. A South Carolina pastor, William Tennent, preached that, "It should be an invariable rule with Christians to regard the hand of God in everything that happens." He explained, "Nations, like individuals, have their vices, which call for punishment." He alluded to the example of Sodom's destruction and warned, "a time of general correction is not far from us."[4]

For the next year and a half, through September 1775, tensions escalated and the storm that had been brewing finally erupted into war. There was nothing inevitable about the war; the British could have revoked the taxes and ended the tyrannical acts. On the other hand, the Americans could hardly be expected to back down from resisting tyranny. Their lives, their property, their liberty, and their sacred honor were at stake, and were pledged "with a firm reliance on the protection of Divine Providence," in the Declaration of Independence.

Many Americans believed, argued, and fought for these natural rights as the "inalienable rights of mankind." If these God-given rights were threatened by a government, the people had the right to overthrow it. It seemed logical to Americans that because they were on the side of freedom and natural rights, God was on their side. Indeed, Thomas Jefferson would later write that his Declaration of Independence was nothing but the common sense of the matter that expressed the American mind rather than aimed for original thought. But thousands of miles away, in mid-August 1775, something else was brewing that would call their belief into question.

Chapter One

TEMPEST BREWING

Throughout the summer of 1775, the sun scorched the desert sands of the Sahara. Easterly jets of wind raced a few miles up over the barren African terrain across thousands of bleak miles. As the winds hurtled toward the coastline, they became highly unstable and broke into pulsing waves. The waves stretched for up to a thousand miles and flew regularly over the shores of the coast every few days. The people of western Africa were left unawares of their existence except for the barest hint of a gentle breeze. But these winds eventually built into an explosive force half a world away.

The blowing winds jetted out over the blue waters of the Atlantic looking for just the right mysterious conditions to grow into a tropical depression. Some became troughs curving counter-clockwise because of the unfelt rotation of the earth. The infant storms needed desperately to feed on warm water if they were to survive.

The summer sun granted their wish, boiling the cauldron of equatorial Atlantic waters past eighty degrees. The heat sucked water right off the gently roiling ocean. It shot upward, cooling as it rose higher and higher. The vapor lifted miles into the air until it condensed into tiny water droplets that plummeted back toward the ocean whitecaps from whence they came.

Dark cumulonimbus clouds formed, menacing any sailors within sight. The intimidating thunderstorm hurled forked lightning bolts while thunder cracked raucously. Heavy downpours inundated hapless ships as the clouds were seemingly wringed all at once by Mother Nature.

Old, weather-beaten captains at the helms of their ships learned to expect these regular storms off the coast of Africa. The winds provided the propulsion necessary to transport their invaluable consumer and human cargoes across the wine dark sea. Frightened slaves were chained together and packed aboard the holds of ships, soon to replace those who were worked to death under sadistic masters in the brutal climate of the Caribbean sugar islands. Captains of slave ships calculated the profits that each piece of human property would bring—if they made it to the islands.[1]

When squalls erupted suddenly near the Cape Verde Islands, sailors likely were not surprised by this common occurrence, despite the troughs that deceptively hid the storms behind crystal clear weather for many miles in front of them. The storms dropped torrential rain on the soaked men and replenished the water that they had skimmed off the ocean. The storms were harrowing, and many men were lost at sea, but the vast majority of ships came through and continued on to their tropical destinations. As bad as they were, most thunderstorms were spent after a few hours. They soon were replaced by more storms, pounding against other ships sailing along the same path.

A few storms survived, however. The growing tempests gobbled up enormous amounts of warm water that was fed into a swirling vortex that spiraled 'round and 'round, its pressure steadily dropping.

The swirling storm bulged into a monster with a giant eye in the middle of it. It hobbled along patiently around ten miles per hour, paralleling the equator, drawing more ferocity before it struck.

The natives of the Caribbean had a healthy respect for hurricanes and an uncanny understanding of nature. According to their beliefs, the wicked god, Hunraken, annually victimized the island people, inflicting them with destructive winds and deadly floods. The natives were terrified whenever he made an appearance. They beat drums, shouted curses, and did everything possible to thwart the god and drive him away. Sometimes they successfully frightened him off; at other times his fury could not be withstood and they suffered the consequences.

The natives depicted the fearsome deity on primitive carvings as a hideous creature with swirling arms, ready to whip his winds and claim his prey. Natives had acquired a great store of knowledge through centuries of experience. Pale foreigners who settled on the tropical paradises, though, did not have the same meteorological understanding despite their advanced technology. Hunraken, however, had no regard for skin color: All were quarry for his wrath.

On August 25, 1775, the evil god's arms stretched out hundreds of miles, packing winds with furious gusts. The god's arms were bands of rain that engulfed the islands of Martinique. Fierce winds bent trees, littering the ground with their tropical fruit. Large waves of clear water collided against reefs and beaches. Buildings and homes were easily ripped apart and blown down. Two days later, the storm descended upon the island of Santo Domingo. Both islands experienced "much damage" as a result of the "violent gale."[2] The dwindling native population kept its traditions alive by ritualistically fighting the god of winds. But the beating drums of the natives were not strong enough to weaken the storm, nor was the small landmass of the islands. Hunraken gorged himself on the tepid waters and increased in intensity.[3]

Falling pressure raised the ocean beneath the storm into a small dome of water that was hurled against the shallow shoreline of any landmass. For every inch the pressure dropped, the ocean lifted a foot. The hurricane created swells that projected far out to lap against the sands of the North American coastline. But swimming was not yet a leisure sport, and no one gathered on beaches for long vacations. Sailors were the only witnesses to the hurricane that was beginning to make its way up the North American coastline. Even if Hunraken spared their lives, though, they could not outrun the storm to warn anyone of its impending arrival.[4]

Interestingly, while the Hurricane of Independence gathered incredible amounts of energy for its assault on North America, the sinister formula of winds and rain began to shape another swirling beast: A second hurricane was slowly forming. The tropical storm soon became organized and started to swirl, assuming its characteristic shape. It voraciously consumed enormous amounts of warm water and burgeoned in size. It followed the Hurricane of Independence and prepared a deadly follow-up blow that promised to be even worse than its predecessor.

The Hurricane of Independence was aimed directly at the American colonies. But for some reason—whether unseen winds, the arms of Hunraken or the hand of God, or a cruel twist of fate—the second tempest followed the Hurricane of Independence for a time but then veered off slightly. It was also on a collision course with the American colonies, but its ultimate destination was still unknown. Perhaps revolutionaries in Virginia and Massachusetts would be punished simultaneously—or chastised to learn virtue—for leading the colonial resistance.

The hurricane might simply have found other prey in America's enemy. Maybe God was directing this ferocious storm against the British to punish them for their tyrannical actions during the last decade. On the other hand, there were a lot of innocents who did not really care one way or another whether America stayed in the British Empire. They were neutral about the matter and just wanted to be left alone to raise their crops or head out to sea to catch the fish that supported their families. It would remain to be seen what the purposes of these two hurricanes were when they ravaged North America soon enough.

In early September 1775, no one in the American colonies knew about or was prepared for the coming storm. Hurricanes were learned about only after they hit. Besides, the attention of the colonists was consumed by matters of taxation and tyranny rather than the weather.

Americans did not believe in the storm god of the Caribbean peoples. Rather, most—Anglicans, Baptists, Congregationalists, Catholics, and Jews, to name a few—believed in the God of Abraham. Their God was a providential God who worked through human agency—saints and sinners alike—and nature. Most of the time, Providence acted through a benevolent confluence of events. At other times, it intervened directly in nature, performing miracles or controlling the weather.[5]

Later, John Witherspoon reminded his patriotic congregation on a Fast Day in 1776 that, "We are told that, 'fire, hail, snow, vapor, and stormy wind, fulfill his word,' in the course of nature…are yet perfectly subject to the dominion of Jehovah." He continued, "The power of divine providence appears with the most distinguished luster, when small and inconsiderable circumstances, and sometimes, the weather and seasons, have defeated the most formidable armaments, and frustrated the best concerted expeditions." Citing the stormy destruction of the Spanish Armada off the coast of England, the minister stated his belief that God would similarly strike down the British foe. He thanked God "for his favors already bestowed on us, respecting the public cause."

Yet Americans were not to "sit with folded hands and expect that miracles should be wrought in your defense," he said. They must renounce sin and corruption and virtuously act with justice, prudence, firmness, selflessness, and patience. Thus, he exhorted them to the virtue that would "make you truly independent in yourselves," thereby correctly fashioning their characters for self-government. Only then, even "while the storm continues, his mercy and kindness shall appear."[6]

The Hurricane of Independence was headed for the American coast. The God of Abraham was seemingly about to chastise his people with a storm to make them righteous enough to become independent and enjoy the blessings of liberty.

Chapter Two

IMPENDING DOOM ON THE OUTER BANKS

On Friday, September 1, 1775, almost all talk in New Bern, the capital of North Carolina, was of the distant war in Boston. That spring, when riders brought the news, they celebrated the whipping the minutemen had given the British at Lexington and Concord. A few months later, they learned of another stunning victory at the Battle of Bunker Hill. The post-riders had been agonizingly slow and frustratingly scant with many of the details. Ship captains coming into port had brought additional word, but rumor still was more common than fact. It stirred heated conversation and rousing orations in New Bern denouncing British tyranny.

The warm summer air that September night was cooled nicely by gusting winds from the Atlantic. The moderate weather on the coast was what attracted the gentlemen planters of the town and caused their annual summer migrations from their tobacco plantations to escape the stifling inland humidity.

They also were drawn by a desire to serve the public in the legislature, though they traditionally devoted a significant amount of time to dancing at balls, attending horse races, and gambling at the card tables. They escorted their wives to important social gatherings and were accompanied by their black servants.

Although New Bern was a small, provincial capital of only a thousand souls, the gentry usually dressed in some of the latest English fashions and imported many fineries. In recent years, however, the price of tobacco fell steadily and the land was exhausted. Many planters were deeply in debt. The British added to their financial woes by taxing them. The planters of New Bern preserved their public reputation and honor by continuing to press their British agents to acquire more goods on credit.[1]

But the war that summer had turned fashion into a political statement. Whereas the wealthy formerly imported their finest clothes from London to display their wealth ostentatiously, many now conspicuously went out publicly in their "simple republican garb" to show their virtuous patriotism. Dressed in their new clothing, the gentlemen used their classical learning from their tutors and academies to deliver speeches in the capital. The speeches were filled with classical allusions to the Greeks and Romans in addition to calls to defend the ancient liberties of Englishmen. Most of all, they denounced British taxes and talked of mobilizing for war. Excited townspeople listened intently, crowding around open windows.[2]

When they were not giving grand speeches, most of the planters and merchants spent time at the docks overseeing the loading of the thousand-pound hogsheads of tobacco. On September 1, the scene at the docks was hectic. The Second Continental Congress had passed a ban on exports going to Great Britain, and the ban was going into effect the following week. The New Bern merchants had only a few more days to trade with the enemy and bring in money before the coming troubled times. They rushed to ship out one final crop of the valuable weed.[3]

Most of the gentlemen planters and merchants had joined an association boycotting British goods. That afternoon, they read in the newspaper of a resolution to confiscate all the firearms of anyone who had refused to join with the boycott and therefore had questionable patriotic credentials. Moreover, those who did not join were ostracized and risked becoming the victims of mob violence, including such painful punishments as tarring and feathering. They were seen as the enemies of American liberty.[4]

The docks were filled with several ships from different ports of call in America and abroad. The colonists had a vigorous coastal trade from Boston, New York, Philadelphia, and Charleston, and New Bern was an important port for lumber, naval stores, tobacco, and provisions. Captains sailed into Pamlico Sound by braving the dangerous currents and shallows of Ocracoke Inlet at the bar. They sailed up the Neuse River with goods to trade at New Bern. At the confluence with the Trent River, several wharves awaited their arrival. West Indian vessels brought sugar, molasses, rum, and sometimes human cargo in the form of African slaves.[5]

Captains and their crews freely shared rumors of war and of the hurricane season. Many sailors were loading the ships with their new cargoes and supplies for the dangerous Atlantic journey to England. One ship that completed its preparations and set sail earlier that day was the brig *Susanna*, commanded by Captain Nichols. He was bound for the island of Dominica. Despite the large swells and approaching storm, the *Susanna* was able to set off and sail out into the Atlantic. It was sailing into the jaws of a monster.[6]

The gentlemen of New Bern often were present at the docks to gather news because they generally had a vested interest in foreign trade, either as planters or as merchants. The sailors occasionally may have whispered comments about the gentlemen, perhaps an old ditty ending with the verse ridiculing them: "As I've often been told/But by his civil robberies/He's laced his coat with gold."[7]

When not at the docks, the wealthy planters and merchants relaxed at home. The houses of the wealthy were made of brick rather than of the typical wood and usually had a second floor topped by a cupola. (Wealthy merchants such as John Wright Stanly could afford to build an opulent Georgian mansion by John Hawks, the same architect who designed Royal Governor William Tyron's palace.) Once arrived home on the night of September 1, they likely pulled out their gilded imported snuffboxes and quaffed a little tobacco. They went inside and dined at the long tables prepared by servants. They hoped that there might be a ball for dancing later in the evening and perhaps some surreptitious card-playing (for the men) over rum punch. Toasts were drunk in support of patriotic ideals, and enthusiastic discussions followed about the latest pamphlets and broadsides against British tyranny.[8] No one expected the destruction the night would bring.

Of course, not everyone in New Bern was wealthy; most were artisans and laborers. On a typical afternoon in the capital, artisans banged away on metal or tinkered carefully on exquisite handmade items. Their shops had large signs hanging by the doors indicating what kind of trade they were plying inside—printers, blacksmiths, carpenters, hatters, coopers, tailors, or wigmakers. Customers haggled over price and some offered a trade because money was hard to come by in the colony. Passers-by could hear German as well as English coming out of open doors as they walked along the cobblestone streets. Closer to the docks and situated on the Neuse River, foul smells were emitted by the tannery that made leather goods from backcountry livestock. A distillery turned imported molasses into rum.[9]

While the artisans, laborers, merchants, and planters went about the town, they saw the loathsome governor's house, Tryon Palace, a stunning example of Georgian architecture and a symbol of royal tyranny. The town had become the capital upon the completion of the home in 1770. The English gardens behind the home had a magnificent view of the Trent River. Tyron had foolishly thanked the people for the "very elegant and noble structure" they built for him, but the commoners saw it as a symbol of oppression and resented building the governor's residence. It contained spacious, ostentatious rooms for the governor's living quarters and meeting rooms for the governor and his council. Yet it had no place reserved for the meeting of the representative assembly. Therefore, the governor raised their taxes to pay for the expensive, elaborate £15,000 building in which they had no representation.[10]

A decade before, the hard-working artisans cried "no taxation without representation" and had joined the Sons of Liberty to protect their right as Englishmen to be taxed only by their consent. They organized into mobs and prevented the landings of ships laden with stamps. The angry mobs forced the resignation of the Stamp Act collector and sent him fleeing for his safety. Afterwards, they drank toasts to "Liberty, Property, and no Stamp Duty."[11]

Although there were constant visitors to the port city, some strangers were noticed right away and given a wide berth. They were the Scots-Irish frontiersmen, who openly carried both their weapons and their fierce pride on their countenance. They were seen as the savage, uncivilized men who lived amidst the anarchy and violence of the western counties. Perhaps some had been former Regulators who hated the oppressive Easterners as much as they hated the distant English. No man ruled them without their consent. They were fiercely independent and self-reliant, and had a generous amount of hatred for the English. They joined the militias on the town green for drill and formation, though they mostly wanted to do some target-practice. When word of war to the north arrived, some had simply started walking through the wilderness toward the action, guns slung on their shoulders.[12]

On the evening of September 1, after finishing their tasks, many sailors probably went about the port town and were instantly recognizable from their distinctive clothes and manner. Their baggy breeches were tarred for protection against the elements. They wore checked blue and white shirts, with blue or gray jackets. If one looked closely, it was evident that the buttons of the jacket usually were carved from hardened cheese or shark backbone. A Monmouth cap completed their look.

If their clothing were not unique enough to mark their profession, sailors had a weathered look from working in the sun and rough hands from their difficult work. Most were tough young men in their twenties, but those in their thirties usually looked a decade or two older because of the rigors of a life at sea. Many had a Jerusalem cross tattooed onto their forearms.

The sailors did not simply walk through New Bern's streets. A life spent balancing on pitching and rolling decks made them sway while swinging their bodies "like a pendulum." Their foreign idioms for sailing terms and their manner of talking was completely indecipherable to any landlubbers who overheard them. Worse was their colorful assortment of cursing, which they acquired in the all-male environment at sea and raised to an art form. Blasphemy was a particular specialty. Any ladies within earshot blushed furiously at the volley of "damned knaves" and worse. Their lurid songs echoed through the night.[13]

The sailors were a free-wheeling lot, living for the moment. They usually were advanced a portion of their wages before a voyage and were paid the balance upon its completion. Either way, they had a pocket full of wages and were eagerly headed to the taverns to spend it generously on alcohol. They may have been defiant and uncouth, but they were a daring, courageous, and independent lot. They lived their life as they pleased, relishing the joys and beauty of a life at sea while enduring its many hardships. They were men—real Sons of Neptune.[14]

On that September evening, bawdy laughter erupted from the windows of the seedier taverns along the wharves. After New Bern became the capital, there were as many as twenty-six taverns to choose from in the town. Sailors, artisans, and some western farmers trickling in to join the militia drank heavily and fought that night. After a day of training in the hot sun, their great thirst was slackened after many rounds. A heavy Scots-Irish brogue was spoken in addition to various dialects of sailors from all over America and Great Britain. If a fiddle was taken out, some customers would have danced a jig while others sang the vulgar lyrics with salacious joy. As glasses of ale and shots of whiskey were poured in great amounts, vociferous political arguments broke out. Insults were hurled and shipmates defended one another from the aggressive Scots-Irish who had recently come in from the frontier spoiling for a fight. Perhaps an eye was blackened, or more seriously, gouged out in dirty fighting in an adjacent alleyway. Pugnacious individuals grew sharpened fingernails and practiced their gouging technique to the horror of moralists and upstanding citizens. Lawmakers were shocked that such "sundry idle and disorderly persons…do make a practice of firing guns and pistols within the…town," and banned the practice.[15]

The First Continental Congress had banned horse racing, cock fighting, and gaming to encourage Spartan frugality and economy over the corrupting vices. But the Scots-Irish were not going to follow the dictates of some distant Congress any more than they were going to pay taxes to Parliament. They were highly suspicious of all authority. Rich planters and powerful politicians alike all were corrupt knaves as far as the Scots-Irish were concerned. They freely played cards and rolled dice, concerned more with whether the sneaky guy next to them was cheating or if anyone had noticed they were cheating themselves.[16]

After wasting most of their pay, the sailors returned to their boarding-houses and vessels in a drunken stupor. The wind was blowing hard and the rain was starting to fall. They took note that a storm was blowing in, but were not in a state to do much about it. Some of the sailors had just enjoyed their last night ashore for a while and were shoving off in the morning. Other sailors had been living and working ashore for a while and were looking forward to casting off again. They negotiated their wage contracts with captains whom they probably knew at least from reputation in one of the Atlantic ports. If the price was right or they were drunk enough, they might have just signed on for a voyage that night.[17]

Most of the citizens, however, were at home with their families. They were artisans who lived in town over their shops or yeoman farmers who lived in the surrounding communities. They were God-fearing people who were much concerned about recent events. Difficult decisions gnawed at them as the wind shook their shutters outside. They hated British taxes and may have joined the Sons of Liberty or participated in the Boston Tea Party the previous year. However, many earnestly wished for peace and to restore good relations with their King. Not many were actually contemplating independence. They were happy to contribute to a shipment of goods and money that was sent in January to relieve the worse suffering of the people of Boston; but leaving their families and marching hundreds of miles to war was an entirely different matter.

For more than a decade, the women of the town had been just as dedicated to the cause of liberty as their husbands and fathers. Back in 1765, the women were inspired by a call for action against the Stamp Act. "Countrymen, shall we be idle, when the general alarm to industry is sounded? No, let the maids trim their spinning wheels, the wives clean their knitting-needles...and we shall presently have little use for the [British] merchants."[18]

Women of nearby Edenton had boldly organized the Edenton Tea Party the previous October under the leadership of Penelope Craven Barker. They pledged "not to drink any more tea, nor wear anymore British cloth," as a "memorable proof of their patriotism."[19] They, like other patriotic women in the American colonies, held to the sentiment expressed in the following poem:

> Stand firmly resolved and bid Grenville to see
> That rather than Freedom, we'll part with our Tea
> And well as we love our dear draughts when adry,
> As American Patriots,—our Taste we deny.[20]

That same day, dozens of Edenton women released a proclamation pledging their "strict adherence" to the resolves of the Provincial Congress and to support the "public good."[21]

On September 1, 1775, a large group of the townswomen might have gone to the home of a minister dressed in their "homespun" clothing. They were there for their spinning bee. They wove homespun clothing at their wheels while they discussed disturbing current events. They drank and exchanged recipes for local herbal teas because they were boycotting British tea. Their actions, however, were not merely limited to the domestic. They may have been acting within their traditional sphere, but they made a significant patriotic contribution to the glorious cause of liberty.[22]

Still, whatever their hopes for reconciliation, many in the capital were dedicated patriots and were beginning to shed their allegiance to the British once shots were fired. North Carolina was one of the centers of the resistance against British rule. On May 31, the Mecklenburg County safety committee had issued one of the most radical statements of American independence of the year. It stated that, "The Provincial Congress of each province under the direction of the Continental Congress, is invested withal legislative and executive powers with their respective provinces." Instead of merely denying the Parliament's right to tax, the resolves repudiated all English authority over the colonies. "No other legislative or executive power, does, or can exist, at this time, in any of the colonies." It was a statement of independence.23

There were some Tories in North Carolina, though never as many as the British imagined. The sight of effigies burning from a tree generally cowed them into silence. The royal governor, Josiah Martin (who had replaced Governor Tyron in 1771), recently had shown just how impotent he was in the face of popular resistance of the patriots. After he dissolved the legislature for the last time in April 1775, the Provincial Congress met and essentially replaced him as the constituted authority and met despite his protests. Governor Martin was terribly frightened by the belligerent actions of the patriots. During the early summer of 1775, he had no troops at his disposal and dismantled the ceremonial cannon in front of the governor's palace in fear that it might be turned against him. His actions, along with rumors sweeping up and down the South that the royal governors were going to free and arm the slaves, further inflamed patriotic mobs who threatened his life.24

Anxious for their safety, the governor sent his family away to New York. Soon after, on July 15, 1775, he fled too, boarding the British sloop, the HMS *Cruizer*, with a handful of loyalists. He would have left a vacuum of authority in the colony but for the fact that he had already been replaced by the patriotic government. From the vantage point of the *Cruizer*, he watched flames lick and smoke pour out of a fort that patriots burned down to the ground in defiance a few days later. In August, he weakly issued a "Fiery Proclamation," denouncing the "evil, pernicious, and traitorous" radicals who now ruled the colony. On the night of September 1, he was at sea.[25]

War clouds were on the horizon. The ominous clouds of the Hurricane of Independence also were beating a path through the night for the North Carolina capital. Through their bold actions, the people of North Carolina had already deposed their governor and achieved some measure of independence from Great Britain. However, the royal governor and his supporters were safely away, while the patriots would suffer a devastating natural disaster.

Chapter Three

FIRST STRIKE: THE HURRICANE OF INDEPENDENCE ROARS ASHORE

The residents of the Outer Banks and New Bern had gone to bed soundly the night of September 1, 1775, unaware that the winds sweeping across the night signaled a hurricane on the way. The swirling monster was less than a hundred miles away, brushing against South Carolina and racing north at roughly ten miles an hour. It was poised to strike the Outer Banks.

The first bands of rain started beating after midnight. People were jolted awake several times by the gusting winds and pealing thunder. When they peeked outside their windows, they could barely see into the darkness. The storm clouds blocked out the sunrise and the intensity of the winds grew with every minute. Around noon, gale force winds soon reached hurricane strength. The weather outside was alarming. It started to dawn on many people that this just might be a "gust" or a "tempest," as hurricanes were commonly called. They started praying.[1]

The trees in town started swaying and then leaning to one direction with the sustained winds blowing them over. Soon, hundreds of trees were uprooted, some smashing into businesses and homes, others falling harmlessly into the streets. Fences were torn up and pointed stakes flew through the air. Thousands of locally made cypress shingles were ripped off roofs. All objects were hurtled through the air with deadly force. Unseen masses struck against the sides of houses, startling the residents inside.

Uninsured tobacco and corn plants were easily blown over, destroying valuable crops and the impending harvest. Livestock nervously mooed and bleated. Some were crushed by falling structures, wounded by flying objects, or drowned in ensuing floods. If they survived, the animals were the only ones who could eat the fallen crops. The livelihood of many small farmers was being destroyed in an instant.

The wind blew furiously, but it was not the most dangerous element of the storm. The ocean swelled and churned underneath the hurricane. It sent thunderous waves crashing against the bar at Cape Hatteras, all the time swelling Pamlico Sound. The natural protective barrier of sand dunes was flattened by the incredible volume of ocean water rolling over them. The ocean soon was beating against the waterfront of the hamlet. The rain was pouring down from the rapidly-turning clouds overhead. Rivers and creeks rose and threatened to flood farmsteads on the marshy, low-lying ground. The Neuse and Trent rivers started to rise and flood New Bern.

The buildings owned by merchants on the wharves were flooded and goods from all over the Atlantic—casks of rum, codfish, salt, tobacco, grains, and clothing all were ruined. Dead fish and mud were deposited on the docks. Large barrels went floating away in the rapid currents.

The initial reports were that the waterfront suffered the worst of the damage. As signs of human settlement were broken up, debris from ships, wharves, stores, farms, and houses littered the colony and washed ashore for miles around. For several days, it was "as yet impossible to ascertain all the damages that have been sustained along the sea coast, and throughout the country; but if we may judge from appearance, it must be very considerable."[2]

The pounding surf and flooding waters were most destructive to the shipping interests that were in port, or even worse, out on the sound and ocean. Sailors were hardy men who were no strangers to foul weather. They instinctively moved to the tasks of making their crafts seaworthy. Any ships in the Atlantic first had their sails furled and then desperately cut away their masts, tempting fate to ride out the storm and save the ships. Crewmembers fought against the mountainous seas and high winds. They could not hear each other's commands above the piercing winds. They worked to save the cargoes on board the boats, as well as their lives. They were injured by equipment being flung against them. Men lost their footing on the wet decks and scrambled to stand again, only to be knocked down by another wave. Men were washed overboard and were immediately drowned and washed away. Their fate was sealed.[3]

Lists were made of several captains known to be in port from distant cities of Boston, Philadelphia, Plymouth, and New York, as well as from North Carolina and "five other vessels not known, are all supposed to be lost, together with their crews, as they have not since been heard of." The great variety of ports of origin testified to the wide-ranging and multinational character of the Atlantic trade. The *Pennsylvania Gazette* was one of the colonial newspapers that listed the numerous "Vessels wrecked at the Bar" and the fate of their crews:

Captain Barber of Pasquotanck—the crew saved.

Captain James of Marblehead—two men saved.

Captain Hastie of Glasgow—one man lost.

Captain Clifton of Whitehaven—four men saved.

Captains Sandelin, Vollantine, and Hackburn of North
    Carolina—all saved.

Captain Clarke of Edenton—four men lost.

Captain Thompson of Glasgow—one man lost.

Captain Cullen Clark of Virginia—all saved.

Captain Parker of Pasquotank—on shore at Hatteras.

Captain Drinkwater—ashore.

Three vessels, masters' names not known—ashore at
    Hatteras.

Captains Collier and Hayman—were drove off but since
    returned.[4]

Ships in New Bern port fared little better. The storm raised white-caps and large waves that violently rocked the boats. Most ships slipped their moorings and were tossed about in port, crashing against other vessels with sickening crunches. Others were simply deluged and sunk with their precious cargoes and invaluable human lives. Boats were thrown by the wind and surf against wharves or deposited in fields unnaturally far from water. Afterward, the *Pennsylvania Gazette* carried a brief account of the first ships that were known to have crashed ashore:

A sloop, Captain Mulford, from New York, drove on Mr.
Ellis' wharf, whereby a large breach was made in her
bottom; a sloop, Captain Dogget, from St. Croix, went
ashore at Green Spring, but did not receive much injury;
sloop *Sukey*, Captain Cochran, is ashore at Bear River; ship
Harmony Hall, Captain Greenaway, and a sloop, Captain
Bell, were drove ashore below Otter Creek, the former of
which has suffered considerable damage.[5]

In the late afternoon, the winds started dying down as the storm abated. The rain slackened. The ocean receded and left behind piles of jetsam as evidence of its destructive power. The residents were relieved that the raging heavens finally did relent. Conditions improved steadily over the next few hours. People slowly emerged from their homes to check on neighbors and friends, and to survey the massive destruction wrought on their town.

New Bern had suffered significant damage but was lucky that it probably did not suffer a direct hit. Even at the time, residents noted that if the hurricane had continued, especially during high tide, the destruction would have been catastrophic. "Otherwise, the swell that must have been thrown into the harbor, would probably have overflowed the greatest part of the town."[6]

Like all port residents along the Atlantic Seaboard, the people of New Bern were concerned about the fate of those who assumed great risks making their living from the sea. Reports spread throughout North Carolina and other colonies that several boats suffered terrific damage and sailors were killed. Newspaper readers learned that many ships were washed ashore. Some crews were never heard of again, nor were the boats ever found.

In the days to come, apprehensive family members, friends, merchants, and fellow sailors who were worried about their loved ones and cargoes eagerly scanned the lists in the newspaper for news. Sailors often took up collections to help those families who lost their husbands and fathers and were consigned to an almost certain future of the desperate straits of poverty. Captains sometimes had to restrain sailors from unselfishly parting with too large a share of their wages. With so many killed by the storm, the need in this case was dire.[7]

During its initial assault against North America, the storm killed almost 200 North Carolinians. The deaths mainly resulted with the storm surge (rather than its impressive winds). Many of those who died probably never knew what happened. Dead bodies were mostly found on the beaches from sunken vessels. "Near 150 lives [were] lost at the bar," as reported by a letter dated from September 9. Sailors had their clothing torn off and considerable violence done to their bodies. Other corpses were found near rivers and on land amidst the wreckage. Thirteen people were reported dead in one neighborhood at Matamuskeet. Some sailors were washed out to sea and their bodies never recovered.[8]

The clean up started soon after the hurricane moved north. Houses, shops, and ships were cleaned out and repaired as much as possible. It took many days for roads to be cleared and made passable again. Communication was difficult and news was hard to obtain. The wreckage was gathered; what was salvageable was kept and the rest was burned.

The funerals began in successive days. Christ Episcopal Church was the only place to worship publicly in the capital. As was traditional, the families of the deceased provided food and drink to anyone from the community who cared to pay their respects (and get a free drink of wine or whiskey). Relatives and friends lamented the cruel fate suffered by loved ones from the act of nature. Many saw the angry hand of God behind the hurricane punishing the wicked for their sins. Sermons were read at Sunday service at Christ Church imploring God's mercy for the sinners and asking for deliverance. Other churches in communities along the coast delivered the same message to their congregations. The ministers also tried to comfort the survivors and the families who lost someone.[9]

Although they were Christians, the people also blamed the influence of heavenly bodies for hurricanes. They were often "attributed to the effect of a blazing planet or star that was seen both from New Bern and here, rising in the east for several nights…its stream was very long and stretched upwards towards the west."[10]

Former Royal Governor William Tyron's reflections on a previous hurricane in 1769 probably represented the North Carolinians' feelings on the night of September 1–2. They thought about how fragile they felt in the face of nature's wrath. People were killed, and life savings were wiped out—all in a matter of hours. "A few days ago so flourishing and thriving," he stated, "It shows the instability of all sublunary things."[11]

The damage from the Hurricane of Independence stimulated the Provincial Congress to consider taking a few actions to help their constituents. In an unusual move, it purposefully delivered disaster relief to a very limited group of victims. It was a relatively small but symbolically important move in the generally self-reliant society. Because the hurricane destroyed a large portion of the year's harvest, the Provincial Congress voted to authorize additional funds to purchase provisions for the gathering militias.[12] The legislature provided an extra allowance of forty shillings for each militiaman.[13] The militias were mustering to head north to relieve Boston and guard their colony against the escaped royal governor who was attempting to raise a counter-revolutionary army.[14] The legislature did not give residents any money to rebuild their homes or to pay for lost boats or destroyed crops.[15]

The revolutionary assembly also declared its intention to offer relief to those who were attempting to ship goods in advance of an approaching September 10 boycott preventing export of goods to Britain. The legislature carefully explained in its resolution that although it generally intended to follow the dictates of the Continental Congress as the lawful authority of the colonies, it would grant the shippers a reprieve because of the "act of God." The congress was not paying a dime to shippers for their losses—it was simply extending the deadline to allow private individuals to ship their goods:

Whereas the time prescribed by the Continental Congress for stopping our exportation to Great Britain and the West Indies expires September 10, and as several vessels were in this harbor and river with cargoes either on board, or in such readiness, as easily to have been shipped within the limited time; but it pleasing the divine disposer of all things to visit us on Saturday the 2nd with a hurricane, by the violence of which some of said vessels are driven on shore, and others so damaged as to stand in need of considerable repairs to enable them to proceed to sea: We, the Committee of the town of New Bern, holding in the highest respect the resolves of the Congress, and determined, as far as in our power, to have them complied with in this district, yet fully persuaded that honorable body never intended that individuals, friendly to American rights, should be distressed, or perhaps involved in irreparable ruin, by a scrupulous observance of any one resolution, when necessary provision had been made for complying therewith, and in which they were defeated by the intervention of the hand of providence, do resolve, that all such vessels which were damaged or driven onshore, or such whole cargoes were provided and lost in the storm, shall be allowed sufficient time to refit, take in, and proceed to sea.

The Provincial Congress reminded its audience that the resolution was not a wholesale invitation to lawlessness by shipping out goods late at will. "Provided nevertheless," it decreed, "That the benefit of this resolve shall not be construed to extend to any vessel or vessels not actually within the bar at the time of said hurricane, and suffering as aforesaid."

In the resolution, the congress publicly acknowledged that the "divine disposer of all things" was responsible for the hurricane. They expressed their dependence upon the will of an omnipotent God. God punished the colonists for their transgressions but was also merciful. After pounding the Outer Banks and North Carolina capital, the *Pennsylvania Gazette* noted that the hurricane "providentially abated" in the late afternoon.[16]

The American struggle for liberty helped provide an appropriate name for the hurricane: the Hurricane of Independence. One of the radical American capitals was the first to feel the wrath of destruction leveled by this hurricane. However, although the patriotic merchants, artisans, farmers, and sailors of the town suffered, the hardest hit was the sailing community. Although many were from New Bern, others were from around the Atlantic: Great Britain, the Caribbean, and other colonies.

Most men who took to sea loved the liberty that their profession offered them, but their multinational character made it difficult to judge why the hurricane struck in that particular place, assuming it had a heavenly design. The superstitious, often irreligious, sailors might have responded to such an idea that God had nothing to do with it. They were the brave ones who took to sea and braved such tempests all the time while landlubbers enjoyed the ease of a life on land.

While the Provincial Congress was passing disaster relief and the residents of New Bern were cleaning up the damage, Captain Nichols was safely piloting the *Susanna* through the Atlantic waters. He had luckily escaped the Hurricane of Independence and was on course for Dominica. Suddenly, on September 10, while Nichols was in "latitude 37°, longitude 67°, he met with a most violent gale of wind that lasted about 12 hours."

The mountainous seas and ferocious winds caught the *Susanna* in a bad way. She was caught at a right angle against the waves, which began to drive her over onto her beams. The waves began to wash over the top of the masts as they neared the water. In a few minutes, the ship would go under, and the crew would die. One man was washed overboard and probably called out for help for a few days before he was dragged under. Men hung on for their lives, while a couple struggled to get some axes. They beat away at the mainmast at a terrific pace, large chunks of wood going flying in every direction. Soon, the mainmast was cut away and crashed into the Atlantic. By this action, "she righted again."

The *Susanna* drifted aimlessly through heavy seas for many hours. She had lost her steerage, rendering the helm useless. The binnacle housing the compass was also washed away. Captain Nichols did not know where he was and had no way of getting anywhere. He had lost one man, and two others were severely injured and needed medical attention. The *Susanna* had barely survived the devastating second hurricane in the Atlantic. Its destination was still unknown.[17]

Norfolk, Virginia, was the next target of the Hurricane of Independence. That port and its waters also contained a confusing tangle of American patriots on land, British warships patrolling the waters, and ships from various ports of call.

Chapter Four

NORFOLK:
AN ATTACK ON BOTH SIDES

The Hurricane of Independence was hundreds of miles across, and was surging forward on a beeline for Norfolk, Virginia. The limits of eighteenth-century communications meant that no one knew a hurricane was about to strike. The outward flow of air from the hurricane created deceptively clear conditions in the path of the storm before it hit.

But, signs of impending doom would have been increasingly apparent as the tempest drew near. It pushed swells far from its mighty center eyewall, striking Virginia beaches not very long after hitting the nearby Outer Banks. The tide and the waves grew, whipping up whitecaps across the ocean's surface. Then, it started to batter the Virginia coast. The wind picked up at a steady pace and did not relent.

Without warning in the morning of September 2, the monster appeared in the distance over the horizon on the Atlantic. The skies darkened, except for the blue and white flashes of lightning, and took on an eerie greenish hue. The ominous wall of clouds and rain moved ineluctably closer and the wind started howling at a piercing level.

It could not be outrun by ship, by horse, by carriage, or by foot. There was no where to go.

The Hurricane of Independence had reached Virginia.

In the eighteenth century, Norfolk was a rising seaport in the Chesapeake Bay. Sailing ships were growing in size and thus were able to transport greater loads across the Atlantic Ocean between North America, the Caribbean, Africa, and Europe. Some new, larger ships could not safely sail in the relatively shallower waters of the surrounding tributaries such as the James and York rivers. Thus, the deeper waters of Norfolk provided an excellent port for sea captains.

The tobacco trade that was so central to life in Virginia caused British merchants to set up shop locally to purchase the crop and then ship it home. Many were Scots from Glasgow, which became a key player in the trade. The Scottish merchants bought the tobacco on consignment, for which they provided wealthy planters access to the world of fashionable consumer goods from England and the Continent. Although the tobacco trade was brisk in Norfolk, it generally was conducted with the mandated tobacco warehouses that lined the major rivers that cut the Virginia coast into three peninsulas.[1]

The soil exhaustion that resulted from raising tobacco caused planters such as George Washington to diversify their plantations and switch production into growing grains.[2] The port of Norfolk thus became a major exporter in the wheat and corn trade.

The town's Scottish merchants generally were Presbyterian. They enjoyed economic liberty and prosperity, but not religious freedom. Despite their growing numbers, the only permitted religion was the official Anglican Church.[3]

The Atlantic System was a complex system of trade with Great Britain and her colonies in America. Americans were supposed to sell raw materials such as tobacco, corn, wheat, fish, and timber for the benefit of the mother country of Great Britain and then to purchase her finished products. In reality, during the early eighteenth century, Great Britain largely left the colonies alone with an unofficial policy of "salutary neglect." The colonies developed quite a trade network with the Caribbean, purchasing its sugar and African slaves.

As Norfolk grew and prospered, it finally petitioned the House of Burgesses for incorporation in 1736. The only other incorporated Virginia towns at that point were Williamsburg and Jamestown. Incorporation was granted.

In 1765, a French visitor to Norfolk recorded his thoughts about the city. He could not help noting its bustling trade. He called it "the most considerable town for trade and shipping in Virginia." Its warehouses along the wharf were filled with lumber, naval stores, and iron. It also had the only major shipbuilding industry in the area.

Norfolk suffered all of the typical problems of an Atlantic seaport. Ships brought smallpox from abroad, threatening the health of local residents. Waves of smallpox arrived in 1738, 1744, and 1746, forcing the authorities to quarantine possible bearers of the illness onboard their ships or in remote parts of town. The weather also affected the seaport, even altering its landscape permanently. On October 19, 1749, a powerful hurricane washed up hundreds of acres of sand (creating Willoughby Spit), and future hurricanes dumped more.[4]

In 1765, the British Parliament passed the Stamp Act, which taxed newspapers, playing cards, and legal documents. Colonists up and down the Atlantic seaboard protested with mobs and legislative resolutions. Merchants also resisted the taxes with widespread smuggling. The British navy stationed a frigate off Norfolk to try to enforce the act and cut down on the illicit trade. Some of its sailors, however, deserted and were harbored in the city.

The Parliament, with rapidly declining trade resulting from the colonial boycott, repealed the taxes with pressure from British merchants. The people of Norfolk welcomed news of the repeal and their gratitude was commemorated by a local artist in a painting showing a prostrate America thanking King George III.

More unnoticed was the Declaratory Act, however, which was passed in 1766. This act reiterated Parliament's sovereign right to tax the colonies and was a harbinger of future troubles.

For a decade, Norfolk sent representatives to the House of Burgesses at the capital in Williamsburg to protest any unconstitutional violation of their liberties so that the American colonies could remain a part of the prosperous British Empire and the port of Norfolk could continue its lucrative trade. When the British passed more taxes, the people of Norfolk sneaked onto British ships in the harbor and held a tea party inspired by their Boston brethren.

Because of the large Tory presence, however, Norfolk was a divided community in the summer of 1775. The hated symbol of tyranny Royal Governor John Murray Lord Dunmore fled from the capital when mobs threatened his life. Norfolk seemed to be a natural place for him to come and stir up trouble and to try to win support from a segment of the local population. Into this tumultuous situation rolled in the Hurricane of Independence.[5]

The hurricane slammed into the Virginia coast in the early afternoon of September 2, 1775. Wind and rain pounded Norfolk as the storm surge brought monstrous waves. Without modern meteorological technology or any detailed contemporary evidence, it is impossible to say exactly how much rain fell, what the exact height of the storm surge was, or what category the storm attained on the Saffir-Simpson Hurricane Scale. In any event, such measurements would have been meaningless statistics to the people who lived through the storm. The damage caused by the storm made it a force to reckon with.

As the initial wind and rainbands alerted the populace that a major storm had arrived, the intensity of the hurricane continued to grow throughout the afternoon as its eye moved ever closer. The *Norfolk Intelligencer* reported that the hurricane was "one of the severest gales within the memory of man, and continued with unabated violence for eight hours."[6] Word later reached Williamsburg that "the devastation at Norfolk was inexpressible."[7]

From the providential view of the hurricane by the people of the time, it is difficult to tell who was meant to experience divine wrath. Norfolk was one of the most loyalist areas of Virginia. British ships abounding with redcoats and royal marines were stationed in American waters. Many of these British and Tories were faithful, churchgoing Christians. On the other hand, many ordinary Virginian patriots opposed royal officials and a great many of the founding fathers led the American resistance of the colonies fighting for liberty from Virginia. God's ways became even more inscrutable.

As John Witherspoon said in another context: "There is an inexpressible depth and variety in the judgments of God, as in all his other works; but we may lay down this as a certain principle, that if there were no sin, there could be no suffering." Both American and British were to, he said, "by distress and suffering be made to hearken to the rod, and return to their duty" to obey the divine will.[8]

The ferocity of the storm surely drove people inside their homes, seeking shelter from the powerful force of nature. They would have been horribly frightened, with rain noisily drumming against their roofs, peals of thunder cracking nearby, and wind screaming through their windows, causing their houses to creak and groan. Flying debris thudded against houses and smashed windows. Residents who lived near the water helplessly saw it rise precipitously and wondered when it would stop. Loved ones huddled together and prayed for God's mercy. Of course, they could do little else against nature's fury.

Norfolk was spared the great loss life that occurred on North Carolina's Outer Banks, but the storm did kill several people. In addition, it wiped out the livelihoods of many of its survivors. "We expect daily accounts of the destructive rage of this relentless hurricane, which has not spared the promising hopes of the year, but broke, leveled, and almost entirely destroyed the ensuing crop of Indian corn," the *Norfolk Intelligencer* explained.[9] Farmers as well as sailors were at the mercy of the elements and could only but pick up the pieces and start over again.

The most easily recognizable and important damage that the hurricane caused in Norfolk was the destruction of its ships. One of the most ubiquitous images of hurricanes in the television age are boats being thrashed about, cut loose from their moorings, and deposited in backyards or parking lots. In Norfolk, boats of varying sizes were subject to the violent seas and winds of the hurricane that tossed them about like nothing but children's toys.

The storm drove ashore "a great number of vessels," which suffered severe damage. The Williamsburg newspaper received reports that, "Four or five and twenty sail of vessels are run on shore there, many of which are irrecoverably gone."[10] The storm surge caused some boats to be "bilged," and, "others can never be got off," or would never again be seaworthy.

Perhaps the most frightened people that day were the sailors who were onboard their ships. They desperately sought to save their vessels because sinking meant almost certain death. It was difficult enough surviving the waves that came crashing over their decks let alone swimming in the thrashing waters. But in doing so, they exposed themselves to the same dangerous elements that were tearing their boats apart. Many sailors lost their lives and drowned while being tossed about and thrown into the rushing water. The *Virginia Gazette* reported that: "From Hampton we learn that they begin to receive melancholy accounts of the loss of lives in the late storm. Mr. Roberts's vessel of Portsmouth was cast away, and every soul on board perished, except the master and a boy. Two ships from Ireland were likewise lost."[11]

There must have been a lot of confusion in the storm's aftermath. Lamentable reports poured in of the human cost of the storm. "All our accounts from the coast are truly deplorable," the *Norfolk Intelligencer* reported, "Out of some whole crews there survive only the melancholy tale bearers of their own irreparable misfortunes."[12]

A few days after the storm, Thomas Jann, master of the ship *Friendship*, advertised in the Norfolk newspaper for recovery of any intact parts of the *Friendship* and another boat. The ad read: "Was cast away from the ship *Friendship*, in the late gale of wind on the shoals of Willoughby Point, all the masts, yards, sails, and rigging belonging to the said ship; likewise a new long-boat about 22 feet keel." Jann promised payment to anyone who could help find pieces of the named ships. "On delivering the whole or any part of them to the subscriber, or to Messrs. Niel Jamieson & Co. at Norfolk, shall be entitled to salvage on the part delivered."[13]

Merchants suffered devastating losses as the storm surge washed away waterfront property and the precious wares stored there awaiting delivery to distant ports. The deadly eyewall of the Hurricane of Independence raised a massive storm surge during this deadly part of the tempest, which was more or less probably centered on Norfolk. Frightened Virginians saw a storm of epic proportions as the ocean rose and deluged the wharves within minutes and caused significant devastation. "The tide rose to a very uncommon height, and made great destruction in the warehouses and among the wharves," the *Norfolk Intelligencer* reported. It made an initial estimate that, "The loss in this harbor alone amounts to several thousands of pounds."[14]

Merchants also experienced losses because they had loaded their wares aboard ships that were getting ready to put to sea. They were rushing to send their goods abroad in order to beat a nonexportation boycott deadline of September 10 that was set by the Continental Congress the previous year. The public was keenly aware of the impending deadline, causing the local newspaper to opine that the hurricane was thus "more particularly felt at this time as many vessels had taken on board part of their cargo, and the remainder afloat, and would have been ready for sea before the tenth of this month."[15] Tobacco was one of the highly valuable cargoes that were lost to the tempestuous seas.

Because the September storm destroyed their cargoes, several Virginia merchants petitioned the Virginia Convention, the acting government in the colony, later that month for exemptions to the boycott deadline. Indeed, Jann submitted such a request on September 13, which Virginia forwarded for consideration to the Continental Congress. It read:

> A Memorial from James Stewart and Samuel Jackson owners of the ship *Friendship*, Thomas Jann, was presented to the Congress and read setting forth "that the said ship on the 28 of August last sailed from Maryland with a cargo of tobacco, but being overtaken by the late storm, she was driven on shoals and much damage and got into Hampton Roads, with the loss of all her masts, and praying that the memorialists may be allowed to unload said ship and that after being refitted she may take the said cargo on board and proceed on her voyage."

The Congress agreed to allow the petitioners to export their tobacco in violation of the boycott once a ship was refitted, or if it was condemned, to transfer the cargo to another ship for export.[16]

Other petitions were received. For example, on August 25, Captain James Dunlop applied to the Caroline County Committee arguing that he had manifest evidence that he sent forty-six hogshead of tobacco to the sloop *Prospect* on the York River, but for some reason the tobacco had not been loaded. The ship sailed up the Rappahannock River, where it remained with the tobacco until September 9 when it was too late to get it onboard the *Prospect*. The Committee allowed Dunlop to export the tobacco on another ship.[17]

The *Prospect*, which traded with London, had been on the York River and "had the good fortune to ride out the storm and has received no injury." Other boats similarly enjoyed good luck. "Some other smaller vessels were drove ashore," the *Virginia Gazette* reported, "but will be got off with little damage." Some captains must have counted their blessings when their boats suffered damage but were largely able to salvage their cargoes—not to mention escape with their lives. For example, "Captain Robertson and Captain McCunn, both lying at Yorktown, and laden with tobacco, were drove ashore, and must unload before they can be got off."[18]

Even the large British man-of-war could not withstand the power of the storm. Once the ships of the mighty British navy were driven ashore, they were vulnerable to further destruction because of conflict with the local patriot population. The *Mercury*, captained by John Macartney, was one of the ships that patrolled Virginia waters. It was a 20-gun ship and gave the British unchallenged domination of the Chesapeake Bay and key rivers. On July 10, the *Mercury* had arrived in the York River to relieve the ship *Fowey*, which was ordered to return to Boston and take aboard the Virginia

Royal Governor, Lord Dunmore. Dunmore refused to sail away and instead stayed in local waters to harass the colonists. Indeed, he provoked them into revolution.

In August, Norfolk was becoming embroiled by Revolutionary fervor during the cases of two merchants, Andrew Sprowle and John Schaw, who were suspected of Toryism. The Norfolk County Committee summoned Sprowle to appear before them and explain "why he suffers the storehouse to be occupied by the soldiery as barracks."[19] He wrote back, claiming innocence and that the soldiers occupied his warehouse without his knowledge. Finding them there, he asked, "What was I to do? Suppose yourselves in my situation. What would ye have done under the guns of two Men of War and sixty soldiers?"[20] The committee ignored his question and reprimanded him for being remiss in not informing it that "his private property had been seized upon, soldiers quartered in his house."[21]

John Schaw, for his part, stood accused of pointing out to Lord Dunmore a fifer of a volunteer company who openly wore a rebel hunting shirt and was consequently seized and brought aboard the British warship, *Otter*. Schaw was thus an "enemy to American liberty" in the words of the Norfolk Committee. An angry mob set upon him, chasing him into a private home where he tried to escape up the chimney but found himself firmly lodged inside.[22] Schaw sent a public apology and promised to conduct himself in the future "as a zealous advocate for the rights and liberties of America."[23]

Captain Macartney of the *Mercury* entered the picture when he composed a letter to Norfolk mayor, Paul Loyall, explaining that he would fulfill his duties to "protect the property of all loyal subjects" and "if it becomes necessary, use the utmost coercive measures in my power." Nevertheless, he promised that he would feel the "utmost pain and reluctance, in being compelled to use violent measures." Ironically, Lord Dunmore rebuked Macartney for his sympathetic feelings for the colonists and accused the captain of being "actuated altogether by principles totally different, and to have principally at heart the making friends among his Majesty's greatest enemies in this country."[24] Dunmore thought it was better to be feared than loved.

The hurricane pushed Macartney's ship "aground, and it is thought will remain so for some time."[25] The *Virginia Gazette* noted that the *Mercury* "lies in two feet water only," and gleefully reported that it remained helplessly "*stuck fast, fast!*" But that was not all.

The British warship did not lay impotent on the shore without some incident with local patriots. Indeed, "Last Monday night there was a good deal of disturbance at Portsmouth between a number of the *Mercury's* sailors and some of the inhabitants of the town." The *Norfolk Intelligencer* recounted the events of a sailor who deserted during the storm. His shipmates pursued him, arousing the ire of locals when they seized random colonists in lieu of the deserter:

> It seems a man belonging to the ship leapt overboard and was swimming to the shore when several muskets were discharged at him. He made the land however and got off among the people, who [assembled] upon hearing the guns. A boat was sent after him, and the marines being told there were a number of men assembled in a house at the water's edge to protect the deserters, broke into it, dragged the master of it out of his bed, struck him, and huddled him into the boat with two or three more gentlemen, who were seized upon in the street, and carried them on board. The Captain, finding there had been some mistake in the matter, immediately discharged them, and, we have no doubt, will upon information make proper examples of such atrocious violators of the peace and personal security of the inhabitants.[26]

Such actions during the storm provided yet more evidence in the minds of the colonists of British tyranny and the danger of the British military to American liberties.

The newspapers could not resist satirizing the hated royal governor during the storm. "Lord Dunmore, we hear," one account went, "keeps cruising about, and at the time of the storm was up in [the] James River on a reconnoitering party."[27] The following week, the *Gazette* reported that the governor "by some accident or other, occasioned by the confusion in which the sailors were," caused him to fall overboard, or in the maritime idiom of the day, "was severely ducked." The editor was pleased to note that fortune saved Dunmore because nature would not drown a man who was destined to be hanged.[28]

Yet another British warship, the *Otter*, washed ashore in Hampton, Virginia, about 16 miles north of Norfolk. "Captain Squire, of the *Otter* sloop, going round to York in his tender, had very near perished in the storm, being cast away upon Back River, near Hampton," the *Virginia Gazette* informed its readers. The event was related to two of the most significant, if contradictory, themes of the American Revolution: rights and slavery.[29]

In August, the Norfolk Committee had objected to Dunmore's and Squire's "most unfriendly disposition to the liberties of this continent, in promoting a disaffection among the slaves, and concealing some of them for a considerable time on board their vessels."[30] Even a hurricane could not frighten white Virginians quite as much as the thought of a slave rebellion. The issue was raised when Lord Dunmore had seized the gunpowder at the Williamsburg powder magazine. "We have too much reason to believe that some wicked and designing persons have instilled the most diabolical notions into the minds of our slaves," the mayor's council protested, "and, that, therefore the utmost attention to our internal security" demanded the return of the powder. Therefore, not only was Dunmore stirring insurrection among their slaves, he was violating one of their most cherished rights: to bear arms. A government armed against its people was the height of tyranny. Some also could easily conclude that Dunmore was arming the slaves with the people's very own powder while denying them the ability to defend themselves against the slave insurrection.[31]

Dunmore's reply explained that he removed the gunpowder to secure it precisely because of word of a slave insurrection nearby. With an empty promise, he offered to return the powder "in half an hour" should another insurrection erupt.[32] Concurrently, the governor threatened to "declare freedom to the slaves," and in a shocking move, he also posted armed slaves as guards at the governor's palace. No plainer evidence could be found in the minds of the colonists of Dunmore's tyrannical intent.[33]

Thus, the angry Hampton mob that descended upon the *Otter* feared it was part of a conspiracy to end slavery in Virginia and offered it no mercy. Squire's vessel "was burnt by the people thereabouts, in return for his harboring gentlemen's negroes."[34] The "gentleman" in question was Colonel Wilson Miles Cary, who officially was still employed by the British as the naval officer for the custom's office of the Lower District of the James River until his patriotic sympathies caused him to lose his position but gain election to the Virginia Convention.[35]

Two of the crew aboard the *Otter* were Cary's runaway slaves, and the ship's "pilot, a mulatto man, was the property of Henry King, Esq. of Hampton." The pilot "after skulking in the woods about 48 hours...found means to paddle off in a canoe," the *Gazette* reported.[36] Cary wrote an open letter to the *Gazette* in which he facetiously gave "my warmest thanks" to Captain Squire "for his very kind and hospitable treatment of my two slaves, Aaron and Johnny, from the county of King and Queen, during their stay on board his ship."[37]

Continuing, Cary wrote that he saw God's hand in the return of his human property, "Providentially, however, on Saturday evening, during the gust, a tender was drove on our shore, upon Back River, commanded by Matthew Squire, Esq., in which came on shore the two fellows above mentioned." Cary narrated their subsequent capture. They "immediately ran off into the woods. On Sunday morning, two of my neighbors brought in to me Aaron, taken up near the wreck; and in the evening, Johnny was delivered me from the captain's division." Two reputable gentlemen signed depositions swearing that they knew Cary to be the owner of the two slaves.[38]

If divine Providence was on America's side in their glorious cause for liberty, and if that liberty was embedded in human nature and thereby universal, it was a terrible test for the endurance of the returned slaves to have a taste of freedom and then lose it through the divine agency of the Hurricane of Independence. George Washington later predicted that as a result of the American Revolution "Mankind will reverse the absurd position that the many were made for the few; and that they will not continue as slaves in one part of the globe, when they can become freemen in another."[39] Perhaps, though, not yet in the tragic case of this poor slave.

Nor was it true in the case of some of Washington's own slaves at the end of the war. During the Yorktown campaign, the British released many slaves into the surrounding woods without any food. Several slaves were dying of smallpox. For those who did not perish, their fate was the same as Cary's slaves when they were returned to their owners. Two captured slaves were sent back to Mount Vernon, having enjoyed only a few miserable months of freedom.[40]

Two months after the hurricane, in November 1775, Dunmore issued a proclamation that sealed Virginia's desire for independence from Great Britain. Dunmore declared that all slaves were "free, that are able and willing to bear arms, they joining His Majesty's troops as soon as may be, for the more speedy reducing this colony to proper sense of their duty, to His Majesty's crown and dignity."[41] Dunmore was not a humanitarian liberator but a strategist trying to rob Virginia of its valuable labor source while building up his own pitifully small forces to quell the rebellion.[42]

As runaways flocked to his banner, Dunmore formed the Royal Ethiopian Regiment. The worst nightmares of a slave-owning society were realized: Their slaves were freed and armed, and they were seeking revenge for their bondage against their owners. The uniforms of the Royal Ethiopian Regiment had the slogan "Liberty to Slaves" stitched onto them (mocking the Virginia militia's "Liberty or Death").[43]

Hundreds of slaves harkened to Dunmore's call for freedom. They were not escaping into the nearby woods to avoid a brutal whipping or a few days of freedom before they returned to their plantation the way that most runaway slaves did in ordinary times. They were running to their freedom. Many would answer the call.

Irate Virginians hurled their vitriol at the governor, calling him "our Devil Dunmore." Richard Henry Lee derided Dunmore as the "African Hero."[44] A mocking poem was published in the *Virginia Gazette*:

> Hail! Doughty Ethiopian chief!
> Though ignominious Negro thief!
> This black shall prop thy sinking name,
> And damn thee to perpetual fame.

Even though Dunmore was freeing slaves from bondage, Virginians labeled him an "arch traitor to humanity." George Washington more moderately named Dunmore "the most formidable enemy America has."[45]

Hearing of Dunmore's Proclamation, the slaves of wealthy planter Landon Carter made good on their escape, but first they "took out my son's gun and one I had there too…They took my grandson Landon's bag of bullets and all the powder, went off in my petty augur canoe." Carter angrily summoned visions of a society run by blacks who used armed force to enslave whites, thereby reversing what he saw as the natural racial hierarchy. He could barely contemplate such a world-turned-upside-down, writing that, "The scheme for the negro command in the southern colonies…a thing so inhuman."

Carter struggled with the contradiction of enforcing his despotic hierarchy over other human beings while he and other patriots were in turn seeking independence from a political hierarchy ruled by a royal tyrant. Essentially, the patriots were arguing that they did not want to lose their rights to govern themselves and be enslaved by the British. Moreover, Carter had to face the consequences of making arguments "for so just a cause as the preservation of the rights of nature impressed on all mankind at their creation."[46]

Captain Squire was lampooned by the press for washing ashore in Hampton. "Master Squire, the *magnanimous* commander of this *mighty* vessel, nearly escaped," wrote the *Gazette*. It further described the ignominious events of that night: "He was obliged to take shelter under the trees that agreeable night." In the morning, Squire made his escape through hostile patriot territory by surreptitiously going "in disguise to some negro's cabin, from whom he borrowed a canoe, by which means he got off."[47]

When the sloop was grounded, Squire's men were not so lucky. A few had gone with Squire to the cabin of a slave, Thomas Finn, while some of the crew stayed with the ship to guard its armaments. On Sunday, September 3, the crew presented some gifts to Finn for his kindness.[48] They paid a price, however, when the people of Hampton arrived on the *Otter* and took "six of her men prisoners, among whom is the gunner."[49]

The angry mob descended upon the ship, plundered, and torched it. "One of the tenders in the same predicament," the *Gazette* reported, "is burnt by some of the people of Hampton."[50] Lord Dunmore, who normally traveled aboard the *Otter*, was most fortunate that he was not aboard ship that fateful night. He would have been captured and what the furious mobs would have done to him is not hard to imagine. The reason given for the burning of the *Otter* was vengeance to punish Squire for "his harboring gentlemen's negroes, and suffering his sailors to steal poultry, hogs, etc."[51] A more detailed newspaper account was unapologetic in rendering a moral judgment against Squire, arguing that he and his men received a just punishment for their tyranny against Hampton. It explained that:

> The men who belong to the *Otter* with Squire at their head, beginning to plunder the neighborhood according to their custom, the people rose, took several of the men prisoners, seized the swivels, small arms, powder, the clothes of the officers who escaped, and the valuable materials belonging to the tender, and then burnt her.[52]

The writer continued in the same vein with a rhetorical question further indicting the officers and sailors of the British Navy. They were supposed to protect the colonists but in his view the British were nothing more than just common criminals, profiting from raids made against the colonists:

> Is it not a melancholy reflection that men, who affect on all occasions to style themselves 'his Majesty's servants,' should

think the service of their sovereign consists in plundering his subjects, and in committing such pitiful acts of rapine as would entitle other people to the character of robbers?[53]

Captain Squire would tolerate no such denigration of his character. On September 13, the *Norfolk Intelligencer* published his letter overtly threatening to seize the printer. "Sir—You have in many papers lately taken the freedom to mention my name, and thereto added many falsities. I now declare, (if I am ever again mentioned therein with any reflections on my character) I will most assuredly seize your person and take you on board the *Otter*."[54]

The publisher of the newspaper was John Hunter Holt, who was a nephew of John Holt, a printer and former mayor of Williamsburg, and a nephew of William Hunter, who had been a printer and assistant postmaster general for the colonies decades before under Benjamin Franklin. Holt instinctively defended his constitutional right to a free press as a basic liberty as a free Englishmen. He did not "conceive that his press is to be under the direction of anyone but himself, and while he has the sanction of the law, he shall always pride himself in the reflection that the liberty of the press is one of the grand bulwarks of the English constitution."[55] He was not intimidated by Squire's threats.

Indeed, Holt openly ridiculed Squire only a week later. "We are informed from good authority that a system of justice similar to that adopted against the devoted town of Boston," he told his readers, was going to be established by the "renowned commodore of the Virginia fleet." Squire had lately "rendered himself the terror of all the small craft and fishing boats" nearby when he seized them, stole their property, and took "honored the passengers…to receive them on board his own vessel." Holt mockingly labeled "this act of generosity" as "obnoxious." He expressed a hope that:

Those who have lived under and enjoyed the blessings of the British constitution, will not continue tame spectators of such flagrant violations of its most salutary laws in defense of private property. The crimes daily committed by this plunderer we would not willingly brand with the odious name of piracy.[56]

Holt was repaid for his biting critique when Squire made good on his promise to punish Holt. In an "illegal and riotous" action in "open violation of the peace and good order," Squire entered Norfolk and seized Holt's press. Holt was not present and thus avoided capture, but a bookbinder and a journeyman printer whom he employed were taken prisoner. The local Norfolk patriot government appealed to Lord Dunmore regarding this "gross violation of all that men and freemen can hold dear."[57]

The people of Norfolk would be greatly disappointed if they thought that Dunmore would do anything about the raid. Squire rendered the people of Norfolk a service, Dunmore publicly rationalized, by ending the "*poisoning the minds of the people*, and exciting in them the *spirit of rebellion and sedition*." Dunmore was blaming the victims for violating their constitutional rights. Moreover, he warned that he would "not be surprised if the military power" was utilized again if the false and malicious aspersions cast against "the characters of his majesty's servants" did not stop. "I requested Captain Squire to seize the types," he freely admitted.[58]

Such open avowals of tyranny even warranted the conservative Virginian leader Edmund Pendleton to inform the Continental Congress of "the degrading and mortifying accounts from Norfolk, where the seizing the printer at noon day and seizing and plundering other in the neighborhood."[59] That same month, the Continental Congress had had enough. Virginian Richard Henry Lee sent his home state an authorization to seize "our inveterate, unprincipled, and well informed enemy Lord Dunmore."[60]

Squire then wrote a letter to the Hampton Town Committee demanding the return of the items that were stolen off the *Otter* during the hurricane. "I am therefore to desire that the king's sloop, with all the stores belonging to her, be immediately returned." The captain enumerated the items, including five muskets, two powder horns, and an anchor, so that there would be no mistake. If they were not returned, Squire warned that "the people of Hampton, who committed the outrage, must be answerable for the consequences."[61] The commander was not exactly winning the hearts and minds of the colonists.

The Hampton Town Committee not only forwarded the letter to Williamsburg, which raised one hundred volunteers in defense, but responded in kind. Calling Squire's allegations "injurious and untrue," the committee argued that the citizens committed no outrages against British property since "The sloop, we apprehend, was not in his majesty's service, as we are well assured that you were on a pillaging or pleasuring party." Essentially, it was not wrong for them to steal from a thief.

The committee pleaded that the people of Hampton were innocent civilians who would have helped Squire and his men if they had only asked for it:

> To that heart which drove you into the woods in the most
> tempestuous weather, in one of the darkest nights, to avoid
> the much injured and innocent inhabitants of this county,
> who had never threatened or ill used you, and who would,
> at that same time, have received you, we are assured, with
> humanity and civility, had you made yourself and situation
> known to them.[62]

The committee stated that the goods in question were either lost in the storm or given to the slave Thomas Finn and therefore were not being held and could not be returned even if the committee wanted to.

Furthermore, the committee had some demands of its own to make. First, Squire must return a slave named Joseph Harris and all of the other slaves held by the British. The slaves, it asserted, were not only the "property of a gentleman of our town," but were more ominously used "in pillaging us, under cover of night, of our sheep and other live-stock." Secondly, Squire had to return "all boats, with their hands," that the British Navy impressed into service. Finally, in a general statement of principles, the committee stipulated that the captain should "not, by your own arbitrary authority, undertake to insult, molest, interrupt, or detain, the persons or property of any one passing to and from this town, as you have frequently done for some time past."[63]

The conflict between the British and the colonists over the "firing on His Majesty's tenders" that were thrown ashore by the hurricane led Dunmore to the fateful step of declaring martial law and calling all Loyalists to his banner in his infamous proclamation of November 7.[64] Later that month, hundreds of patriot soldiers marched from Williamsburg, met up with North Carolina forces along the way, and converged on Norfolk, which Lord Dunmore occupied on November 16. After a foolish attack with great losses on December 8, he abandoned Norfolk and evacuated his troops and Tories. When patriots marched defiantly through the streets, an enraged Dunmore bombarded the city and then launched parties to torch the city, which they promptly did on the first of January. The British, in turn, suffered greatly when their crowded ships, filled with slaves and Tories, experienced outbreaks of smallpox and were forced to throw their dead overboard. In August 1776, Dunmore and his fleet sailed for New York as the war shifted there.[65]

Dunmore would be no stranger to hurricanes. He was appointed the royal governor of the Bahamas during the 1780s—part of the Caribbean islands that were struck by the Great Hurricane of 1780 that killed more than 22,000 people.[66]

The Hurricane of Independence smashed southeastern Virginia's main seaport in September 1775. Within months, the storm of war descended upon Norfolk, where after the first major battle of the colony, its former royal protector laid waste to the city and burned it to the ground. In the meantime, the Hurricane of Independence was preparing to assail the capital at Williamsburg, where the winds of war also had been blowing for some time.

TOBACCO AND GUNPOWDER

A fter hitting Norfolk, the Hurricane of Independence rolled up the peninsula, striking Williamsburg, one of the most important centers of resistance to Great Britain. About forty miles from Norfolk as the crow flies, the storm probably weakened a bit, but it still packed quite a punch. It was continuing its ruinous path and now set its sights on the colony's genteel tobacco planters, many of whom were national leaders in the patriot movement.

The hurricane would have surprised the planters who followed the weather forecasts in their farmers' almanac. The weather predictions that the almanacs published were, of course, at times less than accurate. The 1775 *Virginia Almanack* predicted that on September 2, the "dog days end," meaning a gradual cooling trend after the stultifying humidity of the tidewater summer. Rain was not predicted to come until Thursday, September 7.[1] Needless to say, this prediction was way off.

Almanacs were a font of useful information for their readers who learned everything from advice about when to plant certain crops to information about the royal family's birthdays, which were celebrated with great festivities in the colonies. One such entry read, "Plant Windsor's beans, slip currants and gooseberries. On the day the moon fulls sow onions, and throw in some lettuce and radish seed with them."[2] Much like Benjamin Franklin's *Poor Richard's Almanack*, readers could pick up bits of common wisdom in the form of parables or short verse. The *Virginia Almanack* warned, "HOW difficult a *task* it is for a man to behave himself so in this world as to please ALL the people that inhabit it! A man who makes use of his best endeavors to please *everybody* is sure to please but *very few*, and by that means displease a great many." Other advice counseled humility:

> 'Tis strange! From folly this conceit should rise, That want
> of sense should make us think e're wise. Yet so it is! The
> most egregious elf
> Thinks none so wise or witty as himself![3]

Almanacs also were useful for planters not so much for what the printer actually put on the pages as they were for the blank pages that were provided. Planters could thus record the daily weather, usually noting basic meteorological observations such as the temperature, direction of the wind, and precipitation. The blank pages also were used to record business transactions and even legal documents. Planter John Page and an overseer agreed upon terms of a contract in Page's copy of the almanac: "I agree to live at Paradise as an overseer for Mr. John Page on his allowing 600# of pork and 6 barrels of corn for my provisions & 1/6 of the crops of tobacco & corn & one share of the wheat made there. John Graves."[4]

The almanac certainly did not predict the coming of the Hurricane of Independence. On Saturday, September 2, while Norfolk was bearing the brunt of the storm, the hurricane struck Williamsburg with its outer bands. It hit Williamsburg with full force a few hours later in the afternoon. The *Virginia Gazette* reported that Williamsburg had experienced inclement weather for several previous days: "Every day last week it rained more or less, and sometimes continued chief part of the night." But, then, "On Saturday, it never ceased pouring down, and towards noon the wind began to rise, which increased soon afterwards to a mere hurricane, it blowing most furiously from the N.E. till near to 10 o'clock at night." Unsurprisingly, the strong winds caused large trees "in many places blown up by the roots."[5] The next day, the *Gazette* confirmed that a "great number of trees [were] blown down."[6] Trees and their flying limbs smashed the roofs of houses. Debris left roads muddied and blocked. Residents began the arduous task of cleaning up after the storm passed.

Planters, however, primarily were interested in how their crops fared in the storm. They did not need to read the newspaper to learn that, "Infinite damage has been done to the crops of corn and tobacco, much wheat spoiled in barns...and almost every mill-dam in the country given way."[7] The James and York Rivers, their tributaries, and previously dry streambeds became raging torrents and covered nearby fields in water. This spelled disaster for people who earned their wealth from the land.

The gentlemen planters who assembled at the capital of Williamsburg to fulfill the public service obligations befitting their class were the wealthiest in the colony. They mostly lived on large plantations in grand Georgian homes, where slave labor raised tobacco and carried out a number of other skilled duties. The gentry generally were educated in Europe as well as in the more provincial College of William and Mary in Williamsburg. Holding various local offices, they assumed their "rightful place" in the House of Burgesses, usually after plying the voters full of liquor on election day. They not only spent their time serving the public and managing their plantations, but also gambling, fox hunting, and cock fighting. Theirs was a world of hierarchy—in society, marriage, family, and race—that was ordained by God, in which they stood at the apex.[8]

Williamsburg had been the capital of Virginia since 1699. Francis Nicholson, Virginia governor from 1690 to 1692, moved the capital from nearby Jamestown after a succession of fires burned down the capital, including one caused by the violence of Bacon's Rebellion in 1676. Nicholson was no stranger to violence himself. In 1700, he stood on the deck of an English man-of-war for three hours while it exchanged short-range broadsides with a French pirate ship that attempted to assail Hampton Roads.

While Nicholson served as the Maryland governor and visited Virginia as a trustee of the College of William and Mary, he and Edmund Andros, who succeeded Nicholson as Virginia Governor from 1692 to 1698, feuded and traded insults. One time, their dispute stooped to blows when a melee broke out in which Nicholson punched Andros in the face. Nicholson received a horse-whipping from swordsman Colonel Daniel Parke, who was a supporter of Andros.

After selecting Middle Plantation, near Bruton Parish Church, located between the James and York Rivers, as the site for the new capital, Nicholson used his amateur, yet skilled, town planning knowledge to design the layout of the new capital with fellow Virginian Theodorick Bland. They designed the broad ninety-nine-feet-wide and mile-long main avenue, named Duke of Gloucester Street (after Queen Anne's son), with the Wren building at the College of William and Mary and the House of Burgesses at either end, and the Governor's Palace situated between on an expansive green. The town was laid out with gracious residential plots, many of which were owned by Virginia's elites. An ample number of shops, taverns, and boarding houses lined the main avenue. A coffeehouse, racetrack, and theater offered entertainments to the swollen crowds who were in the capital during the sessions of the General Court and House of Burgesses.[9]

The town of Williamsburg that the storm battered was experiencing a tempest of its own. From the Governor's Palace on Christmas Eve 1774, Governor Dunmore wrote to William Legge Lord Dartmouth, secretary of state for the Colonies, that the Virginians were forming into "outrageous and lawless mobs," and warned that they were "arming a company of men…to be employed against government." Dunmore pushed Dartmouth to consider punishing the Virginians with a blockade of their ports and starving them into submission.[10] Virginians were outraged when they read this letter, which was published in the newspaper. The Virginia Convention did not need much further proof of British tyranny in the spring of 1775 when Dunmore issued a proclamation forbidding the election of delegates to the Second Continental Congress and King George III assented to a bill that banned the trade of Virginia and four other colonies.

But what most thoroughly alarmed the people of Williamsburg was Dunmore's seizure of gunpowder from the magazine and its keys on April 21, 1775. Fearing the patriotic mobs, he thought it "prudent to remove some gunpowder…where it lay exposed to any attempt that might be made to seize it, and I had reason to believe the people intended to take that step." Accordingly, fifteen marines from a warship on the York River sneaked into the magazine in the middle of the night to take possession of the powder. Beating drums awakened militia members from their sleep, and they mobilized to protect their right to bear arms against a tyrannical government while moderate patriot leaders pleaded with Dunmore to return the powder and the keys. The rotund, conservative speaker of the House of Burgesses, Peyton Randolph, mollified an assembled crowd to return home.[11]

Dunmore promised to return the powder but then stimulated a crisis that was even worse. A few days later, he threatened "by the living God" to "declare freedom to the slaves and reduce the City of Williamsburg to ashes," if he should suffer any "insult or injury."[12]

Dunmore had raised a tumult with his actions that could not be easily reined in. In Fredricksburg, forty miles north of Richmond, several hundred militiamen were drilling and made ready to march on Williamsburg because of the missing gunpowder. Two companies under the command of Captain Hugh Mercer advanced on the capital until Randolph, who was concerned about further tensions, advised them to turn back. They did so, but considering the "just rights and liberty of America to be greatly endangered by the violent and hostile proceedings of an arbitrary ministry," these "minutemen" promised to be ready "at a moment's warning, to re-assemble."[13] The intransigent Dunmore told Dartmouth that, "I shall remain here until I am forced out."[14] That time would come sooner than he thought.

Firebrand revolutionary Patrick Henry, upon hearing news of the battles of Lexington and Concord, also whipped up a group of men—this one from his home county of Hanover—to march on Williamsburg to recover the gunpowder. Henry led them until he was satisfied with a royal payment of £330 for the missing powder. He soon set out to take his seat at the Second Continental Congress in Philadelphia but not before the governor declared him an outlaw.[15]

Henry had been at the center of resistance to British taxes for a decade, starting with his response to the Stamp Act taxes as a freshman burgess who had been in the assembly all of nine days when he rose to give a momentous, though divisive speech. On May 29, 1765, Henry introduced resolutions in the House of Burgesses protesting the Stamp Act.

With shocking candor, he attacked the king as a tyrant bent on destroying the liberties of the colonists. "Julius [Caesar] had [his] Brutus, Charles had his Cromwell," he declared, and hoped that "some good American would stand up in favor of his country." The conservative Speaker of the House of Burgesses, John Robinson, interrupted Henry, yelling, "Treason!" But Henry told his mostly outraged listeners that he was motivated to speak by "the interest of his country's dying liberty."[16]

Randolph is supposed to have lamented, "By God, I would have given one hundred guineas for a single vote!" after the House passed several of Henry's resolutions claiming that the colonists were "entitled to all liberties, privileges, and immunities…as if they had been abiding and born with the realm of *England*."[17] In response, the royal governor, Francis Fauquier, dissolved the Burgesses, confirming that Britain was prepared to deny the colonists self-government.[18]

The Stamp Act was not enforced in Virginia because its tax collector, George Mercer, resigned for fear of his life. Richard Henry Lee, a member of the burgesses who was becoming increasingly radical, denied that the British could tax the colonists "without the consent of [their] representatives." He mobilized a procession that burned effigies of Mercer and British Prime Minister George Grenville. Lee derided Mercer in the *Gazette*, saying in Mercer's voice that he planned to "fasten the chains of slavery on this my native country…It was the inordinate love of gold, which led me astray from honor, virtue, and patriotism."[19]

On March 23, 1775, Henry rose on the floor of the second session of the Virginia Convention to give the most important speech of his life. Descriptions of Henry were filled with classical allusions. Describing his oratory, Thomas Jefferson said that Henry "spoke as Homer wrote."[20] John Adams heard that Henry was the "Demosthenes of the age."[21] The assembly met in Richmond at St. John's Church away from the reach of British warships, under the chairmanship of the ever steady Randolph. Speaking extemporaneously, with the windows open to allow the crowd outside to listen to the proceedings, Henry argued that the colony must arm in self-defense. He stated with breathtaking oratory:

> For my own part I consider it as nothing less than a question of freedom or slavery.... Ask yourselves how this gracious reception of our petition comports with these warlike preparations which cover our waters and darken our land. Are fleets and armies necessary to a work of love and reconciliation?...If we wish to be free—if we mean to preserve inviolate those inestimable privileges for which we have been so long contending—if we mean not basely to abandon the noble struggle in which we have been so long engaged, and which we have pledged ourselves never to abandon until the glorious object of our contest shall be obtained, we must fight! I repeat it, sir, we must fight!...There is no retreat but in submission and slavery! Our chains are forged! Their clanking may be heard on the plains of Boston! The war is inevitable—and let it come! I repeat it, sir, let it come![22]

Henry then made a hurricane analogy: "The next gale that sweeps from the north will bring to our ears the clash of resounding arms!" He finished with the famous "As for me, give me liberty, or give me death!" as he plunged an imaginary dagger into his heart.[23]

One witness exclaimed after hearing such sweeping rhetoric, "Let me be buried on this spot!" Another said it was "one of the most bold, vehement, and animated pieces of eloquence that had ever been delivered."24

When Henry set out for Philadelphia in the spring, assembled crowds cheered him, and he was escorted across the Potomac with "repeated huzzas."25

The Virginia Convention soon selected representatives to the Second Continental Congress. They were alarmed with events in distant Boston and closer to home in Williamsburg. Lord Dunmore called the Burgesses into session to read Lord North's offer of reconciliation, and then bolted in the middle of the night with his family. Mobs raided the Governor's Palace and seized the remaining muskets from the foyer, while their representatives met for the last time in the capitol before they formed the extra-legal Virginia Convention and moved to Richmond.

The Hurricane of Independence struck simultaneously with the political eclipse of Williamsburg, which arguably was the most significant colonial capital. The storm damage in Williamsburg was considerably less than in New Bern or Norfolk because it was not a port city lying astride the sea. Williamsburg suffered the fierce winds and torrential rain, but not the lethal storm surge that swamped other towns. It is not surprising then that there were no reported deaths in the capital. Although the residents did not notice, the storm weakened imperceptibly as it began to pass over land. The eye was beginning to disintegrate, rapidly draining power from the tempest. That did not mean, however, that people farther north could rest easy.

Chapter Six

LANDON CARTER: DIARIST AND PLANTER-PHILOSOPHER OF THE NORTHERN NECK

The hurricane thundered northward as the afternoon of September 2 progressed. Landon Carter was a planter living at Sabine Hall, a plantation on Virginia's Northern Neck, situated between the wind-swept waters of the Rappahannock and Potomac rivers. Carter left detailed written evidence of his experience during the hurricane, as he lost his crops but searched for the storm's larger philosophical meaning.

Carter was the scion of Robert "King" Carter, a merchant planter who grew fabulously rich off the Atlantic tobacco trade: At the time of his death, "King" Carter had more than seven hundred slaves and claims to hundreds of thousands of acres of land. Carter was schooled in England and held a number of local offices until his election to the House of Burgesses in 1752.[1] As a planter-statesman, he believed that growing the finest tobacco was the measure of an honorable and virtuous man, and that serving the public was the highest calling to which one could aspire.[2]

Carter had been a consistent and fervent opponent of British taxes for a decade, beginning with the Stamp Act. Carter was responsible for writing the Virginia petitions to King George III and to Parliament seeking the repeal of the unconstitutional taxes. He believed that constitutions were the fundamental source of basic rights and needed to be held "as sacred as possible." Therefore, the designs of a corrupt British ministry to alter the traditional rights and constitutional liberties of the colonists had to be thwarted.[3]

In December 1764, the House of Burgesses unanimously adopted Carter's petitions, which claimed the colonists had the rights of Englishmen and the British liberty that "was secured to them and their descendents, with all other rights and immunities of British subjects." Taking an even more expansive view of rights and liberty, the Burgesses pronounced they were entitled to the "freedom which all men, especially those who derive their constitution from Britain, have a right to enjoy." Therefore, they claimed that, "It is essential to British liberty that laws imposing taxes on the people ought not to be made without the consent of representatives chosen by themselves." If this basic right were not protected, "The inhabitants of the colonies are the slaves of Britons."[4]

Later, Carter was upset that Patrick Henry's fiery oration had trumped his sober contribution in defending American liberties, and claimed that he was the one who blew "the first breath for liberty in America." Thomas Jefferson, who saw both men in action in the Burgesses, thought Henry the more eloquent speaker. Carter's speeches were, "like his writings, dull, vapid, verbose, egotistical, smooth as the lullaby of the nurse, and commanding, like that, the repose only of the hearer."[5] In 1774, Carter paraphrased Henry's most memorable phrase, but with less dramatic effect, when he stated that he was "resolved to be free or cease to exist…[for] he who is to take my liberty from me must be an equal enemy of my life."[6]

When the Declaratory Act reiterated parliamentary authority

over the colonies after the repeal of the Stamp Act in 1766, Carter labeled it a "bill of might." He thought that the British "devils" had sunk into a "universal state of dissipation" when Parliament passed a new round of taxes in 1767. A year later, he began to see that the "desire [for] independence" would be the result of British tyranny. In the wake of the Boston Tea Party, Carter was a "hearty" supporter of the Virginia nonimportation association boycotting British goods and warned that King George III was "one grand corrupter of mankind." After Royal Governor Lord Dunmore left Williamsburg and tried to stir up the slaves against their masters, Carter called the British "butchers." In short, he said, the British were violating the "rights of nature" and introducing "the most hateful of iniquities, a tyrannical despotism in the king who rules in Great Britain with money, and would govern America with an iron scepter."7

In addition to being a patriot, Carter fashioned himself a man of science in the eighteenth-century world of Enlightenment. He read the latest agricultural tracts from England and even penned some ideas himself. With that knowledge in mind, he observed, measured, experimented, and recorded while conducting a scientific enterprise to master nature. He experimented with new crops and tried to find ways to eradicate pests in an elusive quest to control nature. He made daily meteorological observations, but he could not command the weather. Rather, he was more of a victim of nature than its master.

Carter often looked on helplessly as his crops died when a frost came too early, the heavens deluged the ground with too much rain, or too much heat brought uncontrollable insects. He confided to his diary that he had less control than he desired and that, "The farmer is nothing without weather." Weather was a matter of chance, and he was its pawn. The farmer had little choice but to "always feel the weather and rejoice when it is good and be patient when it is unseasonable."[8]

Yet, Landon Carter was also a man who believed in God. Nature was not a blind force, but rather was guided by the hand of divine Providence who created the world and continued to intervene in its affairs.[9] He was a devout Anglican who believed that humans were dependent upon the sovereignty and will of God. He begged God for forgiveness of his sins, thanked God for his blessings, and strove to be virtuous to win divine favor. Carter believed that misfortune had to be endured with humility and a faith that a just God rewarded the virtuous.[10] Both his scientific and religious views are evident in his chronicle of the Hurricane of Independence as it struck his plantation.

At Sabine Hall, Carter recorded probably the most thorough eyewitness account of the hurricane. It had been raining a lot over the past week, he jotted down, but this was something different. "I thought the two spare pages [of his diary] in the last month, as it had rained ever since Sunday last, would have been enough to set down the rainy days; but it is not, for it rained all last night and all this day very much and now it blows and rains, the wind at Northeast and bids fair for a Gust."[11]

As a diarist who kept track of the weather, he had careful records about the arrival of hurricane season and their typical intensity. He remembered some previous storms of a similar nature. He wrote, "I have known four such spells in my observation and all in August, that is, old style, and all began moderately for several days and then at last began to tear away. But, I, though, hope otherwise." A hurricane would be very bad news indeed. But, despite his hopes, the storm that was brewing was one—and a terrible one.

Carter's careful observations about wind direction leave no doubt that he experienced a hurricane. "About half after three o'clock the much suspected Gust began," he began, writing in the midst of the storm, "It has now struck six, and I wish I could say there were any signs of its abating. The wind is from North to Northeast and sometimes to Northwest with prodigious flows that drive vast sheets of rain before it, and makes everything shake almost to their foundations." He felt as if the house were coming down around him.[12]

Then, in the middle of the storm, he waxed philosophical, reflecting on God's divine mercy and judgment. As an expression of his Christian faith, he thought that sinful humans should place themselves in God's hands:

> We have but one hope, and that is in a merciful good. It is true we can't plead for protection from any goodness of ours; but his mercy has always hitherto exceeded his judgments and may it do so now. It is only hoped we are not incorrigible offenders; our frailties often overbear us; but is not his wisdom satisfied that our hearts are good towards him; and though man is blessed with reason, yet how often is imperfection divested of all reason.

Carter seemed to be recording events as they happened, and had the wherewithal to write down his thoughts in his diary even in the midst of a hurricane. But, still he did not have control. He regretted not being as thoroughly prepared as he would have liked since some flooding was occurring. "Half past nine, a dreadful time, Gust harder and all the weather side of my house in a float. I am obliged to get up. If the window sand bags or some such thing had been thought of before night, this leaking might in a great measure [have] been prevented."[13]

Finally, during the middle of the night, the storm died down and moved off to the north and northeast. "The violent Gust began to abate about two o'clock in the night." With a thousand worries on his mind, Carter did not sleep very well that night, even though in the middle of the night, there was not much he could do to inspect the damage. He had to wait until the morning light to begin assessing the toll the storm took on his farm.

Weather was not the only problem facing the great Virginia planters who raised tobacco. Simply growing the crop was an exceedingly difficult task and one that often vexed the planters.

The "noxious, stinking weed," as King James I called it, was unlike most other crops in that it demanded year-round labor and careful attention. After the twelve days of Christmas and the holiday from work for the slaves were over, the intensive planting began as tobacco seeds were sown with animal or ash manure and covered with branches to protect against frost. Because of the vulnerability of the plants, ten plants were planted for every one eventually cut.

In late spring, running slaves carried the seedlings to their fields and planted them during wet weather to avoid damaging their roots. Slaves worked all summer to weed the fields and fight against pests. The slaves then "topped" the tobacco in order to prevent flowering, which would draw nutrients away from the valuable leaves.

In September, during hurricane season, the slaves would cut the plants according to the planters' judgment. This was a critical decision because if the leaves were too moist, they would rot on the ships crossing the Atlantic. Conversely, cutting them when they were dry meant that they would become brittle and disintegrate.

The "harvest" did not mean the end of work for the slaves because the tobacco had to be cured in special curing barns to dry. If the weather were too rainy, special fires would be lit to prevent rot—hopefully without burning down the curing barn. Slaves then stripped the leaves from the stalks and hung them to dry before they were pressed and loaded into thousand-pound hogshead barrels for the trip to England or Scotland. The process generally was not completed before the next year's crop was laid.[14]

The management of the tobacco crop on the plantations reflected on the planters' personal honor. Expertly grown tobacco that fetched a high price meant that the planters were skillful and would win recognition. Thus, they would earn a public reputation for virtue among their fellow planters. This fame and honor was in many ways more valued than the income derived from selling the tobacco.[15] Not completely, however.

Planters were voracious consumers of luxury goods from Great Britain as they sought to emulate the lifestyles of fashionable Europeans. Great amounts of goods were conspicuously consumed to adorn their great houses. George Washington, for example, put in an order for sterling silver forks with ivory handles, pewter plates engraved with his crest, a carriage, and a fashionable summer cloak and hat for his wife Martha.[16]

Because they sold their tobacco on consignment to the English or Scottish factors at increasingly lower prices, the planters' buying sprees left them in growing debt. During the 1760s, merchants demanded payment, and planters understood the action as a threat to their individual honor and autonomy. When Parliament simultaneously taxed them, the planters more readily accepted Whig ideas of independence, liberty, and rights opposed to enslavement. The planters in the House of Burgesses passed boycotts and pursued more frugal and simple republican lifestyles.[17]

The hurricane affected the planters' consumer orders from their British mercantile agents. On September 15, 1775, John Norton explained that he had sent seven hogshead of tobacco down the York River "to go on board the *Prospect* to your address." Before the boat could even get to the Chesapeake, the hurricane struck. "Unluckily before they could be got aboard, a violent storm arose, which drove the flat ashore, and entirely ruined the tobacco." Having been able to salvage only one of the barrels, he nevertheless arranged for the purchase of a "small stove" for his son and a list of other goods.[18]

Other planters, such as George Washington, diversified their crops so that they would be independent men. Washington stopped growing tobacco in the 1760s to escape the cycle of debt and to place his finances on firmer ground. Nevertheless, although wheat farmers could avert the kind of debt experienced by tobacco planters, no farmers could avoid the power of the hurricane. Because of the storm, "There is hardly a possibility of getting any grain [from the] ground for the use of the inhabitants of this city."[19] The wheat that already was harvested was "spoiled in barns."[20] Hunger, as well as British tyranny, threatened Virginians in the late summer of 1775.

The economics of the plantations were seen through moral lenses. The luxury, debt, and greed of Virginia tobacco planters were seen as major character flaws and as the path to allowing oneself to become enslaved both by material possessions and British creditors. Conversely, wheat planters maintained their virtue and independence. Yet, as John Witherspoon reminded his audience, divine Providence usually saw fit to punish both the corrupt and the righteous who were "apt to grow remiss and lax in a time of prosperity and seeming security."[21]

Carter was relieved that the hurricane was over, and admitted that he was afraid for his safety and that of his dependents, including his slaves. "It carried every terror with it that could be conceived." And, although he had learned that, "It cost me my mill-dam again, to rebuild waistgates and all, a vast damage," he was, in fact, happy to be alive. Everyone on his plantation had made it through the storm alive—even the slaves in their shabby dwellings. Carter praised divine Providence for intervening to protect them. "Without a most merciful God to preserve us, it made me doubtful whether anything would have [with]stood it. I can't therefore be but thankful and greatly rejoice. Wind now every way, sometimes down. Poor man indeed! But the Lord is gracious and merciful."[22]

The next day, Sunday, September 3, Carter's overseer, John Purcell, toured the plantation to survey the damage and reported his findings back to his boss. Purcell informed Carter that the "fodder [was] all gone, corn quite flat, tobacco leaves all broke off and drove about, all the fences down everywhere." As Carter noted in his diary: "In short, one general destruction except my houses, people, and cattle." Although he was relieved that their survival was "a great mercy," he worried that none of the "food is safe for them."[23]

With the storm abated, Carter had calmer moments for reflecting on God and why nature had wrought such evil. He thought that humans stood powerless before God's omnipotence and, like an eighteenth-century Job, believed that humans could not question God's ways. Unlike the French philosopher Voltaire, who openly spurned Judaism and Christianity after the devastating 1755 Lisbon earthquake and tidal wave, Carter believed that the hurricane was not only a lesson of God's omnipotence but also of divine goodness and mercy:

> I dare not murmur because I was at the time in a trembling doubt whether the whole existence of the creation here would be of a moment's duration. God gave and God hath taken away and blessed be the name of the Lord. Let the impious, the blaspheming mortal stand forth and deny now there is a good or his omnipotence when but a 12 hours of wind and rain can tear up the very foundations of man's invention and man himself, were it not for the

unspeakable mercy of God.[24]

Carter saved his anger for thinking about his life as a planter, launching into a monologue about the uncertain nature of agriculture. Thomas Jefferson may have waxed eloquent about the yeoman farmer "as the chosen people of God, if ever he had a chosen people."[25] Unfortunately, the agrarian ideal did not usually match the harsh reality. Although Carter also celebrated the pastoral ideal, reading classical works about agriculture by the Roman poets Horace and Virgil, he also knew that planters were at the mercy of the elements that could destroy their livelihoods in an instant no matter how much skill or care was employed all year. He pondered in his diary:

> May I not in such a situation ask who can be said to be worth anything? Certainly not the man who tills the ground in Virginia, for let his crop be ever so promising, as they never with any propriety can be fit to be secured before this season of the year in which Gusts are generally experienced if at all. How then can the trader rate his value when the laborer cannot produce anything to deal with?…Lands may be mortgaged, but if they can't be worked to a profit, as we see they rarely can, what can be his security as the value of his possessions?

In other words, planters could not count their chickens before they hatched, and were subject to forces beyond their control.

The damage to Carter's mill-dam greatly concerned him. Hearing from his grandson, who had recently arrived at Sabine Hall, Carter learned that, "All the mills to be heard of [were] carried away with this Gust." He probably also would have read in the newspaper that "almost every mill-dam in the country given way."[26] Of course, this was of little consolation to anyone who was so affected. Fixing it was of such importance that Carter ordered "every male hand I have to go to work directly to repairing my dam." Classically educated, he used his knowledge of geometry to draw up plans for his slaves to work from for the repair.

Weeks later, Carter wrote in a highly agitated state that the rain was not letting up, thereby delaying repair on his mill-dam. He reported that there was a "vast rain indeed, a mere Northeast Gust again." The relentless wet weather was affecting the health of his slaves. The patriarchal Carter asked, "What chance do my poor people stand who have been all while in the rain?" Even though they had "a bottle of rum," Carter noted, "One of them, Ambrose, is come up very sick."[27]

Carter's inability to escape his difficulties caused him to make another theological reflection upon his situation. "How vast and tremendous is omnipotent power that mere natural causes uncontrolled by him shall be capable of effecting such destruction to his creation. And when he bids them be still, how obedient they are…I still hope it only a natural change and that it will be so, far from being an instrument of divine wrath that his mercy will restrain the violence of its most natural cause." Frustrated, he lamented that his crops and trade had suffered because of the weather for two years without end.[28]

There were few people who pursued personal virtue and demanded it of all others around him quite as much as Landon Carter. Because of his Christian belief in the fallen nature of humans, Carter argued that all humans had to master their corruption and passions. This was the basis of personal and public virtue. No longer enslaved to self-interest, the virtuous were truly independent. Therefore, a virtuous citizenry could govern themselves in a free society. "Independence," he wrote, was the "base or footstool on which liberty can alone be protected."[29]

In early September 1775, Carter faced the forces of an omnipotent God and was spared. He stoically and piously passed the test because of his submission to God's will. His faith and virtue seemed to win God's mercy and favor as he believed.

Carter always held fast to his faith that God was on America's side in the American Revolution. It was not that the Americans were more virtuous than the British, for Carter lamented the lack of public virtue that actually made republican government a dangerous experiment. God favored America "not from any peculiar goodness in us, but in the cause we are engaged in."[30]

The Hurricane of Independence moved off to the north along the Atlantic Seaboard. It bore down on the other centers of Revolutionary activity where delegates met on the state and national levels to protest politically and where patriots picked up their muskets to fight for their freedom in the Continental Army. Following the path of the storm, Virginia sent its best sons to do both.

Chapter Seven

THE STREETS OF ANNAPOLIS

After crashing into North Carolina and Virginia, the Hurricane of Independence rolled over the Northern Neck of Virginia. As night fell upon the Chesapeake Bay on the night of September 2 and in early morning hours of September 3, the coastal land denied the hurricane of the warm waters that powered it. Its intensity weakened and its speed increased. Its distinctive eye fell apart, and it began to collapse.

Nevertheless, the hurricane still generated powerful gusts likely in the neighborhood of 70 miles per hour. Whitecaps were kicked up in the bay, thrashing against each other and endangering the crews of any boats caught unawares. Torrential rains caused flash floods as creek beds and river banks filled suddenly and water swept into low-lying areas. Howling winds and flashing lightning startled thousands of people awake in their beds. And the hurricane still packed enough of a wallop to do significant damage to buildings and crops. The storm set its sights on Maryland's capital, Annapolis: the center of Revolutionary activity in the state.

Annapolis was the brainchild of Francis Nicholson, the same royal official and architect who designed Williamsburg. Nicholson was appointed as the royal governor of Maryland in 1694, in the wake of the colonial reorganization after the Glorious Revolution that brought William and Mary to the throne of England. Immediately upon assuming office, he lobbied the state legislature to move the capital to Annapolis from St. Mary's on the Potomac.

The assembly agreed that Annapolis was a suitable location for the new capital. It rested on the Severn River, which flowed into the Chesapeake Bay. With access to the Atlantic for international trade, Nicholson chose the site for its excellent harbor. The city had natural economic advantages, and proper city planning could add to its political and cultural importance.

Seeking to impress visitors and connect the various activities of the city—politics, religion, trade, and residential space—into a united and aesthetically pleasing whole, Nicholson laid out the design. Wharves and merchant-houses were placed near the waterfront to facilitate trade. A broad avenue containing two circles led to the central features of the city. The smaller circle housed St. Anne's Parish, whereas the ceremonial state house was perched visibly atop a knoll in the second circle. Radial and diagonal roads converged on these centers of religious and civic life. Adjacent to the important meeting places and centers of power were the genteel homes of the wealthier elites located in the heart of town, Bloomsbury Square, which was named after the fashionable London area. There also were several nearby open public gathering spaces, including the square for the market house. The design of Annapolis copied the layout of the continental European capitals, though on a much smaller scale and with a small design flaw: The statehouse circle did not run on an exact straight line to the waterfront but instead took a dog-leg turn.[1]

Nicholson based his plans on Baroque architectural principles and emulated the style of Christopher Wren. Wren was a London "Renaissance man" who had proposed an audacious plan to redesign London after the Great Fire of 1666. He was an architect, mathematician, and scientist who embodied the idea of the enlightened man:

> For a man to arrive to its utmost perfection, he should be almost as universal as the orator in Cicero, and the architect in Vitruvius: but certainly some tincture in history, the optics, and anatomy are absolutely requisite, and more (in the opinion of our author) than to be a steady designer.[2]

Wren was a founder of the Royal Society, which was a scientific body established to make "philosophical enquiries" and contribute to promoting "useful arts and sciences" for the general diffusion of knowledge for the good of humanity. Wren took credit for inventing a weather gauge that measured rainfall, barometric pressure, and humidity. It even had a tipping-bucket to make periodic measurements of rainfall without overflowing.[3]

On the night of September 2, 1666, a fire started to blaze in London. The "dreadful flames" spread quickly among the wooden buildings of the capital, causing a "miserable and calamitous spectacle." The fire fed on dry, hot conditions, and a "fierce Eastern wind" caused it to consume churches, residences, hospitals, monuments, and public buildings indiscriminately as it leaped "in a prodigious manner from house to house and street to street, at great distance one from the other, for the heat had even ignited the air."

The nightmare conflagration burned for five days. Night turned into day because, "All the sky were of a fiery aspect, like the top of a burning oven, and the light seen above 40 miles round about for many nights." The blaze destroyed more than 12,000 homes, creating an unbelievable "noise and crackling and thunder of the impetuous flames." Adding to the din was "the shrieking of women, and children, the hurry of people, the fall of towers, houses, and churches." It was like a "hideous storm." In the end, seven eighths of London lay in smoldering ruins.[4]

Yet, thanks to Christopher Wren, London became a phoenix rising out of the ashes. King Charles II appointed Wren as Surveyor of the King's Works with the goal of restoring the capital symbolic of the king restoring the monarchy after the civil war of a decade before. They wanted to glorify the monarchy and win fame by building lasting monuments.

Wren had traveled on the continent and was influenced by its architecture and city-planning. He visited Paris and witnessed the extensive building program of French finance minister Jean-Baptiste Colbert under King Louis XIV. He disappointingly met only briefly with the Italian genius Bernini who was in Paris to sculpt a bust of Louis XIV, the Sun King. Wren was taken by the design of the Louvre but was not impressed by the excessively ornate, courtly architecture of the palace at Versailles. He thought it too "crowded with little curiosities of ornaments" and lacked enduring beauty.[5]

Although the dazzling splendor of the layout of Paris inspired him, Wren was even more influenced by the classical revival of Dutch Republic minimalist architecture. He created an ambitious rebuilding plan for London with radial streets superimposed on a grid, with several main streets diverging from St. Paul's Cathedral. St. Paul's had been scheduled for renovations even before it was gutted by the Great Fire because it was a decaying old structure and had been battered by a lightning strike a century before. Only days before the fire, Wren inspected the cathedral and found it in dismal condition. He dismantled the ruined church with explosive powder until frightened residents mistook it for an earthquake, so he then used a massive battering ram.[6]

Through the turmoil of the death of Charles II, the rise of the Catholic James II, and the bloodless Glorious Revolution under William and Mary, Wren directed the excruciatingly slow progress of St. Paul's Cathedral. Wren conferred with his scientific partner, Robert Hooke, at their favorite London coffeehouse and decided to borrow from Byzantine and Islamic architecture in adding a coppered dome topped with a cupola. When completed in 1711, the cathedral was inscribed with the motto "resurgam" (I shall rise again) to symbolize the rebuilding of London.[7]

As with its European counterparts, the Annapolis state house was the architectural focal point of the city as well as the heart of civic life for the entire colony. The first state house was completed in 1697, shortly after the capital moved to Annapolis. Because Benjamin Franklin's invention of the lightning rod was decades in the future, the state house had no protection and was struck in 1699, killing one of the delegates inside and starting a fire in the structure. In 1704, another fire caused significant damage and the place was gutted. Construction of the new building began the following year and was not completed until 1709.

Despite its grand design and prospects for growth, Annapolis still was just a provincial capital and remained a quaint little town of only about a thousand souls by 1765. (In contrast, the port city of Baltimore had experienced rapid growth, climbing to a population of more than 6,000 people by the start of the Revolution to become one of America's largest cities.) One visitor to Annapolis was rather unimpressed by what he saw: "The houses are old, ill-built, but two new ones as I could see now building and but very little trade stirring." Even so, trade expanded after the French and Indian War ended in 1763, and the gentry were having elegant homes built during this increasingly prosperous time.[8]

During the next decade, other visitors were more sanguine about the city's qualities. Although it was primarily a civic capital dominated by politicians and lawyers who gathered for the courts, dozens of merchants set up shop in Annapolis for the tobacco, grain, and iron trade. It also had a group of skilled craftsmen—silversmiths, dressmakers, cabinet-makers—who supplied the luxuries that the wealthy desired.

Virginian George Washington was one such admirer of Annapolis and all of the diversions it offered for the gentry. A frequent visitor, he was one of many notables from Virginia and Maryland who gathered for the annual Race Week and bet heavily on their favorite horses while commoners showed off their livestock in competitions at the county fair. He enjoyed his favorite pastimes, attending the balls, the theater, and many dinners.[9]

Many others testified to the growth of the city, such as one British official who wrote favorably of Annapolis in a letter home. "In a few years Annapolis will probably be one of the best built cities in America, as a spirit of improvement is predominant…There are few towns of the same size in any part of the British dominions that can boast a more polished society." He later wrote home on the eve of the Revolution that, "We are making considerable advances towards perfection."[10]

As Annapolis was undergoing its mini-renaissance, the elites decided that the state house, which had gradually entered into a state of disrepair, would simply not do. By the time of the imperial crisis with Great Britain, it was a dilapidated old building and too small to conduct political business. Consequently, it was razed and plans for a new structure were drawn up after the Assembly voted to erect a new state house with the modest goal of it being "equal to any public edifice on the American continent."

In 1772, the last royal governor of Maryland, Sir Robert Eden, laid the cornerstone for the new state house. The following year, the

Assembly instructed Charles Wallace, the project manager, to affix an iron rod pointed with silver or gold at least six feet above the cupola and to cover the roof in copper rather than slate. Work proceeded slowly because of significant delays due to the dearth of artisans who would fight in the Revolutionary War.

The prosperity of the 1760s and 1770s occurred in spite of Revolutionary activity in Annapolis. Although Annapolis was far from the main centers of resistance, many patriots in the capital supported the growing opposition to British taxes. However, even as local patriots fought against foreign tyranny, some people in Maryland struggled against domestic tyranny as they fought to practice their religion freely.

In 1765, native Annapolitan Zachariah Hood was visiting London when Parliament passed the Stamp Act on the colonies. Hood received an appointment as distributor of the stamps for the colony—a decision he would soon live to regret. After sailing across the Atlantic, he soon discovered the passionate hatred of the colonists against the tax. Mobs assembled on the docks and refused to let Hood come ashore, taunting and threatening him with bodily harm. The mobs, thirsty for violence, then marched through the town and tore down the house Hood intended to use for his office. Frightened for his life, Hood fled and resigned his office.

Not everyone was pleased by the rioting. Many elites frowned upon the "lower orders" for their spontaneous acts of rebellion. The wealthiest man in the colony, Charles Carroll of Annapolis, thought that, "The clamor of the people out of doors proceeds from their ignorance, prejudice, and passion." His son, Charles Carroll of Carrollton, felt the same about the unrestrained passions of the mob though he opposed British taxes. Unless the colony's "best men" established law and order, he warned that, "Injustice, rapine, and corruption in the seats of justice will prevail, and this province in a short time will be involved in all the horrors of an ungovernable and revengeful democracy and will be dyed with the blood of its best citizens."[11]

In spring 1774, Parliament passed the Coercive Acts to punish Boston for the Boston Tea Party. In May, Annapolis was roused to action when it received word of the suffering of their beleaguered brethren in Massachusetts. On June 22, sympathetic to Boston's plight, delegates met in an extra-legal convention and immediately elected representatives for the meeting of the Continental Congress in Philadelphia in September, agreed to a boycott of British goods, and formed its own committee of correspondence. Carroll of Carrollton hoped "to defeat the pernicious design of the British administration" against American liberties.[12]

In October 1774, Annapolis joined the other colonies in open defiance of British authority. When a merchant named Anthony Stewart imported tea through the capital in violation of the boycott, Annapolis patriots went wild. They distributed pamphlets protesting the arrival of the tea and angrily met in taverns, their tempers flaring. Under the cover of darkness, a furious mob boarded his vessel, the *Peggy Stewart*, and threatened Stewart, warning that "we will…commit to the flames, or otherwise destroy, as the people may choose, the detestable article which has been the cause of this our misconduct." Other radicals yelled that if he "did not immediately set fire to the Brigantine that his house and family would be in danger that night."[13]

The mob made good on its threats. They menaced Stewart enough that he actually ordered that the ship be run aground at the tip of Annapolis, Windmill Point. The ship had its white sails raised and colors flying in the breeze, when Stewart "voluntarily set fire to the tea." But, unlike the Boston Sons of Liberty who dumped the tea and departed peacefully, the Annapolis mob cut a wide swath of destruction in the Severn River. In a few hours, "In the presence of a great number of spectators…the vessel was consumed." The mob probably bid farewell to the ship with a steady round of "huzzahs."[14]

Although such passionate violence shocked the patriotic elite, they organized formal resistance to British policies, especially in the wake of news of the battles at Lexington and Concord. In July 1775, the Maryland Convention convened as an "Association of Freemen," proclaiming that they were "firmly persuaded that it is necessary and justifiable to repel force by force, do approve of the opposition by arms to the British troops…And we do unite and associate, as one band, and firmly and solemnly engage and pledge ourselves to each other, and to America." The storm of revolutionary fervor divided Annapolis between loyalists and patriots, causing many to depart in fear to the sound of the beat of war drums. One observer reported, "Annapolis is daily more and more deserted…Agriculture is neglected; the voice of peaceful industry is heard no more; and the military science is the universal study."[15]

One loyalist, Rev. Jonathan Boucher, tutored George Washington's stepson, Jacky Custis. When he publicly supported Great Britain and an Anglican bishop in America, he made many patriotic enemies. Moreover, he refused to give a sermon asking his congregation for a collection to support Bostonians after the Coercive Acts. He preached with loaded pistols laying on the Bible cushion at the pulpit because he lived in such fear of mobs that assembled at his church. Before he left America just after the Hurricane of Independence struck Annapolis, he used the Fifth Commandment advising his congregation to obey Britain just as they were enjoined to obey their parents. God did not, he counseled, give them just order and rule to turn them loose at the whim "only of their own unruly wills."[16]

The tempest of revolution ironically brought greater harmony among the citizens of Annapolis under the umbrella of expanding liberty. Ever since the Glorious Revolution, Roman Catholics had experienced severe civil repression at the hands of the monarchy and its representatives in Maryland. Catholics could not vote, hold office, practice law, bear arms, serve in the militia, send their children to Catholic schools, or even worship publicly. As late as 1773, in a particularly nasty dispute with a Protestant critic who insulted him by calling him a "papist by profession," Charles Carroll of Carrollton warned that he was "prepared to blow out his brains."[17]

As the Maryland elites met to decide about how to react to British tyranny, internal religious disputes continued to cause disunity and waste the talent of Catholic elites. Because of his religious liability, Carroll was banned from participating in the Maryland Convention and the First Continental Congress, but he attended both meetings as an observer. He participated fully in the Second Continental Congress in 1775, however. Finally, in 1776, the Maryland Constitution guaranteed religious freedom and ended the tumult of civil strife.

An advocate of religious liberty, George Washington understood the reasons in human nature for the profusion of religious sects in America. He said that, "The mind is so formed in different persons as to contemplate the same object in different points of view. Hence originates the difference on questions of the greatest import, both human and divine." Whether for his own practice of Anglicanism or for the Catholic faith of his acquaintance, Charles Carroll, or any other faith, it was the duty of limited government to abstain from violating one of the fundamental rights of all people—liberty of conscience and the right to worship one's god how one chose. "The liberty enjoyed by the people of these states of worshipping Almighty God agreeably to their consciences, is not only among the choicest of their blessings, but also of their rights."[18]

America would never be free of religious conflict, particularly in the decades after the Revolution, during which many of the states struggled over disestablishment of their official churches. But instead of the experience of religious wars that had wracked Europe for centuries and the severe repression of dissenting groups in the colonies, the citizens of the American new order for the ages enjoyed the fruits of religious liberty. As Charles Carroll said, "Freedom and independence, acquired by the united efforts and cemented with the mingled blood of Protestant and Catholic fellow citizens shall be equally enjoyed by all."[19] Religion was not meant to be pushed out of the public square. Indeed, George Washington argued that religion undergirded virtue and thus good citizenship and republican government. In his farewell address, he stated:

> Of all the dispositions and habits which lead to political prosperity, religion and morality are indispensable supports. In vain would that man claim the tribute of patriotism, who should labor to subvert these great pillars of human happiness, these firmest props of the duties of men and citizens.[20]

As seen during the time of the Hurricane of Independence, the American people largely were a devout people who believed in God, even as they were a religiously pluralistic society in which all could worship God according to the dictates of conscience. Whether for Baptists in Virginia or Catholics in Maryland, this was a revolutionary and welcome change for people of all faiths and contributed to civic harmony.

However, not everything was calm in Annapolis as the Hurricane of Independence approached.

On the night of September 2, 1775, the Hurricane of Independence swept into Maryland and made a beeline for the capital.

The people did not know that the hurricane was weakening. All they knew was that a ferocious storm had blown in from the south with no warning, bringing with it great gusts of wind and sheets of rain. The *Maryland Gazette* reported, "On Saturday night last, we had a most violent storm from the north-east, which for several hours blew a mere hurricane, with heavy rain."[21]

Few were foolish enough to venture outside in the dark, and most huddled in their homes for protection. The relentless wind pounded buildings until large and small pieces were ripped asunder and joined the mass of deadly debris whipped around by the hurricane. Trees blew over into the streets. Several inches of rain were dumped onto the capital and muddied the roads. Carriages were thrown about, shattered into pieces, and scattered about the streets. Lightning flashes provided momentary glimpses of the damage and caused additional devastation. The beautiful capital was marred by the storm.

Merchants suffered losses down on the waterfront when rising waters destroyed their stored goods. "The water rose three feet perpendicular above the common tide," the *Gazette* reported, as the hurricane brought the storm surge up the Chesapeake Bay and Severn River. Merchants and traders who operated several blocks into town also had their goods damaged. The market house could not withstand the sustained winds of the hurricane and was simply "blown down" with a horrifying crash. It would take several days to clean up.[22]

As the storm ripped through the town, Annapolis merchants were as concerned as Virginia merchants had been about their goods, especially because of the impending boycott of British goods set for September 10. Charles Carroll of Annapolis worriedly wrote his son, asking, "Did our tobacco from R. Creek get on board in time?"[23]

The weather in late August already had inundated Maryland with rain for days before the hurricane hit. Carroll told his son that he feared

that the soggy weather would "prevent your coming up," and reported
that it prevented the slaves from "pulling the hemp." The flooding river
was "too high for my men to work," and the tobacco "in the low
grounds is drowned."[24] The hurricane only caused more chaos to
planters by ruining their crops. "The damage sustained in different
parts of the province, we are told, is very considerable."[25]

The Hurricane of Independence did not spare the unfinished
state house. In downtown Annapolis, the hurricane followed the
Baroque street design straight to the state house. When the storm
hit the state house, it suffered immense damage. "A great quantity
of the copper on the state house was torn up," by the sustained
winds, the *Gazette* reported.[26] Hundreds of pieces of copper
sheeting were jarred loose and sent flying as deadly objects into the
city. Many trees, fences, and homes probably had one of the sharp-
tipped pieces of metal embedded in them.

A decade later, merchant Charles Wallace remembered the great
"Gust" that blew that night and the damage it caused to the
state house. Wallace explained to a friend that, "The September
Storm of 1775 blew off the roof." Because it was too late in the year
to complete repairs, "the building lay open near the whole winter."
Thus exposed to the elements for months, further damage was done
to the recently renovated building. The consequence was that, "the
work of the upper rooms, which was entirely finished, was totally
destroyed." A lightning strike sometime in the next two years caused
further delays, and the state house was not finished until 1779.[27] It
was somewhat of a miracle that it was completed at all considering
that it seemed as if nature was conspiring against it, in addition to
the problems that the raging Revolutionary War caused.

Chapter Eight

LIGHTNING AND ENLIGHTENMENT

Even before the hurricane hit in 1775, the Maryland Assembly had been concerned about the ability of the state house to weather storms such as the Hurricane of Independence. As a result, the legislature had become interested in the increasingly popular lightning rod that was being installed on public buildings and churches in America and Europe. In 1773, to guard "as far as may be against any accident from lightning," the assembly ordered the builder to "fix place and secure in the best manner an iron rod pointed with silver or gold of six feet at least above the height of the cupola of the said building and conducted at least six feet in the ground."[1]

The lightning rod was the invention of the Revolutionary scientist and statesman, Benjamin Franklin. Franklin won international renown as a scientist during the Enlightenment. Through his publications and travels, he became part of a cosmopolitan community of scientists who made significant discoveries. They wrote letters to each other and published their findings in scientific journals.

The Enlightenment was rooted in the Scientific Revolution of the seventeenth century during which Sir Isaac Newton postulated that the natural laws of the material universe operated like a giant clock and were discoverable by reason. This undermined the classical and medieval understanding of the universe as a living organism that needed consistent attention by God.[2] Scientists thus set out to experiment and classify knowledge into a systematic understanding of the world. They measured progress by the advances in science to conquer superstition and master the forces of nature.[3]

The scientists were not always very successful in either venture, however. As Virginian Landon Carter found out, control over nature was at best elusive. Meanwhile, even during an enlightened age, people continued to believe in witchcraft, alchemy, and astrology. Sir Isaac Newton himself saw no contradiction of science and superstition and became preoccupied by alchemy, while Kepler and Galileo dabbled in horoscopes.[4]

Indeed, astrology was widely popular in the eighteenth century. The front cover of the 1776 *Virginia Almanack* listed its meteorological and astrological contents as "containing the lunations, conjunctions, eclipses—judgment of the weather—rising and setting of the planets." Within its covers, it reconciled astrology with religious beliefs in the following poem:

> The ANATOMY of the HUMAN BODY,
> As governed by the TWELVE CONSTELLATIONS.
>
> This page to all the characters directs,
> Of signs and planets, also their aspects
> They quickly may be learnt; and, being known,
> The ground work of ASTROLOGY's your own.
> Then study next their natures, and from thence

Observe their various wond'rous influence.

Yet ever mind, there are but nature's laws,

And reverence GOD, the prime o'er ruling cause.

Not all were convinced. The *Almanack*'s skeptical publisher issued a challenge to his readers to prove the veracity of astrology over human lives. "Now, I challenge all the *astrologers* and *conjurers* throughout the whole continent of America to demonstrate, that all the whimsy-headed opinions which different men retain of different actions, together with their being so vastly different as different times, etc. one from another. I say, I call upon them ALL to prove, that they are (wholly) owing to the *starry* influences!"[5]

As a young man in Philadelphia, Franklin was interested in this world of ideas. He organized a mutual improvement and debating society for personal growth and civic betterment. In 1743, he developed a "Proposal for Promoting Useful Knowledge among the British Plantation in America," which in 1745 became the American Philosophical Society, imitating the British Royal Society and its European counterparts. The stated purpose of the society was to provide an outlet for scientists to develop their ideas. "[Among] men of speculation, many hints from time to time arise, many observations occur, which if well-examined, pursued and improved, might produce discoveries to the advantage of some or all of the British plantations, or to the benefit of mankind in general." Members of the society were also encouraged to share their knowledge with others in their enlightened circle, communicating their "observations, experiments, etc., to receive, read, and consider such letters, communications, or queries as shall be sent from distant members." Members published their findings in quarterly scientific journals.[6]

Franklin believed that the purpose of science was to benefit all of mankind rather than to profit personally from his inventions. Franklin became one of the wealthiest men in the colonies, with revenues coming from his printing house, property rents and speculations, government positions, and paper mills, which enabled him to retire at a young age.7 He believed that science, rather than politics, should engage the pursuits of a man of leisure, as he told a friend:

> You see I am in a fair way, of having no other tasks than such as I shall like to give myself, and of enjoying what I look upon as a great happiness, leisure to read, study, make experiments, and converse at large with such ingenious and worthy men as are pleased to honor me with their friend-ship or acquaintance, on such points as my produce some-thing for the common benefit of mankind, uninterrupted by the little cares and fatigues of business.8

For example, he never applied for a patent on his "Franklin Stove," allowing others to freely copy and improve upon his design. The lightning rod likewise was freely placed atop tall buildings. Of course, Franklin's motives were not completely disinterested. The international acclaim he won was all the payment he needed, winning such praise as, "He snatched lightning from the sky and the scepter from tyrants."9

Franklin was an inveterate meteorologist who made observations from an early age. On the long journey across the Atlantic after a trip to England in 1726, the young printer noted in his journal that he witnessed two eclipses: one each of the sun and moon. Onboard the ship, he dutifully recorded the temperature, winds, and precipitation each day. In 1732, he began publishing his annual *Poor Richard's Almanack* combining meteorological predictions with his famous satire and wit.

Franklin made a significant contribution to meteorology when he accurately charted the path of a hurricane. On the night of

October 22, 1743, he stepped outside his Philadelphia home to observe a predicted eclipse of the moon when stormy weather frustrated his hopes to witness the spectacle. "There was an eclipse of the moon at 9 in the evening, which I intended to observe, but before 8 a storm blew up at N.E. and continued violent all night and all next day, the sky thick clouded, dark and rainy, so that neither moon or stars could be seen."10

Greatly disappointed, Franklin was informed that his brother in Boston had seen the eclipse that night. Several hours after hitting Philadelphia, the hurricane struck Boston and caused widespread damage. It toppled trees, flooded the seaside wharves, and swept away houses. The curious Franklin had previously thought that the storm had come to Philadelphia *from* Boston and was surprised to hear otherwise. Curious about the coincidence, Franklin began to make "inquiries from time to time of travelers," correspond with New Englanders, and comb through the newspapers to collect data about hurricanes.11

Satisfied with his observations, he offered some conjectures about the movement of hurricanes. Franklin proposed "it to be a constant fact" that hurricanes follow a northeasterly direction.12 This was quite an achievement because hurricanes were greatly misunderstood at the time. No one before this understood the path of hurricanes: All people knew was that they suddenly blew in as if from nowhere and laid waste before moving off. The gaping ignorance was seen in the fact that many eighteenth-century accounts believed that the eye of the hurricane was actually a dividing line between two different storms, though of mysteriously equal fury. Franklin's discovery later became known as the "law of storms."

Franklin's Eclipse Hurricane, as the storm was later named, produced another important first for hurricane watching. Harvard College Professor of Mathematics and Natural Philosophy John

Winthrop recorded the first measurement of the barometric pressure of a hurricane. As the Eclipse Hurricane passed overheard, Winthrop took measurements and wrote in his journal: "NE by N worst in years—great damage on land as well as at sea. Barometer 29.35...Storm abated about 7 p.m. Barometer lowest at 2 p.m."[13]

Franklin's meteorological science oftentimes ran up against engrained religious beliefs. When earthquakes rocked New England in 1727 and 1755, the Puritans found solace in religion and looked to atone for their sins to appease divine punishment. They heard sermons or read newspapers that expressed such sentiments as, "'Tis *sin*, and that *only*, that enkindles the anger of almighty God, and causes Him *to march through a land in indignation*."[14]

Unlike the Puritans or Virginia planter Landon Carter, Franklin preferred to understand the weather scientifically rather than plead for divine mercy. Franklin rejected such ideas. Among the founders, he was perhaps the most unorthodox in matters of faith and was truly close to the Deism, which has erroneously been used to describe the religious beliefs of the founders across the board.[15] He usually proposed a purely natural understanding of the elements. "Surely the thunder of heaven is no more supernatural than the rain, hail, or sunshine of heaven, against the inconvenience of which we guard by roofs and shades without scruple."[16] But, like many Enlightenment scientists, Franklin believed that God gave humans reason to discover scientific truths and natural law. "It has pleased God in his goodness to mankind at length to discover to them the means of securing their habitations and other buildings from mischief by thunder and lightning." Armed with this knowledge, humans therefore could reasonably guard themselves against the deadly discharges from the heavens. Franklin even had the support of the usually envious John Adams who thought that people had wrongly criticized Franklin's lightning rods as "an impious attempt to rob the Almighty of his thunder, to wrest the bolt of vengeance out of his hand."[17]

Franklin's God, moreover, was not the distant clockmaker who had no regard for humans. Either out of a prudential act of statesmanship or with a twinkling of faith, Franklin would later ask for prayers by a chaplain to invoke divine aid for compromise at the Constitutional Convention. He stated his belief in a Providence that governed human affairs:

> The small progress we have made after four or five weeks close attendance and continual reasonings with each other—our different sentiments on almost every question, several of the last producing as many noes as ays, is methinks a melancholy proof of the imperfection of human understanding. How has it happened, Sir, that we have not hitherto once thought of humbly applying to the Father of lights to illuminate our understandings? In the beginning of the contest with Great Britain, when we were sensible of danger we had daily prayer in this room for the divine protection—our prayers, Sir, were heard, and they were graciously answered. All of us who were engaged in the struggle must have observed frequent instances of a superintending providence in our favor. To that kind providence we owe this happy opportunity of consulting in peace on the means of establishing our future national felicity. And have we now forgotten that powerful friend? Or, do we imagine that we no longer need his assistance? I have lived, Sir, a long time, and the longer I live, the more convincing proofs I see of this truth—that God governs in the affairs of men...Is it probable that an empire can rise without his aid?...We shall be divided by our little partial

local interests; our projects will be confounded, and we ourselves shall become a reproach and bye word down to future ages. And what is worse, mankind may hereafter from this unfortunate instance, despair of establishing governments by human wisdom and leave it to chance, war, and conquest. I therefore beg leave to move—that henceforth prayers imploring the assistance of Heaven, and its blessings on our deliberations, be held in this assembly every morning before we proceed to business, and that one or more of the clergy of this city be requested to officiate at that service.[18]

The motion actually was rejected, but perhaps the Convention did receive the blessings of Providence (and the aid of a reflective Fourth of July holiday) when it was able to hammer out compromises over a two-house national Congress.

Many other scientists and theologians were perfectly willing to use hurricanes and lightning to reconcile a providential and natural view of the universe. Newton himself believed that nature was designed by God. Theologian Jonathan Edwards reconciled his Christian faith with his natural observations: "Before, I used to be uncommonly terrified with thunder, but now, on the contrary, it rejoiced me. I felt God, so to speak, at the first appearance of a thunderstorm; and used to take the opportunity, at such times, to fix myself in order to view the clouds, and see the lightnings play."[19] Puritan minister, Increase Mather, examined storms and earthquakes to "offer one level of explanation in terms of second [natural] causes, but also to insist that the Providence of God whether working through nature or outside its confines is ultimately inexplicable to the world."[20]

For his part, Franklin complained to Winthrop, wondering how long people could "hold out against the evidence of new knowledge that does not square with their preconceptions, and how long men can retain a practice that is conformable to their prejudices." For example, Roman Catholic priests throughout Europe blessed and rang church bells to ward off dangerous storms. One cleric noted that the bells stirred the faithful "to pour forth their prayers, by which they win from God the turning away of the thunderbolt." But the prayers did not always work. Lightning struck countless steeples, killing hundreds of unsuspecting bell-ringers, leading Franklin to wonder incredulously, "Yet still they continue to bless the new bells and jangle the old ones whenever it thunders. One would think it was now time to try some other trick."21 The "trick" was his lightning rod.

Franklin was fascinated with lightning, eagerly reporting stories in his newspaper, the *Pennsylvania Gazette*. One story told the tale of a young lad who was sitting on a porch and suddenly struck down and badly burned "from the side of his face to the calf of his leg." The lightning bolt descended from the sky, splitting the chimney, shattering the roof, and breaking a rafter in two. It then smashed a window and melted its lead framing, finally hitting the unfortunate boy. Another lightning strike traveled down a similar path in a different home, crashing down into the cellar without causing injury except to "a full hogshead of rum" and "several hundred weight of butter in tubs." There might have been a rather pleasant odor wafting up.

Franklin rather enjoyed using the story of a lightning strike that showed some humor without hurting anyone. He heard that in New York, a flash hit near a young man. It did not injure him but melted "the pewter button off the waistband of his breeches." Not above a little ribald humor, Franklin joked, "'Tis well nothing else thereabouts was made of pewter."22

Other lightning strikes caused considerably more damage and

prompted scientists such as Franklin to look for a way to shield people and property. In 1769, for example, a lightning bolt struck an ammunition magazine in Brescia, Italy, resulting in a massive explosion that rocked the town. More than a thousand people were killed in the blast.[23]

Lightning was a little understood natural phenomenon that struck with impunity, but some structures seemed to be more susceptible than others. Franklin was especially interested in "preserving houses, churches, ships, etc., from the stroke of lightning." He hoped that his knowledge could be "of use to mankind." He thought that the solution might be to "fix on the highest parts of those edifices upright rods of iron, made sharp as a needle" that were grounded and would harmlessly disperse the lightning, preventing "that most sudden and terrible mischief."[24]

From the periphery of the empire, he ordered a Leyden Jar, which stored electricity, and then conducted electrical experiments and communicated his findings to his European friends. More playfully, Franklin wowed dinner guests with his parlor tricks, sending small shocks around circles of people with joined hands or else giving ladies who were game a charge with which they could give an "electric Venus," or shocking kiss.[25] "Repeating them to my friends and acquaintance, who, from the novelty of the thing, come continually in crowds to see them," drew him away from his engrossing experiments, he complained.[26]

Sometimes, experiments went wrong and reminded him to pay respect to the forces involved. Trying to kill a turkey with an electrical shock, he almost became its victim as his horrified guests looked on. He recounted:

> The flash was very great and the crack as loud as a pistol...it raised a round swelling where the fire entered as big as half a pistol bullet by which you may judge of the

quickness of the electrical fire…I then felt a universal blow throughout my whole body from head to foot which seemed within as well as without; after which the first thing I took notice of was a violent quick shaking of my body…I had a numbness in my arms and the back of my neck, which continued till the next morning but wore off. Nothing remains now of this shock but a soreness in my breastbone which feels as if it had been bruised.[27]

In June 1752, Franklin carried out his legendary electrical experiment. During an impending thunderstorm, he and his son, William, raced outdoors to the cover of a cow shed. Franklin carried a kite with a piece of metal wire attached to the top. A key dangled from some ribbon tied to the kite's twine string, which Franklin held. The sky grew ominous with dark storm clouds, and a strong wind lifted the kite rapidly to a great height. The clouds opened up and dumped their rain, sending an electrical charge through the string and lighting the key with sparks.[28]

On that stormy night, Franklin "snatched lightning from the sky" and gave birth to the lightning rod.

Not everyone was pleased. In 1755, earthquakes flattened Lisbon, sending a murderous tidal wave crashing into the destruction and shaking New England. New Englanders went scurrying into churches. Some thought that Franklin just might be responsible for the tremor. A Boston minister, Thomas Prince, accused Franklin of encouraging Bostonians to erect so many lightning rods that they drew enough electricity to build up in the earth and cause the mighty quake. At the same time, Prince thought that God was punishing Boston for trying to evade lightning's divine chastisement—but there was no escape.[29]

Despite such thoughts, many towns across Europe and America

attached Franklin's rod atop their tallest buildings, including cathedrals and public buildings. In Europe, rods were mounted on St. Mark's Basilica in Venice, Voltaire's home, and the Prussian Ministry (against the wishes of the enlightened despot Frederick the Great).[30] The controversial invention was at the center of a debate surrounding Christopher Wren's great masterpiece, St. Paul's Cathedral. Franklin joined a committee appointed to consider securing the church with a lightning rod and explain why, "If points are *so essential* to our safety," what was preventing "having them on that capital edifice?" The embattled Franklin explained:

> The dome and the whole roof of the church were *covered* with lead, from whence a number of large leaden pipes descended into the common sewers…This being agreed to, none of the committee thought it necessary to propose points. Dr. Franklin would not propose them for a dwelling house so covered, unless where some timid inhabitant dreaded the noise of an explosion, which a pointed conductor might give a chance of preventing.[31]

By 1768, with twelve years of experience, the rod had proven effective across the Atlantic in the colonies. "Among the great number of houses furnished with iron rods in North America," Franklin stated, "several have been evidently preserved by their means." Even though a "number of houses, churches, [and] barns," were struck by lightning, "not one so guarded has been materially hurt."[32]

Franklin, perhaps to his wife's horror, put a lightning rod on his own house. During hurricane season in 1752, Franklin "erected an iron rod to draw the lightning down into my house," and attached some bells to give notice of an electric charge. He then gave orders to his wife and children to "catch some of the lightning" for him when the bells rang if he were not at home. Poor Deborah Franklin must have jumped every time she heard those infernal bells ring.[33]

Benjamin Franklin proved that some limited control over nature—or at least its effects—was possible. Lightning strikes and hurricanes still would occur, but Franklin was a pioneering scientist who made many important discoveries about them through observation and experimentation. His study of nature led to practical discoveries about saving property and lives through knowledge and technological devices.

Through his many significant discoveries about the natural world, Franklin was able to demystify some of the popular superstitions about nature. Although he never adopted a mechanistic world view that excluded God's providence, his kind of scientific reasoning gradually would take hold of the American mind. It is much less commonplace for Americans today to ascribe God's hand in hurricanes and other natural disasters than it would have been in the eighteenth century.[34]

In 1786, when the Maryland assembly voted to add a great dome to the state house, it hired Simon Retalick, an ironmaster, to craft and install a new lightning rod. While delegates from twelve states met in the Constitutional Convention in nearby Philadelphia, Retalick forged a rod that was the largest constructed during Franklin's lifetime. It measured twenty-eight feet tall, and withstood a severe hurricane in 1787. In fact, it has stood for more than two hundred years.

At the end of the war, the Annapolis state house was the site of one of the most moving, and important, moments of the American Revolution. In late 1783, General George Washington received word of the arrival of the final peace treaty with Great Britain. After reoccupying New York and saying a tearful goodbye to a few of his assembled officer corps, he slowly made his way through Trenton, Philadelphia, and Baltimore to fulfill his promise to be home with Martha by Christmas.

In New Jersey, the site of his headlong retreat from British forces in 1776, banners and flags waved to thank the victorious general. In Philadelphia, church bells tolled, ships fired their cannon, and toasts were raised—all in rounds of thirteen to celebrate the independence of the thirteen colonies. No amount of praise seemed too much. One poem read:

> Let WASHINGTON'S immortal name,
> Loudly swell the trump of fame;
> That gallant Chief, long press'd with care,
> Whose bosom never knew despair!
> Him shall the just historian's pen
> Shortly proclaim the First of Men:
> His wond'rous deeds the muse engage
> And deathless live from age to age!

After an elegant dinner at Philadelphia's City Tavern, Washington traveled to Annapolis for his retirement.

"This event will put a period not only to my military service, but also to my public life," Washington wrote his brother, "as the remainder of my natural one shall be spent in that kind of ease and repose which a man enjoys that is free from the load of public cares."[35]

Washington arrived in Annapolis to surrender his military commission to the civilian authority of Congress. Thomas Jefferson was embarrassed that Congress might not have a quorum to be able to receive the general. But Washington was escorted by a welcoming committee and his presence was announced with more thirteen-gun salutes. The next morning, he thanked the people of Annapolis for the "affections of a free people." With carefully staged theatrics by Jefferson, Washington entered the State House dressed with great dignity in his blue military uniform.

At the appointed moment, he arose and addressed the Congress solemnly. The room was silent. Washington's voice cracked as he choked back tears as he tightly gripped his prepared speech. There was not a dry eye in the State House. "Happy in the confirmation of our independence and sovereignty, and pleased with the opportunity afforded the United States of becoming a respectable nation," Washington said, as he resigned his position as commander-in-chief. He humbly argued that victory was won because of the "rectitude of our cause, the support of the supreme power of the Union, and the patronage of Heaven." He thanked his countrymen and officers for their aid during the war. He finished his speech with faltering words to the weeping audience:

> I consider it an indispensable duty to close this last solemn act of my official life, by commending the interests of our dearest country to the protection of almighty God, and those who have the superintendence of them, to his holy keeping. Having now finished the work assigned me, I retire from the great theatre of action; and bidding an affectionate farewell to this august body under whose orders I have so long acted, I here offer my commission, and take my leave of all the employments of public life.[36]

Like Cincinnatus, the Roman general who surrendered his dictatorial powers to the Senate and returned to his plow, Washington voluntarily gave up his powers to the republic. He presented the parchment of his 1775 commission to Congress and left for

Mount Vernon to spend Christmas with his family at Mount Vernon.[37] With his public retirement, he helped to create the American republic by setting the precedent of civil supremacy over the military. King George III correctly predicted that, "If he does that, he will be the greatest man in the world."[38]

The last moments of the American Revolution were less tumultuous than its beginning in 1775 when the Hurricane of Independence left Annapolis and raced into Philadelphia. At the time, members of Congress were involved in making fateful decisions about the war. George Washington had recently departed Philadelphia and arrived in Boston with his new commission to lead the Continental Army. Philadelphians were riding out the storms of nature and war in America's largest city.

The Hurricane of Independence had passed through Annapolis, where it wrought damage against the capitol, the site of Revolutionary debate in the colony. At Philadelphia, some of the most influential American statesmen were gathering to continue preparing for the coming war. If divine providence could have been interpreted to be disciplining tiny Annapolis, the meeting of national significance in Philadelphia would receive that much more of a greater rebuke.

Chapter Nine

THE COLONIES UNITE IN PHILADELPHIA AGAINST BRITISH TYRANNY

B ack in the late spring and summer of 1774, twelve colonies agreed to send representatives to Philadelphia to attend a general congress—the First Continental Congress—to formulate a response to the Coercive Acts, especially a continental boycott of British goods. The colonies were, if possible, even more diverse in their character than the pluralistic Philadelphia society to which they traveled. But they were united by their resistance to British oppression and love of liberty. If they did not join together in a common cause, Boston would be doomed and the budding rebellion snuffed out by redcoats.

Philadelphia was chosen for its central location on the eastern seaboard to reduce the travel time in carriages over bumpy roads. The distance was nonetheless too great for Georgia, which decided not to send delegates and was otherwise engaged in a war with Creek Indians. But there was perhaps another reason why Philadelphia was chosen.[1]

Philadelphia was arguably America's most important city and commercial center. Its merchants, artisans, sailors, and farmers were thoroughly integrated into the Atlantic trade. Goods passed from the agricultural hinterland through the bustling city and onto the holds of ships to ports all over America, Europe, and the Caribbean, and back. All groups consequently bristled at British trade regulations, even if they differed in their proposed remedies.[2]

By the time the delegates were traveling to Philadelphia in the late summer of 1774 it was a thriving, rapidly growing metropolis, quickly surpassing its rival port of Boston. It was as close to an unofficial national capital as America could come, and the perfect meeting place for the First Continental Congress.

On August 28, 1774, delegate John Adams wrote a letter to his wife and confidant, Abigail, from Princeton, New Jersey, while he traveled through the colonies on his way to Philadelphia. At the College of New Jersey (later Princeton), he met with the college president, John Witherspoon, and several professors who received him politely. Adams heard Rev. Witherspoon, who was a fierce advocate of American liberty from the pulpit, give a sermon.

Witherspoon had emigrated to Princeton from Scotland a half-dozen years before and was a product of its Enlightenment. He would become the only clergyman to sign the Declaration of Independence and he formed a circle of patriots centered around the college. Adams wrote admiringly that, "Dr. Witherspoon enters with great spirit into the American cause. He seems as hearty a friend as any of the natives—an animated Son of Liberty."[3]

Adams was journeying from Boston to Philadelphia on his way to the meeting of delegates from twelve colonies called in response to the Coercive Acts that Britain imposed to punish Boston for its Tea Party. Abigail received word that her beloved John "met with great hospitality and kindness in Connecticut."[4] Adams explained that he (and the other delegates) had had opportunities to meet with the "most eminent and famous men" in the colonies and that the Massachusetts delegation had been "treated with unbounded civility, complaisance, and respect."[5] In New Haven, "All the bells in town were set to ringing, and the people—men, women, and children—were crowding at the doors and windows as if it was a coronation. At nine o'clock the cannon were fired, about a dozen guns I think."[6]

Adams had been on the road since setting out from Braintree more than two weeks earlier on August 10. He had been worried when he heard someone tell that "they wash miserably at New York, the Jerseys, and Philadelphia too in comparison of Boston, and am advised to carry a great deal of linen." Ever concerned about people's opinions of him, he deliberated over his clothing. He wondered "whether to make me a suit of new clothes at Boston or to make them at Philadelphia."[7]

Adams told Abigail that the people of the other colonies had a favorable spirit and considered "our cause as their own." He was optimistic about the chances for the upcoming Congress. "Tomorrow," he reported, "We reach the theater of action."[8]

As Adams climbed aboard the carriage for the ride across the Delaware River into Philadelphia, he was anxious thinking about his participation in the Congress. For several months, Adams was concerned that, "I might appear with less indecency before a variety of gentlemen, whose educations, travels, experience, family, fortune, and everything will give them a vast superiority over me." He brushed up on his reading in law and history, and he seemed to be more concerned about whether the other delegates thought highly of him than whether he would make a meaningful contribution.[9]

After crossing the Delaware on a ferry at Trenton, Adams and the Massachusetts delegation rode steadily through the countryside. Adams enjoyed the summer's ride and noted the landscape, recording in his diary, "The scenes of nature are delightful here." By nightfall, they reached the outskirts of the city and stopped for lodgings.

After dinner, a number of congressional delegates and Philadelphia dignitaries rode out to meet the travelers. Adams and the others were "introduced to all these gentlemen and most cordially welcomed to Philadelphia."[10] The Massachusetts delegation was, after all, representative of the heroes who had struggled for a decade against British tyranny in Boston, which was often the center of the maelstrom in the imperial conflict.

They rode into the city the next day, and Adams was duly impressed by what he saw. He took in some sights as he rode into Philadelphia. The first thing he probably saw was the spire of Christ Church that towered above the city, which soared 196 feet into the air, standing above a cupola topped with a weather vane. Erected in 1725, Christ Church was an elaborately designed church, copied from Christopher Wren's London churches. In 1772, the *Pennsylvania Packet* proudly announced that it, "in point of elegance and taste, surpasses everything of the kind in America."[11]

Because the travelers were "dirty, dusty, and fatigued as we were, we could not resist the opportunity to go to the tavern." Adams went to the City Tavern, on Second Street between Walnut and Chestnut, several blocks from where the commoners gathered at less reputable establishments near the docks. The City Tavern had opened its doors only the year before to the gentility of Philadelphia who subscribed and sought more polite forms of entertainment.[12] Adams, with little exaggeration, called the tavern, "the most genteel one in America," and thought that the "supper appeared as elegant as ever was laid upon a table."[13] The dinner was interrupted by introductions and political conversation among the men of different colonies who were getting to know each other.

The next day, Adams "walked a little about town." He was struck by the regularity of the town's grid layout. Philadelphia was the largest city in the colonies with a growing population of 25,000 people, surpassing both Boston and New York. It was a bustling city of commerce with a thriving port that had numerous warehouses. The waterfront was the place through which goods came from the West Indies and Scots-Irish immigrants passed on their way to farms on the Pennsylvania frontier. Artisans, merchants, free blacks, Quakers, Presbyterians, and beggars mixed freely in the streets of this remarkably diverse city. He thought Philadelphia "elegant."[14]

As he walked, Adams smelled the stench of a large urban area, but he was used to it and did not consciously note it. Garbage and horse manure filled the streets. Livestock and other animals roamed freely, adding to the filth and spreading diseases that frequently passed through the city indiscriminately.

Adams's tour around Philadelphia included a trip to the local hospital, where he saw a number of cells with "lunatics." He even seemed to have recognized an old client of his whom he saved from a whipping for stealing horses. Adams thought the woeful sight "a dreadful scene of human wretchedness," taking pity on the patients. He was dazzled by Dr. William Shippen's display of anatomical drawings of the human body.[15]

On Friday, September 2, after dining at delegate Thomas Mifflin's home, Adams and his colleagues went to the City Tavern to meet part of the illustrious Virginia delegation. They appeared to be "the most spirited of any," with Benjamin Harrison claiming that he would have walked to Congress if necessary for the patriotic cause. Caesar Rodney of Delaware declared that "more sensible, fine fellows you would never wish to see."[16] Adams thought Richard Henry Lee was "a masterly man," while Peyton Randolph was a "large, well looking man."[17]

Adams informed Abigail that the Massachusetts delegates were just as highly praised as the Virginians:

The Massachusetts councilors and addressers are held in curious esteem here, as you will see. The spirit, the firmness, the prudence of our province are vastly applauded, and we are universally acknowledged the saviors and defenders of American liberty.[18]

Maryland's Charles Carroll thought that they were "as moderate as any—nay the most so." Indeed, John and Samuel Adams were cautiously (if somewhat deceptively) downplaying their thoughts about independence to win over the others to their cause. Consequently, Joseph Reed observed that next to the Virginians, "the Bostonians are mere milksops."[19]

As Adams and the other delegates waited for the official opening of the Congress on September 5, 1774, they made the social rounds, receiving invitations to several dinner parties. At one party, Adams recorded, they ate "an elegant supper, and we drank sentiments till 11 o'clock." With a disapproving tone, he wrote that Lee and Harrison drank a lot and were "very high." Many were drunk because of the endless round of toasts to the firmness of the colonies, the wisdom of Great Britain, America's freedom, the friends of America, constitutional rights, and the union of Britain and the colonies. One delegate raised his glass with an explosive toast: "May the collision of British flint and American steel produce the spark of liberty which shall illumine the latest posterity."[20]

Part of the Virginia delegation was still en route to Philadelphia. On August 30, the most unlikely pair of fiery orator Patrick Henry and stanch conservative Edmund Pendleton arrived at Mount Vernon. They were entertained that evening by Martha and George Washington, with the men probably discussing the prospects for the meeting in Philadelphia. The next morning, they set out for the short trip, with Washington accompanied by his manservant,

William Lee. They traveled through Annapolis, stopping at taverns for dinner and lodging at some of Washington's favorite haunts.[21]

The trio arrived in Philadelphia on Sunday, September 4, just in time for the next day's opening meeting. Washington lodged with Dr. Shippen for the night. When Washington joined the Congress on Monday morning, he was already a committed patriot. Only a few days before, he made his ideas clear to his friend Bryan Fairfax: "An innate spirit of freedom first told me," he wrote, that the British taxes and repression "are repugnant to every principle of natural justice." Because the petitions that the colonists had sent to the king for a decade were treated with the "utmost contempt," Washington decided that, "The crisis is arrived when we must assert our rights, or submit to every imposition that can be heaped upon us; till custom and use, will make us as tame, and abject slaves." Only unity and firmness could prevent the "systematic plan" of tyranny against the colonists. Thus, Washington came to the meeting in Philadelphia as a supporter of the patriotic cause—including war, if necessary.[22]

Washington cut an imposing figure immediately among Congress. Silas Deane said that Washington had "a very young look and an easy, soldier-like air and gesture."[23] Adams was told that Washington pledged to "raise 1000 men, subsist them at my own expense, and march myself at their head for the relief of Boston."[24]

The representatives from twelve colonies gathered at the City Tavern at ten in the morning. Formal introductions were made and the delegates' credentials were read and accepted. They also sized each other up. Adams humorously thought that Caesar Rodney was the "oddest looking man in the world," with a face that was "no bigger than a large apple."[25]

The Carpenters' Guild of Philadelphia offered their spacious chamber hall, complete with a well-stocked library, for the gathering of notables. The delegates walked the short distance from the tavern to Carpenters' Hall, where they assessed the offer. "The general cry was that this was a good room," Adams recorded, with only a few dissenters in the first vote of the Congress.

Then, Thomas Lynch of South Carolina arose and nominated Peyton Randolph as the president of the Congress. Lynch said:

> There was a gentleman present who had presided with great dignity over a very respectable society, greatly to the advantage of America, and he therefore proposed that the Honorable Peyton Randolph, esq., one of the delegates from Virginia, and the late Speaker of their House of Burgesses, should be appointed chairman and he doubted not it would be unanimous.

Indeed, the question was put to the assembly, and Randolph was chosen unanimously.[26]

Other assessments were just as favorable for the leader of the Virginia patriot cause. Silas Deane thought that Randolph was the right man for the leadership. Deane wrote, "Our president seems designed by nature for the business. Of an affable, open and majestic deportment, large in size, though not out of proportion, he commands respect and esteem by his very aspect, independent of the high character he sustains."

Thomas Jefferson, who knew Randolph well, thought him, "a most excellent man; and none was ever more beloved and respected by his friends." Randolph was "somewhat cold and coy towards strangers, but of the sweetest affability when ripened into acquaintance." Jefferson thought that Randolph had a logical mind and was well read in the law. Randolph's patriotism was also beyond dispute, but he moderated the radicals to avoid unrestrained passions from bursting forth. Jefferson wrote, "Although sound in his principles, and going steadily with us in opposition to the British usurpations, he with the other older members, yielded the lead to the younger…tempering their ardor, and so far modulating their pace as to prevent their going too far in advance of the public sentiment."[27]

Before the Congress convened, Randolph had led a procession of dignitaries down Williamsburg's Duke of Gloucester Street to Bruton Parish Church for a service on an appointed day of fasting and prayer in support of Boston. After being selected as the first Virginia delegate to the Continental Congress, a large crowd escorted him to the Raleigh Tavern, entertained him at "a most splendid dinner," marched him to his house, and gave him three cheers "to show their tender regard for their speaker," and "his many essential services towards this country."[28]

His home overlooking the governor's green was also the spot where Thomas Jefferson's "A Summary View of the Rights of British America" was first read in August 1774. Jefferson was riding down from Monticello when he became ill and returned home. He sent his treatise, which would become the basis for the Declaration of Independence, to Williamsburg anyway. It was met with a welcoming reception from those who heard it at the Randolph house and then earned international recognition as it was reprinted and made Jefferson famous.[29]

Jefferson wrote a petition to the king of the "united complaints of his majesty's subjects in America; complaints which are excited by many unwarrantable encroachments and usurpations, attempted to be made by the legislature of one part of the empire, upon those rights which God and the laws have given equally and independently to all."[30] Jefferson later joined Congress in the following spring, replacing Randolph when he returned home to attend the Virginia Convention.

John Adams was impressed not simply with Peyton Randolph but by the whole assembly of men. They were a well-educated and experienced lot: Most were lawyers, had been to college, and were active locally in the resistance to British policies. Even taking a swipe at his more democratic Massachusetts, Adams told Abigail that, "There is in the Congress a collection of the greatest men upon the continent in point of abilities, virtues, and fortunes. The magnanimity and public spirit which I see here make me blush for the sordid, venal herd which I have seen in my own province."[31]

So much greatness assembled in one room was not always a good thing, however. A few weeks later, Adams told Abigail that, "This assembly is like no other that ever existed. Every man in it is a great man, an orator, a critic, a statesman." The problem was that every question that was raised caused a lot of egotistical grandstanding so that "business is drawn and spun out to an immeasurable length." Adams sardonically jested that if it "should come to a resolution that three and two make five, we should be entertained with logic and rhetoric, law, history, politics, and mathematics" that the answer were true.[32]

More than pride divided the Congress. Patrick Henry was bold enough to assert, "I am not a Virginian, but an American." Few others shared Henry's sentiment, however. The colonies were too different from each other to be strongly unified. The Congregationalist, democratic New Englanders had relatively little in common with the hierarchical Anglicans on the plantations of the South. During the French and Indian War, Benjamin Franklin had proposed a plan of union at an assembly in Albany, but it failed miserably.

Local allegiances continued to divide the colonists at Philadelphia. Adams rightly understood the nature of the problem. "Fifty gentlemen meeting together, all strangers, are not acquainted with each other's language, ideas, views, designs. They are, therefore, jealous of each other—fearful, timid, skittish." This gulf led to a tedious pace of business—"slow as snails"—he thought.[33]

The Continental Congress even had trouble deciding on prayers for its sessions. Religious differences were almost too great for any prayers to be said. Adams described the furor over religious divisions:

> When the Congress first met, Mr. Cushing made a motion that it should be opened with prayer. It was opposed by Mr. Jay, of New York, and Mr. Rutledge, of South Carolina, because we were so divided in religious sentiments, some Episcopalians, some Quakers, some Anabaptists, some Presbyterians, and some Congregationalists, that we could not join in the same act of worship. Mr. Samuel Adams arose and said he was no bigot, and could hear a prayer from a gentlemen of piety and virtue, who was at the same time a friend to his country.

They finally compromised on an Episcopal clergyman whose extemporaneous prayer "filled the bosom of every man present." His prayers for America, Congress, and Boston "had an excellent effect upon everybody here."[34] The minister, Philadelphia Anglican priest Jacob Duché, borrowed from Psalm 35, in which God protects his chosen people from their enemies.[35] Duché later became the Congress' first chaplain and told the members in July 1775, "Go on, ye chosen band of Christians."[36]

Adams praised Duché, but the delegate was not above a little religious prejudice. He attended a Roman Catholic Mass in Philadelphia and recounted "the poor wretches fingering their beads, chanting Latin not a word of which they understood; their Pater Nosters and Ave Marias; their holy water; their crossing themselves perpetually...Here is everything which can lay hold of the eye, ear, and imagination—everything which can charm and bewitch the simple and ignorant. I wonder how Luther ever broke the spell."[37]

More importantly, the delegates had a debate over the fundamental source of their rights in preparing a Declaration of Rights. Richard Henry Lee stated that, "The rights are built on a fourfold foundation—on nature, on the British Constitution, on charters, and on immemorial usage." Moreover, Lee argued that they should "lay our rights upon the broadest bottom, the ground of nature" to secure life and liberty. John Jay of New York agreed, saying, "It is necessary to recur to the law of nature."

Others contested this view and thought that American rights "are well founded on the British Constitution, and not on the law of nature." Joseph Galloway of Pennsylvania told the Congress, "I have looked for our rights in the laws of nature—but could not find them."[38]

They settled upon a Declaration of Rights that claimed the right to life, liberty, and property from natural law, the British Constitution, and colonial charters. As free people, they could be taxed only by their consent.[39] It would be another year before Thomas Jefferson asserted more forcefully and eloquently, "We hold these truths to be self-evident, that all men are created equal, that they are endowed by their Creator with certain unalienable Rights, that among these are Life, Liberty, and the pursuit of Happiness." These rights were derived from "the Laws of Nature and Nature's God."

The delegates in Philadelphia had to overcome this disunity; resistance to British tyranny provided the means to unite.

On Friday, September 16, 1774, in an important but lesser known event than his famous April 1775 ride, silversmith Paul Revere came thundering into Philadelphia with explosive news. Revere brought a copy of the declaration of the legislature of Suffolk, Massachusetts, for Congress to consider. The Suffolk Resolves asserted that the British were following a tyrannical plan to enslave the colonies and advocated direct resistance:

Whereby the streets of Boston are thronged with military executioners; whereby our coasts are lined and harbors crowded with ships of war; whereby the charter of the colony, that sacred barrier against the encroachments of tyranny, is mutilated…We resolve that no obedience is due from this province to either or any part of the acts above-mentioned, but that they be rejected as the attempts of a wicked administration to enslave America.[40]

The Congress responded favorably to the radical set of resolves and "earnestly recommend to their brethren a perseverance in the same firm and temperate" resistance to the "murderous acts."[41] John Adams was pleased that "America will support Massachusetts or perish with her."[42]

Revere later rode back into Philadelphia with frightening news. On October 6, he reported that British General Thomas Gage was preparing for war, erecting fortifications around Boston. Not yet ready for war, Congress weakly compromised on advising the people of Massachusetts to conduct themselves peacefully and avoid provoking the redcoats.[43]

The main accomplishment of the Continental Congress was agreeing to commercial resistance against Great Britain. The Congress unanimously adopted a plan not to import goods from Britain as of December 1. More contentious was a nonexportation agreement. The Virginia planters informed the Congress that, "Tobacco is not [shipped] until the next year."[44] As a result, they refused to agree to any plan that did not allow their valuable tobacco crop to be sent to Britain. The ban on exports would not take effect until September 10, 1775—in the middle of hurricane season.

The boycott included a call for nonconsumption of British goods and urged buying exclusively American products. The

Congress was promoting simplicity and Spartan republican morality and virtue, encouraging "frugality, economy, and industry." Rejecting corrupt British luxury that led to tyranny, it sought to discourage "every species of extravagance and dissipation." Assailing some of George Washington's favorite pastimes, Congress disapproved of horse racing, gambling, cock fighting, and theater. As a result, Americans would be more moral and capable of self-government.[45]

Adams was of a divided mind about his own pleasurable consumption of the culinary delights of Philadelphia. The Puritan in him felt guilty about eating "a most sinful feast again!" He enjoyed "everything which could delight the eye, or allure the taste," and sampled from the table including "curds and creams, jellies, sweet meats of various sorts, twenty sorts of tarts, fools, trifles, floating islands, whipped syllabubs, etc., etc.—parmesan cheese, punch, wine, porter, beer, etc., etc."[46]

On the other hand, Adams rather delighted in the tempting treats. Starting at four o'clock in the afternoon, he feasted upon "ten thousand delicacies" and for hours drank copious amounts of Madeira, Claret, and Burgundy to wash them down. He told Abigail that he went home "fatigued to death" with the dinner parties, but "yet I hold out surprisingly." Something that helped was consuming the local Philadelphia beer and porter. He thought the porter "as good as any that comes from London" and hoped to introduce it to Massachusetts because it was better than the local punch and cider.[47]

Having completed its business, the Congress adjourned on October 26, 1774. It agreed to reassemble on May 10, 1775, unless the British satisfactorily responded to America's grievances thereby making another meeting unnecessary. On the evening of October 26, as it later would after signing the Constitution on September 17, 1787, the members of Congress met for a scrumptious celebratory dinner at the City Tavern. Washington's description of the later event could easily have described the 1774 adjournment: "The business being thus closed, the members adjourned to the City Tavern, dined together and took a cordial leave of each other."[48] Anxious to get home, they began the journey over the next day or two. If they were anxious to attend to their personal affairs and resistance in their home colonies, they were perhaps even more nervous about opposing the mighty British Empire. They were choosing a path fraught with many dangers.

Chapter Ten

THE RADICAL, THE PRESIDENT, AND THE GENERAL IN PHILADELPHIA

The American petition to the king was summarily ignored. Parliament declared Massachusetts in a state of rebellion in February 1775. King George III told Lord North that "blows must decide whether they are to be subject to this country or independent." The king was right.[1]

Not everyone in Britain agreed with the king. Some members of Parliament wanted to reconcile with the colonies, allowing them to tax themselves and preserving their rights as Englishmen. Edmund Burke, for example, rose in Parliament on March 22, 1775, to plead for conciliation and explain why the Americans would never submit to force:

> In this character of the Americans, a love of freedom is the predominating feature which marks and distinguishes the whole: and as an ardent is always a jealous affection, your colonies become suspicious, restive, and untractable whenever they see the least attempt to wrest from them by force,

or shuffle from them by chicanery, what they think the only advantage worth living for. This fierce spirit of liberty is stronger in the English colonies probably than in any other people of the earth.[2]

As the delegates to the Second Continental Congress arrived in Philadelphia that spring, they received alarming word that militiamen had battled British forces marching through Lexington and Concord. In early May 1775, Benedict Arnold joined with Ethan Allen and his riflemen to seize Fort Ticonderoga in upstate New York. The erupting battle lent a new urgency to the dealings of Congress as it began to prepare for war.

In April 1775, Peyton Randolph learned that he was declared a rebel by King George III. Randolph was blacklisted along with John and Samuel Adams, John Hancock, John Dickinson, and Henry Middleton. British General Gage received blank commissions from England for their arrest. They were to be executed if captured. They were literally risking their necks for the cause of freedom.[3]

In the spring, Randolph presided over the Virginia Convention and received the most votes to represent Virginia for the impending meeting of the Continental Congress. Riding with Benjamin Harrison and Edmund Pendleton, Randolph departed from his home in the middle of Williamsburg with an honor guard to prevent his arrest. Detachments of the militia cavalry escorted the esteemed delegation all the way through Virginia until they reached the Potomac River. When they crossed, "about 250 of the first gentlemen in this part of the country...gave them three cheers, and returned home." As a measure of their fame, they were immediately joined on the Maryland side by two militia companies from that colony.[4]

Randolph presided briefly over the Congress and then returned home in late May to attend the meeting of the Virginia General

Assembly. Boston's John Hancock succeeded Randolph as president of the Congress. On his return trip home, a Williamsburg cavalry detachment rode out to meet Randolph and was joined by the infantry two miles from the capital to bring him safely home. Upon his return, "The bells began to ring…there were illuminations in the evening, and the volunteers, with many other respectable gentlemen, assembled at the Raleigh [Tavern], spent an hour or two in harmony and cheerfulness, and drank several patriotic toasts."

The next morning, Randolph received an address from the militia:

> We, the members of the volunteer company in Williams-burg…are exceedingly alarmed to hear, from report, that the same malevolent demons, from whom have originated all the evils of America, are now exerting their utmost treachery to ensnare your life and safety…MAY HEAVEN GRANT YOU LONG TO LIVE THE FATHER OF YOUR COUNTRY, AND THE FRIEND TO FREEDOM AND HUMANITY!

Randolph patriotically replied that, "Such unjust and arbitrary proceedings would bring down on the authors of them the resentment and indignation of every honest man in the British empire."[5]

In late April, John Adams set out from his Braintree, Massachusetts, home, once again leaving Abigail to care for their home and children, this time near the war zone. He met up with the rest of the Massachusetts delegation in Hartford, Connecticut. In New York, Adams was struck by the joyous welcome. "It would take many sheets of paper to give you a description of the reception we found here. The militia were all in arms, and almost the whole city out to meet us."[6] John Hancock was a bit flustered and embarrassed by all the attention:

Persons appearing with proper harnesses [who] insisted upon taking out my horses and dragging me into and through the city, a circumstance I would not have had taken place upon any consideration, not being fond of such parade.[7]

When they arrived on the outskirts of Philadelphia several days later, they were "met five miles out of town by a great number of gentlemen and military companies, one of riflemen." Feted by the people of Philadelphia in honor of their fighting at Lexington and Concord, they were "escorted by music to City Tavern."[8] Adams disingenuously complained of "the unnecessary parade that was made about us," and in reality basked in the glory.[9]

During the spring, George Washington attended the Virginia Convention held in Richmond, where he witnessed Patrick Henry proclaim "Give me liberty or give me death." As the crisis with Britain steadily worsened, Washington made preparations for war. In Virginia, he was chosen as commander of five regiments that were raised. He also purchased several items for war, including a tomahawk and books on military science.[10]

Chosen second in the balloting behind Peyton Randolph, Washington was elected to the Second Continental Congress. He traveled to Philadelphia, retracing his path from the previous autumn, though by this time war had erupted. On May 4, 1775, he climbed aboard his carriage with Richard Henry Lee and began the grave journey.

Washington arrived and was appointed to several committees to address the war needs of America. With Philip Schuyler of New York and Samuel Adams, among others, he sat on a committee "to consider of ways and means to supply these colonies with ammunition and military stores and to report immediately" and another to estimate the money necessary to support an army.

Washington had ample military experience fighting in the French and Indian War and against the Indians on the frontier in the 1750s, unlike Henry Knox and Alexander Hamilton who learned their artillery craft from books. Nonetheless, on one of his many shopping excursions for his wife and himself, Washington walked down to a local bookshop and purchased five military books.

Everyone, it seemed, was infected with the martial spirit. Adams told Abigail that he witnessed a "very wonderful phenomenon" in the city streets:

> A field-day, on which three battalions of soldiers were reviewed, making full two thousand men, battalion men, light infantry, grenadiers, riflemen, light horse, artillery men with a fine train, all in uniforms, going through the manual exercise and the maneuvers with remarkable dexterity.[11]

He also was taken with Washington's dignified, commanding presence. Adams dreamed, "Oh that I was a soldier! I will be. I am reading military books. Everybody must, and will, and shall be a soldier." Fortunately, these dreams quickly passed.[12]

Congress began its sessions by immediately debating Richard Henry Lee's "proposals for raising an army." Even conservative John Dickinson, who preferred reconciliation to war, raised the war cry. He thought that Congress should start making "a vigorous preparation for war" and a "vigorous prosecution of it."[13] Britain, Dickinson angrily stated, had begun the war with "the butchery of unarmed Americans. He admitted that it would be difficult to make peace with the mother country while "her sword is opening our veins."[14]

Congress began mobilizing for war. On June 14, it approved a plan to raise a Continental Army made of troops from all the colonies to support Boston. On June 15, Washington was made the commander of "all the continental forces, raised, or to be raised, for the defense of American liberty."

There was little doubt that Washington would be selected to lead the Continental Army. The famous hero of the French and Indian War pulled out his musty uniform and wore it conspicuously while attending sessions in Congress. He possessed a martial dignity and remained silently above the political fray in Congress after his arrival. He was a known supporter of republican liberties, though he was not a passionate firebrand like Patrick Henry. A member of Congress was deeply impressed by Washington and described him as "discreet and virtuous, no harum scarum ranting swearing fellow but sober, steady, and calm. His modesty will induce him I dare say to take and order every step with the best advice possible to be obtained in the army."[15]

A Virginian, Washington was a symbol of intercolonial unity. Expressing a common sentiment in Congress, Adams viewed Washington as "a gentleman whose skill and experience as an officer, whose independent fortune, great talents, and excellent universal character would command the approbation of all America and unite the cordial exertions of all the colonies better than any other person in the Union."[16]

As a member of the House of Burgesses and experienced war commander, Washington was familiar with civil-military relations. This convinced Congress that it could entrust him with power over a continental army. Still, because of the fear of standing armies and tyranny, Congress reminded him of his subordination to its civilian authority. It directed him to follow "such orders and directions from time to time as you shall receive from this or a future Congress of the said united colonies."[17]

Because the delegates thought Washington could lead the army with skill, prudence, and patriotism, Congress unanimously selected him commander-in-chief. Washington accepted with a sense of gravity and great humility. He told Congress:

> I am truly sensible of the high honor done me in this appointment, yet I feel great distress, from a consciousness that my abilities and military experience may not be equal to the extensive and important trust. However, as the Congress desires it, I will enter upon the momentous duty and exert every power I possess in their service and for the support of the glorious cause. I beg they will accept my most cordial thanks for this distinguished testimony of their approbation...I, this day, declare with the utmost sincerity, I do not think myself equal to the command I am honored with.[18]

In addition, Washington refused the proffered salary because he did not wish to profit by service to his country and asked only that his expenses be reimbursed. John Adams admired this selfless act and thought, "His views are noble and disinterested." Washington possessed the necessary classical republican virtues to command an army of citizen-soldiers.[19]

Nevertheless, Washington was apprehensive that poor leadership on his part or a humiliating defeat would ruin his honor. Revolutionary physician Benjamin Rush related that Washington bemoaned the potential consequences of his appointment to fellow Virginian Patrick Henry. "Remember, Mr. Henry, what I now tell you: From the day I enter upon the command of the American armies, I date my fall, and the ruin of my reputation."[20] On the other hand, Washington feared that refusing the appointment would demonstrate a dishonorable lack of patriotism.

Like great historical figures of the past, Washington decided to serve the public in a cause higher than himself. Washington later stated that, "The establishment of civil and religious liberty was the motive which induced me to the field."[21] In letters home, he explained that he saw the hand of Providence in his service. He thought he had the characteristics necessary for good leadership: a firm belief in the cause for liberty, a faithful adherence to his duties, and integrity. Also, he could win the immortal fame he aspired to by leading the patriot army.[22] At the same time, he distanced himself from any accusation of being motivated by selfish ambition. "It is an honor I by no means aspired to—It is an honor I wished to avoid…a thorough conviction of my own incapacity and want of experience…May God grant therefore that my acceptance of it may be attended with some good to the common cause and without injury to my own reputation."[23]

Before he departed to take command of the army, Washington wrote home to several people using a storm metaphor to explain his decision to accept. "I am now embarked on a tempestuous ocean from whence, perhaps, no friendly harbor is to be found." He was bidding adieu to "every kind of domestic ease."[24]

Adams used similar sailing imagery to describe his impatience with the pace that Congress was moving. "America is a great unwieldy body," he wrote, "Its progress must be slow. It is like a large fleet sailing under convoy. The fleetest sailors must wait for the dullest and slowest."[25]

Washington left for Boston to great acclaim on his way out of Philadelphia. Adams was part of the escort and related that he and several members of Congress had "this morning been out of town to accompany our generals, Washington, [Charles] Lee, and [Philip] Schuyler, a little way on their journey to the American camp before Boston…a large troop of light horse in their uniforms; many officers of the militia besides, in theirs, music playing, etc., etc. Such is the pride and pomp of war."[26]

Only two days after Washington accepted the appointment as commander of the newly created Continental Army, British General William Howe assaulted American militia forces at the Battle of Bunker Hill. The resulting carnage meant that war had come to America: There would be no reconciliation. Washington was going to break the siege of Boston and he promised his wife Martha (like many other soldiers marching off to war) that he would be home by Christmas, saying, "I shall return safe to you in the fall."[27]

Nevertheless, as late as July, at least some members of Congress still held out the possibility of resolution and peace even as Congress explained its reasons for taking up arms. John Dickinson and Thomas Jefferson (who had replaced Peyton Randolph as a delegate) jointly penned the "Declaration of the Causes and Necessity of Taking up Arms." Congress explained that, "Honor, justice, and humanity forbid us tamely to surrender that freedom which we received from our gallant ancestors, and which our innocent posterity have a right to receive from us." With the aid of "divine favor," Americans would fight to "exhibit to mankind the remarkable spectacle" of a people defending their liberties.[28]

Conversely, Dickinson and other moderates in Congress sent a final petition, known as the Olive Branch Petition, to the king for harmony between Britain and her colonies. With humble supplication to the crown, the Americans pledged their fealty and asked for reconciliation with the hope that "measures may be taken for preventing the further destruction of the lives of your majesty's subjects; and that such statutes as more immediately distress any of your Majesty's colonies may be repealed."[29]

One adopted son of Philadelphia needed no further proof of British tyranny and wanted no petitions. Benjamin Franklin had sailed back to America back in March after a decade in Britain and a humiliating send-off when he was verbally abused by the Privy Council. In July, while Congress wrote petitions to King George III, Franklin penned a letter (which he did not actually send) to his life-long friend in England. Furious, he wrote: "You are a member of Parliament and one of that majority which doomed my country to destruction. You have begun to burn our towns, and murder our people. Look upon your hands! They are stained with the blood of your relations! You and I were long friends. You are now my enemy, and I am, Yours, B. Franklin."[30]

Before the Second Continental Congress wrapped up its business, it voted for a day of "public humiliation, fasting, and prayer," because their work so far was "so peculiarly marked, almost by direct interposition of Providence, that not to feel and acknowledge his protection would be the height of impious ingratitude." Because of God's "desolating judgments," Congress called on the nation to fast and pray to "beseech him to forgive our iniquities." Members of Congress attended services on July 20, 1775, at the Anglican Church of Rev. Jacob Duché (who read their first prayer the previous year) in the morning and Francis Alison's Presbyterian meeting in the afternoon. John Adams heartily approved of the day's national significance. "Millions will be on their knees at once before their great Creator, imploring his forgiveness and blessings, his smiles on American councils and arms."[31]

There were a million things to be done and yet members of Congress decided to adjourn for a time. They trusted Washington to take control of the army in Boston while it enjoyed a short recess. Besides, the delegates were desperate to escape the oppressive heat and horseflies of Philadelphia in August, and had spent too much time away from their homes and families. On August 2, 1775, Congress wrapped up its business and adjourned until September.

Although many members of Congress feared the outcome of the storm of war, none could have known that the storms off the coast of West Africa were forming into a hurricane.

A few weeks later, King George III declared all of the colonies to be in open rebellion and ignored Dickinson's Olive Branch Petition. The King soon gave a speech to Parliament announcing that the colonists "now openly avow their revolt, hostility, and rebellion." He was moving to "put a speedy end to these disorders by the most decisive exertions."[32]

The King's proclamation meant trouble for the colonists and their chosen representatives in Philadelphia. They could expect to face the full might of the combined forces of the British Army and Navy. Any leaders who were caught would be executed. The odds were overwhelmingly against the colonists, who mustered a great deal of courage to continue on their chosen path of war and rebellion. They would need a miracle to be victorious. Thus they declared just how dear liberty was to them.

On August 27, Peyton Randolph, accompanied by George Wythe and Thomas Nelson, Jr., and their wives, set out from Virginia for Philadelphia to take their seats in Congress again. Riding such a long distance in carriages during the eighteenth century was hardly a pleasant experience and was guaranteed to make riders' bottoms sore. Soggy roads and blocked paths were a common occurrence, but the Virginians had no idea what they were really in for.

Along the way, they encountered a series of mishaps as they experienced the effects of the Hurricane of Independence moving up the Atlantic seaboard. In Maryland, their carriage broke down and delayed their journey. A kindly gentleman learned of their plight and offered a replacement, which they graciously accepted.

They were riding through high winds, pounding rain, and mud-clogged roads when their second carriage also was demolished, this time by an unskilled (and probably drunk) driver who smashed into a tree. They finally arrived in Philadelphia a few days later windswept, waterlogged, and a little worse for wear.[33]

Chapter Eleven

STRIKING THE SECOND CONTINENTAL CONGRESS

O n the night of Saturday, September 2, 1775, soon after ripping off the roof of the Annapolis state house and delaying the travel of part of the Virginia delegation, the Hurricane of Independence smashed into the City of Brotherly Love. The fact that the Hurricane of Independence was hitting the capital of the united colonies could not have been interpreted as a favorable sign from above. Unlike the coastal capitals, Philadelphia did not have both Americans and British present who would muddy interpreting the hurricane as heavenly punishment against the tyrannical enemy. The tempest struck the symbolic center of the rebellion, where its assembled statesmen made their fateful decisions regarding their freedom and self-government.

Much like the rest of the mid-Atlantic, the Philadelphia press reported, "All last week we had squally weather and rain." But, just as in Virginia and Maryland, the weather took a turn for the worse. "On Saturday evening it began to blow hard at N.E. and S.E. and by midnight increased to a hurricane."[1]

Philadelphian Phineas Pemberton was an amateur meteorologist who took weather measurements, including barometric pressure with his new weather instrument. The notes he jotted in his diary were consistent with the findings in the press: "September 3—Stormy and showery. A violent gale from NE to SE the preceding night with heavy rain, lightning, and thunder." Perhaps too occupied by the dangerous gust howling in the dark to make observations, he read the rising pressure of the barometer at 29.50 inches at eight o'clock the next morning with great relief. Rising pressure was a sign that the stormy weather had passed. That evening, after the hurricane swept away any bad weather, Pemberton recorded that the skies cleared and there were "flying clouds and wind with sunshine at times."[2]

Many structures in the city were protected from the lethal lightning strikes by hometown-hero Benjamin Franklin's lightning rods. The lightning flashes revealed the awful tempest that was blowing through the city. But they may have brought relief to a few who looked out their window during the storm and saw the elevated spire of Christ Church protected from the elements, unharmed.

The Delaware and Schuylkill rivers swelled during the storm to abnormally high levels. Heavy downpours of rain flooded the city at the confluence of the two rivers, and the water rose to dangerous heights. The hurricane "raised the tide in our river higher than has been known there several years." Pemberton also observed "a remarkably high tide in the Delaware this morning."[3]

The flooding was sure to wreak havoc upon the interests in the city so dependent upon its port. Luckily, few people were out in the night while the rivers continuously rose in the dark. Creeping steadily up and overflowing their banks, the flooding rivers spilled into the cobblestone streets, which were already saturated from the heavy rains. They flooded several businesses. Along the waterfront, fierce winds whipped the choppy waters against buildings, causing significant damage to merchandise in warehouses and storefronts. The tempest "has occasioned much damage in the stores on the wharves, among sugar, salt, and other perishable articles; wood, staves, plank, &c. was washed off the wharves."

Merchants, sailors, and fishermen lost their livelihoods when the fierce winds pounded the boats in the harbor. The hurricane simply was still too powerful for the boats to withstand its fury. Under the constant wind, the boats were rocking and thrashing about in the rivers. During the night, "Many boats and small craft were sunk or beat to pieces." With their goods ruined and no boats to ship them out on, many merchants suffered heavy losses in the storm.[4]

Ships that were out on the rivers fared even worse and caused a great fright. "We hear that no less than 30 sail of vessels are ashore in our river, among which are the ship *Caesar*, captain Miller; brig *Rachael*, captain Clay, at Reedy Island, the brig *Betsy*, captain Douglass, at Rombay Hook, the other were chiefly river craft, many of which are drove so high on the shore that they will be hardly worth the expense of launching."

The flood caused by the storm also affected smaller towns and settlements outside Philadelphia. In addition to the wind damage, the hurricane destroyed farmers' crops and killed their livestock. The powerful floods permanently altered the landscape by instantly eroding the surrounding river banks and environment. "We hear that the above storm has done considerable damage along the river, by breaking the banks of the meadows, drowning cattle, etc."[5]

Philadelphia was spared the damage that was sustained by such oceanfront cities as Norfolk. No lives were reported lost; nor would any more lives in America be lost to the Hurricane of Independence. The storm continued to weaken as it moved over land.

From the pulpit the next day, ministers might have spoken of the great gust from only hours before as a lesson for how the people must ask for divine mercy. Most people, though, began cleaning up the debris or accounting for lost items destroyed or missing due to the storm.

Life quickly returned to normal in the aftermath of the Hurricane of Independence. Congress assembled, and aside from perhaps some informal exchange of harrowing tales of traveling to Congress or the gust of a few days before, no comment was made. The hurricane did not seem the bad omen for the American cause that it could have been. From the view of Philadelphia in September 1775, the Revolutionary War was progressing rather well, with the Americans actually fighting the British to a stalemate up north.

The members of the Second Continental Congress soon began debating the course of America in its war with Great Britain. The hurricane did not wash away their troubles or momentous decisions that had to be made, such as whether to declare independence—a decision that would be made by the following summer as the British chased Washington across New York City and into New Jersey in headlong retreat. He encountered a nor'easter that swelled the Delaware River and masked his daring attack on Christmas night. The nor'easter was perhaps one critically important sign of Providence protecting the crumbling American army during its greatest test in the Revolutionary War. Still, Washington and his valiant citizen-soldiers proved that to win those blessings, they had to act with firmness and bravery in facing the trials of the Almighty. If anything, the Hurricane of Independence was only a sign of the greater tempest to come.

But both the disastrous Battle of New York and the stunning victories at Trenton and Princeton were in the future. For now, New Yorkers were assembling their forces for war and facing enemy ships in their surrounding waters. The men-of-war could not effect the conquest of New York by themselves, but they were intolerable symbols of British tyranny. Moreover, if the Continental Army did not decisively defeat the British in Boston, it probably was only a matter of time before the redcoats swept down into the important port city with enough troops to assert their authority and squash the incipient rebellion.

Chapter Twelve

THE HEROIC COLLEGIAN: HAMILTON IN NEW YORK

Under the cover of darkness during the night of August 23, 1775, as the Hurricane of Independence gathered strength in the Caribbean, a young New York college student joined several of his fellow students and citizens to do their patriotic duty. They assembled to carry out the wish of the assembly that "the cannon should be removed from the battery." The British warship *Asia* was patrolling New York harbor that night. The captain of the colonial artillery, John Lamb, posted several men to cover those who recovered the guns. They also were stationed to prevent a landing of redcoats. The minutes ticked by slowly as the men nervously peered into the darkness, searching for any sign of the *Asia*.

After about an hour, the British finally discovered the rebel plot that was afoot. After the colonials exchanged some musket fire with some British soldiers on smaller ships, the *Asia* wheeled into position broadside facing the Battery. In the stillness, the man-of-war unleashed a thunderous barrage against the shore with her nine-, eighteen-, and twenty-four-pound guns. Periodically, she tried to pummel the rebels with piles of grapeshot. The drummers added to the din by playing their war beat. The militiamen on shore did their best to return fire with their muskets, but to no effect.

As cannon balls smashed through houses and punctured the roof of Fraunces Tavern, the young man and his comrades scurried to complete their business, remaining cool under fire. He courageously helped to rescue several cannon from the Battery. Three rebels were hurt in the exchange of fire. The heavy bombardment finally drove off all the patriots. When Hercules Mulligan left his weapon back at the fort, the college student "went for it...with as much unconcern as if the vessel had not been there."[1]

The rebels escaped with twenty-one pieces of artillery that were mounted on carriages. Wisely, in the aftermath of the short battle, "women and children have been continually moving out of town with their most valuable effects."[2] The brave young man was an immigrant who was already fervently dedicated to the American cause of liberty. His name was Alexander Hamilton.

Even as a young man living on the Caribbean island of St. Croix, Hamilton sought glory on the battlefield of war that led him to accomplish such valiant acts as he did that night in New York. He dreamed of leaving his provincial island backwater to make his mark. He wrote his friend:

> My ambition is prevalent that I condemn the groveling and condition of a clerk or the like, to which my fortune condemns me and would willingly risk my life though not my character to exalt my station. I'm confident, Ned, that my youth excludes me from any hopes of immediate preferment nor do I desire it, but I mean to prepare the way for futurity. I'm no philosopher, you see, and may be justly said to build castles in the air.

With a mixture of youthful exuberance and naiveté, he stated, "I wish there was a war."[3]

On St. Croix, Hamilton was part of a very important link in the transatlantic trade network for sugar and slaves. Hamilton worked in the mercantile house of Beekman and Cruger, which imported colonial goods from New York and Philadelphia and exported them to Africa in exchange for slaves. He worked hard and quickly learned about trade, bookkeeping, currency exchange, sailing, and management. In late 1771, Nicholas Cruger left for New York, entrusting fourteen-year-old Hamilton with running the firm for five months.[4]

The presumptuous young man energetically seized control of the operation and ran a tight ship—maybe too tight. He insolently reprimanded his boss for shipping items of poor quality from North America: "Your Philadelphia flour is really very bad," he informed Cruger, "It could not have been very new when it was shipped."[5] Hamilton contemptuously dismissed Captain William Newton, who delivered a boatload of dying mules that could not be sold. In Hamilton's estimation, Captain Newton seemed "to want experience in such voyages."[6] Hamilton ripped into Cruger's brother, who was previously advised by Hamilton to arm the ships against raiders, but, "How he came to neglect it I don't know."[7] Cruger excused Hamilton's brashness because he recognized the young man's genius and knew that he was meant for better things.

Hamilton received his opportunity in 1772 when Reverend Hugh Knox, a classically-trained Presbyterian minister who attended Princeton University, moved to St. Croix to evangelize the island people, bringing them the religious revival called the Great Awakening that had swept the colonies in the previous decades. Knox represented a "New Lights" denomination that made emotional appeals for conversion.

Knox wanted to be a "patron who draws genius out of obscurity" and quickly found a willing subject in Hamilton. Knox opened his impressive library to Hamilton, who now had access to a broad range of classics. Through their conversations, Knox fired Hamilton's religious fervor and republican ideals from the Scottish Enlightenment.[8]

On August 31, 1772, a hurricane devastated the island of St. Croix. It was a turning point in Hamilton's life, propelling him to America. At the precocious age of fifteen, he wrote a letter to the *Royal Danish American Gazette* that grandly described his frightening experience in apocalyptic terms. "It began at dusk," he wrote, "and raged very violently till ten o'clock." The eye of the massive storm passed, giving a momentary reprieve until the worst part of the storm followed. In the darkness, the wind returned "with redoubled fury and continued so 'till near three o'clock in the morning." Thinking about that frightening night, he wrote, "Good God! What horror and destruction."

Young Hamilton's description of the destruction was chilling. It seemed to him as if "a total dissolution of nature was taking place. The roaring of the sea and wind, fiery meteors flying about it in the air, the prodigious glare of almost perpetual lightning, the crash of the falling houses, and the ear-piercing shrieks of the distressed were sufficient to strike astonishment into angels."

With considerable eloquence, Hamilton saw death personified riding in the winds. "Death comes rushing on in triumph veiled in a mantle of tenfold darkness. His unrelenting scythe, pointed, and ready for the stroke. On his right hand sits destruction, hurling the winds and belching forth flames. Calamity on his left threatening famine, disease, and distress of all kinds." With considerable understatement, he wrote, "How gloomy the prospect."

Death, indeed, had been in the hurricane. The aftermath was a pitiable sight to any observers who saw the people suffering in such deplorable conditions. Hamilton noted that, "A great part of the buildings throughout the island are leveled to the ground, almost all the rest very much shattered; several persons killed and numbers utterly ruined; whole families running about the streets, unknowing where to find a place of shelter; the sick exposed to the keenness of water and air without a bed to lie upon, or a dry covering to their bodies; and our harbors entirely bare. In a word, misery, in all its most hideous shapes, spread over the whole face of the country."

The chaos and desperation were reminiscent of the scenes of suffering in the recent disasters in New Orleans and Asia. Hamilton wrote, "Hark the bitter groans of distress. See sickness and infirmities exposed to the inclemencies of the wind and water! See tender infancy pinched with hunger and hanging on the mother's knee for food! See the unhappy mother's anxiety. Her poverty denies relief, her breast heaves with pangs of maternal pity, her heart is bursting, the tears gush down her cheeks. Oh sights of woe! Oh distress unspeakable. My heart bleeds, but I have no power to solace!"

In the wake of the storm, Hamilton reflected on what was truly important in life. He called on his fellow islanders to give generously to relieve the suffering of their neighbors. "O ye, who revel in affluence, see the afflictions of humanity and bestow your superfluity to ease them. Say not, we have suffered also, and thence withhold your compassion. What are your sufferings compared to those? Ye have still more than enough left. Act wisely. Succor the miserable and lay up a treasure in Heaven."

The survivors saw no end in sight for their suffering. Hamilton even felt guilty that he had lived through the hurricane and bemoaned his own condition while others were much worse off. He slipped into the language of the King James Bible to express his lamentations. With self-loathing, he flagellated himself for his joy at being alive. "Oh vain mortal! Check thy ill timed joy. Art thou so selfish to exult because thy lot is happy in a season of universal woe? Hast thou no feelings for the miseries of thy fellow creatures? And art thou incapable of the soft pangs of sympathetic sorrow? Look around thee and shudder at the view. See desolation and ruin where'er thou turnest thine eye. See they fellow-creatures pale and lifeless; their bodies mangled, their souls snatched into eternity."

In Hamilton's eyes, the hurricane was not a random event. Fired by the religion of the Great Awakening under Knox's tutelage, the young man saw the hand of Providence in the storm. He thought that God was punishing the people of St. Croix for their sins and reminding them of his omnipotence. Hamilton seemed to be delivering a written sermon for the readers that resembled the language of Jonathan Edwards' "Sinners in the Hands of An Angry God." Hamilton wrote:

> Where now, oh vile worm, is all thy boasted fortitude and resolution? What is become of thine arrogance and self-sufficiency? Why dost thou tremble and stand aghast? How humble, how helpless, how contemptible you now appear. And why? The jarring of elements—the discord of clouds? Oh! Impotent, presumptuous fool! How durst thou offend that Omnipotence, whose nod alone were sufficient to quell the destruction that hovers over thee, or crush thee into atoms? See thy wretched, helpless state, and learn to know thyself. Learn to know thy best support. Despise thyself, and adore thy God.

The alternative to sin was clear: Trust in God. All the survivors could do, in Hamilton's view, was to seek God's divine mercy and forgiveness for their sin:

Let the earth rend. Let the planets forsake their course. Let the sun be extinguished and the Heavens burst asunder. Yet what have I to dread? My staff can never be broken—in Omnipotence I trusted. He who gave the winds to blow, and the lightning to rage—even him have I always loved and served. His precepts have I observed. His commandments have I obeyed—and his perfections have I adored. He will snatch me from ruin. He will exalt me to the fellowship of angels and seraphs, and to the fullness of never ending joys.

Hamilton took umbrage in the mercy of God. The God who was punishing them also brought relief by ending the storm. "See, the Lord relents. He hears our prayer. The lightning ceases. The winds are appeased. The warring elements are reconciled and all things promise peace. The darkness dispelled and drooping nature revives at the approaching dawn. Look back, oh, my soul, look back and tremble. Rejoice at thy deliverance, and humble thyself in the presence of thy deliverer."[9]

Hamilton was no ordinary fifteen-year-old. Knox recognized that such a prodigy as Hamilton needed real academic training that the tiny island could not afford him. Knox and Cruger therefore arranged to fund a scholarship for Hamilton to attend Princeton, and Knox wrote several letters of introduction for his young protégé. He later wrote to Hamilton, "I have always had a just and secret pride in having advised you to go to America and in having recommended you to some of my old friends there."[10]

In late 1772, Hamilton sailed for America and landed in Boston, where the American Revolution had been building for a decade. He made his way to New York to see the merchants who held his scholarship money. However, when President John Witherspoon of

Princeton University rejected Hamilton's demand for studying in an accelerated program, he attended King's College in New York, even though it was a center of Anglicanism and Tory sentiment. In these cities, he witnessed the widespread resistance to British rule among the colonists, especially among merchants and seamen.

The city in which Alexander Hamilton found himself was perfectly suited to his youthful ambitions. New York was a major trading port with a population of more than 20,000 people. It was blessed with a deepwater port for the thousands of ships that sailed in and out of the harbor every year. It was an energetic city of commerce and prosperity, connecting the agricultural hinterland of upstate New York with the international market. Merchants tried to meet the insatiable European desire to sweeten their coffee, tea, and cocoa with Caribbean sugar or to wear fashionable furs from Canada. They also loaded the ships with rum, flaxseed, barrel staves, pig iron, and grain in massive quantities.

John Adams described what he considered the undesirably fast pace of life in New York: "There is no modesty, no attention to one another. They talk very loud, very fast, and altogether. If they ask you a question before you can utter three words of your answer, they will break out upon you again—and talk away."[11]

There were visible signs of commerce everywhere in the city. The unmistakable tall masts and billowing sails of ships laden with goods filled the East River harbor. The waterfront housed the Merchants' Exchange where traders gathered worriedly to check the prices of their goods as they tried to outguess the market. Artisans labored away in nearby shipyards and tan yards. Goods were hawked in local markets, stored in warehouses, or loaded and unloaded on the docks.

The poor lived in stinking dwellings and drank at seedy taverns. Fights erupted among drunken sailors in the streets, which were lined with abundant whorehouses where prostitutes plied their wares to sailors whose pockets were filled with their pay. Cutthroats and thieves searched out potential victims from among the crowds. Smallpox and other diseases frequently swept through this part of town—as did British Navy press gangs grabbing unfortunates to serve unwillingly aboard their ships.

Merchants, to be sure, lived in wealthier parts of the city or bought large estates out in the country. They attended the theater and dined at establishments such as Fraunces Tavern. Dressing fashionably, they followed the latest European tastes.

Merchants performed many different economic roles. They acted as wholesalers and retailers for the local and international markets, importing and exporting an endless variety of goods. Seeking to diversify their wealth and keep their investments active, they owned the ships that traveled the oceans with their goods. They acted as bankers, leading money for other commercial activities. And, sometimes, they insured ocean voyages, which were threatened with storms, piracy, and losses stemming from other causes.[12]

At other times, merchants made extra money smuggling their goods. Merchants and ship captains went to great lengths conspiring to evade British trade regulations. Secret doors in ships and houses masked chambers filled with illicit goods.

In the wake of the French and Indian War in 1763, a severe economic depression struck New York. Poor weather led to dismal agricultural crops that negatively impacted the economy, including the import-export activities of the merchants. British trade regulations and American boycotts further caused trade to collapse and demand for artisan goods to wither. Ravages of cholera and hunger further exacerbated the suffering and anger of New Yorkers.[13]

Despite their social distinctions, the suffering merchants and artisans formed a broad coalition that resisted British tyranny. When

Parliament passed the Stamp Act, these colonists organized the Sons of Liberty and went into the streets for a decade of turbulent street riots and demonstrations of Revolutionary fervor. They marched in the streets for their liberty, and more often than not, fought violently with the redcoats stationed in New York who were visible symbols of British tyranny.

The New York Assembly denounced the tax by appealing to the principle of "no taxation without representation." New Yorkers could not be taxed by a distant Parliament 3,000 miles away without their consent. It was, therefore, unconstitutional to "impose taxes upon the subjects *here*, by laws to be passed *there*." On May 24, 1764, the Assembly warned that "if the colonist is taxed without his consent, he will, perhaps, ask a change."14

A more moderate response from New York merchants included a boycott of British goods to apply economic pressure for repeal. The Stamp Act deeply affected merchants whose goods, legal documents, and land deeds were taxed. Moreover, as ship owners, their captains needed to have their bills of lading and clearance papers stamped before sailing. Merchants spearheaded the boycott, with hundreds agreeing to nonimportation at a meeting in a coffeehouse on the night of October 31, 1765. They pressured others not to buy British goods.

People began appearing all over New York in "homespun" clothing, ostentatiously displaying their patriotism and rejecting British luxuries. "All pride in dress seems to be laid aside, and he that does not appear in homespun, or at lest a turned coat, is looked on with an evil eye." There was a movement to produce and buy manufactured goods in America rather than importing them from Britain. As for British goods, "Shopkeepers will buy none...merchants will not clear out a vessel." The boycott had its desired effect—British imports to America plummeted, and British merchants cried foul.15

Another form of moderate resistance was the Stamp Act Congress that assembled in New York. Delegates from twelve colonies traveled to New York and stayed at the houses of merchants while they deliberated on the proper response to the Stamp Act. They declared that, "It is inseparably essential to the freedom of a people, and the undoubted right of Englishmen, that no taxes shall be imposed on them but with their own consent."[16] The Congress symbolized the growing unity among the colonists that answered Benjamin Franklin's cartoon "JOIN OR DIE" back in 1754 while pushing his failed Albany Plan of Union. In the face of British oppression, colonists began to be united by the idea of liberty.[17]

James McEvers was a New York merchant who had sought a lucrative royal appointment as stamp collector but quit his position even before any stamps arrived in the city. Hearing of terrible violence in other colonies, McEvers told the lieutenant governor of New York, Cadwallader Colden, to hide the stamps in Fort George and find some other fool to fill the position. The merchant feared that, "My house would have been pillaged, my person abused, and his Majesty's revenue impaired." He thought the hatred of the populace would be detrimental to his business as would the possibility of having his £20,000 worth of inventory in his warehouses destroyed.[18]

More violent reactions however erupted all over the city as thousands of New Yorkers protested the tax and forcibly prevented its collection. On the night of October 23, 1765, a ship bearing stamps had to be escorted by the British Navy as it sailed off lower Manhattan and dropped anchor off Fort George, protected by the battery's guns. A mob of two thousand enraged New Yorkers assembled by torchlight to protest the landing of the stamps.

A week later, the day before the tax was scheduled to take effect, "A mob in three squads went through the streets, crying 'liberty,' at the same time breaking the lamps and threatening particulars that they would the next night pull down their houses. Some thousands of windows broke. Major James of the artillery threatened to be buried alive."[19]

The next day, the mob became even more threatening. Two thousand artisans, sailors, and merchants gathered with clubs, thirsty for violence. They broke into the governor's coach house and stole a chariot. They pulled the chariot with an effigy of Colden perched atop through the town to the gates of Fort George where there was a tense standoff with loaded cannon aimed at the screaming mob. Three hundred carpenters threatened to use their expertise to tear down the gates and assault the troops within. Within sight of the frightened troops, the crowd erected a gibbet to hang the effigies and then burned them and the carriage in a wicked bonfire. The mob proceeded to ransack the house of Major James, the commander of the garrison, breaking windows, tearing down walls, and looting wine and other valuables.[20]

Colden read an anonymous message warning that if he took action against the people, "you'll bring your grey hairs with sorrow to the grave, you'll die a martyr to your own villainy, and be hanged…upon a signpost as a momento to all wicked governors, and…every man that assists you shall surely be put to death."[21]

Over the next few months, more stamps were quietly slipped into the city, though very little revenue was actually collected. Mobs paraded more effigies, with the likenesses of British commander Thomas Gage and Prime Minister George Grenville, through the streets until they went up in smoke. The Sons of Liberty continued to menace local stamp collectors and those from other states who had sought refuge in New York. Also threatened were any New Yorkers who were even presumed to have dealings with the British. As long as the British persisted in attempting to collect the tax, there was no end in sight to the chaotic violence.[22]

The following year, New York received word from merchant ships bringing news from England of the repeal of the Stamp Act. It seemed as if the American boycott had had its desired effect. British merchants were deprived of a huge source of trade and pressured Parliament for the repeal. Although it admitted the failure of the Stamp Act, Parliament passed the Declaratory Act professing to legislate for the colonies "in all cases whatsoever." New Yorkers greeted the repeal of the hated taxes with the tolling of bells, the making of toasts, and the firing of rounds of cannon.

The patriotic storm did not abate with the repeal of the Stamp Act, however. The British antagonized many colonists, including New Yorkers, by stationing troops there in peacetime. The troops originally were intended to enforce the Proclamation Line of 1763, which was intended to prevent further American settlement west of the Appalachian Mountains after the French and Indian War. When those troops were used to quell the violent mobs, the colonists saw them as a repressive standing army in time of peace contrary to the British constitution.

General Thomas Gage, commander-in-chief of British forces in America, settled in New York in 1764. He had fought with General Edward Braddock and a young George Washington at the disastrous battle at Fort Duquesne during the French and Indian War, where Braddock was killed and Washington rallied the troops despite having horses shot out from under him and several bullets pierce his coat. Gage then served as governor of Montreal before coming to New York.

Commander Gage and his forces could not control the city's merchants and artisans who stood at the middle of the furor with the redcoats. The British Navy routinely swept the docks that netted castaway sailors and innocent colonists who were taken in the raids. In July 1764, an incident erupted in New York Harbor when several well-known fishermen who supplied the local markets were seized and brought on board a British ship. When the captain went ashore a few days later, a mob descended upon his barge and burned it. The navy quickly released the fishermen to avoid further trouble.

But there were more confrontations since the British kept impressing sailors not just from New York but from almost any ship that happened to be in New York Harbor. With furious mobs protecting their own, it became a dangerous business for British captains to appear onshore for long—one officer was "pretty roughly handled by some of the populace."[23]

American shipbuilders and sailors were further incensed when British troops took scarce jobs while they were off duty. The Americans hated the competition for jobs while the depression raged. Drunken fistfights broke out in the waterfront taverns and streets as insults were frequently exchanged and tempers escalated rapidly. Merchant seamen felt bitter toward the customs officials and their taxes, with trade suffering under the weight of a boycott and depression.

Anger was directed not only at the redcoats but at the New Yorkers who employed them while the unemployed locals struggled to feed their families. "Whosoever seriously considers the impoverished state of this city, especially of many of the poor inhabitants of it, must be greatly surprised at the conduct of such of them as employ the soldiers, when there are a number of [city people] that want employment to support their distressed families."[24]

One thing the New York Assembly and residents refused to do was to quarter the British troops as ordered to do by Great Britain. The Quartering Act of 1765 required the colonists to supply barracks and provisions for the redcoats. About fifteen hundred British troops were in New York, and the assembly complained that it could not afford to comply with the act because of the depression. Moreover, it steadfastly rejected the demand to pay for the very troops that took away their liberties. The assembly explained that it would be "guilty of a breach of [the] most sacred trust" of the people if it quartered the troops.[25]

The violence continued. Liberty poles, which were massive logs erected with scrawled patriotic messages, were the focus of much of the tension. New Yorkers proudly and defiantly raised them near British barracks while holding celebrations for liberty. Having endured daily taunts and violence, the troops usually responded by tearing or cutting them down with an axe. In the heat of a night in August 1766, a mob of almost three thousand amassed when word spread that a Liberty Pole had been knocked down. The crowd hurled curses and projectiles at the British troops, who affixed bayonets to protect themselves and made ready to charge. A bloody clash was barely averted.[26]

In 1767, Parliament passed a new round of taxes—the Townshend Acts—that came closely on the heels of the repeal of the Stamp Act. Merchants patriotically announced another boycott of British goods even though they were hurt by the ensuing precipitous decline in trade. Unity among the colonies started to break down, however, when each colony would only agree to the boycott if the other states followed it as well.

New York merchants sent petitions to England to protest the taxes, but they were summarily ignored. Even more galling than the rejected petitions and taxes were the new regulations that affected their purses and violated their constitutional rights. A Board of Customs Collections was established in the colonies and officials were authorized to search the warehouses and homes of merchants for smuggled goods without evidence.[27]

Mobs, of course, took to the street to protest the new taxes. In November 1768, in solidarity with Bostonians, New Yorkers paraded effigies of Royal Governor Francis Bernard of Massachusetts and of the Boston sheriff and then burned them. In early 1770, the tension and violence that had occurred in New York throughout the previous half-decade exploded. Only weeks before redcoats would fire on a crowd in Boston and kill five colonists, a major battle erupted in New York.

In January, the colonists and the British each issued pamphlets debating the issue of British soldiers working in their spare time. The exchange of words escalated to brawling in the streets when the British tried several times to assault a liberty pole standing on the green, including by filling the pole with gunpowder to blow it to pieces. Several nights later, the redcoats not only chopped the pole down but cut it into several pieces.

On January 19, 1770, in what would be called the Battle of Golden Hill, thousands of New Yorkers angrily poured into the streets, spoiling for a fight. The British obliged them. Cornered troops, withstanding threats and hurled rocks, heard the command, "Soldiers, draw your bayonets and cut your way through them!" Cutting and slashing, they indiscriminately attacked the crowd. Women and children were among the victims who were wounded. Sailors and fishermen lost fingers and received deep gashes across their faces. One was killed.[28]

The melee claimed injured victims on both sides until the greatly outnumbered British beat a hasty retreat, fighting their way with reinforcements into their barracks. The Battle of Golden Hill was over, though the crisis remained. Like a thumb in the eye of the British, a patriotic mob numbering in the thousands soon defiantly erected an iron-reinforced sixty-foot liberty pole that was impervious to British saws.[29]

Simultaneously, a constitutional crisis broke out when revolutionary leader Alexander McDougall was arrested in early 1770. McDougall was a member of the merchant class who helped to lead the resistance against the British. As a young man, he joined the crew of a ship and eventually earned the command of an eight-gun sloop for the Royal Navy. While battling and seizing ships from Britain's foes, he won enough prize money to begin a respectable career in commerce. McDougall diversified his interests to expand his wealth and sold St. Croix sugar for Caribbean planters (and had indirect ties to Alexander Hamilton). He owned ships that transported many of his goods and owned a tavern on the New York waterfront. He also speculated in land.

When he was arrested and imprisoned for publishing a libelous Revolutionary tract, McDougall's followers supported his patriotic cause. Evoking the arrest of John Wilkes in 1745 for Whiggish literature in England, the Sons of Liberty feted McDougall. Forty-five of them drank (a whopping) forty-five toasts to McDougall and American patriotism. Forty-five supporters ate forty-five pounds of meat with him on the forty-fifth day of the year (February 14) in 1770.[30]

In the autumn of 1773, after word arrived in America that Parliament passed the Tea Act, merchants, sailors, and ordinary New Yorkers boycotted imported tea. A group called the Liberty Boys praised ship captains and merchants whose "prudent conduct in refusing the freight of the East India Company merits the approbation and applause of every well wisher to the liberties of this or any other country."

Isaac Sears was a merchant who helped lead the resistance of this group of New Yorkers. He was a peddler as a youth, and learned to hawk his wares. After apprenticing at sea, he became a captain who traded in some of the most significant Atlantic ports from Halifax to New York to the West Indies. He was a privateer for the British during the French and Indian War, amassing enough of a fortune to make investments (and marry into a merchant family) in trade, ships, and taverns after the war.[31]

Sears and other merchants mobilized the Sons of Liberty and a group calling itself "The Mohawks" to warn the governor that ships arriving with tea better not unload their cargo or there would be trouble. McDougall even made an overt threat, asking, "What if we prevent the landing and kill the governor and all the council?" A member of the council advised the ships' captains that thousands were massing on the city's wharves and attempting to land the tea would thus expose "the lives of your crew as well as your ship to destruction by an exasperated and irresistible multitude."[32] The governor learned the truth of this when a mob shortly burned his house to the ground after thoroughly looting it. On December 21, the ubiquitous Paul Revere rode into New York spreading word of the Boston Tea Party.

The *London* sailed into New York the following spring loaded with eighteen boxes of tea. New Yorkers were tripping over themselves to be the first to dump the tea. A crowd beat the Mohawks (including several sea captains led by McDougall) to the tea and threw it overboard to wild cheers from hundreds of people who gathered on the docks. Fortunately for the captain, he decided to vanish before he was next.[33] One New Yorker stated that, "The political sky at this place is cloudy." He might have said "stormy" instead.[34]

When the New York delegates departed later that year for Philadelphia to join the First Continental Congress, citizens accompanied them with "colors flying, music playing, and loud huzzas at the end of each street." There was a procession down to the wharf near the Merchants' Exchange. While the delegates pulled away, the Battery fired its cannon in salute. The jubilant crowd lingered in nearby taverns to toast the work of the Congress, their liberties, and "the good of the common cause."[35]

The trade bans on Britain that the Continental Congress passed further inflamed passions in New York. Some frustrated loyal merchants, such as James Beekman, bridled under the trade restrictions and complained to their British agents that they could not ship their goods. Beekman averred that, "The present state of our public affairs has put a total stop to trade." Several patriotic merchants and sea-captains refused to ship troops and military supplies to Boston for the British. It was not hard to see why. Public threats were issued against any who would aid and abet the enemy. "Should any miscreant aid the enemies of this country to subvert her liberties, he must not be surprised if that vengeance overtakes him, which is the reward justly due to parricides."[36]

This was the riotous condition in which Alexander Hamilton found New York City when he came to King's College. The patriotic fervor running through the city soon swept up the young immigrant. Hamilton attended and spoke at a Sons of Liberty meeting where a liberty pole was raised. He supposedly gave an inspired speech to the assembled crowd, denouncing the "Intolerable" Acts (as the colonists labeled the Coercive Acts) and calling for a boycott of British goods. Americans must defend their liberty, he warned, or "fraud, power, and the most odious oppression will rise triumphant over right, justice, social happiness, and freedom." The crowd was electrified by his words and rooted the fiery young man on with the cheer, "It's a collegian!"[37]

In late 1774, Samuel Seabury, a New York Anglican minister and Loyalist, issued an abrasive attack upon the assembled Continental Congress. Seabury published a series of pamphlets under the pseudonym, "A. W. Farmer" (i.e., "a Westchester farmer"). The Continental Congress was a "venomous brood of scorpions," he charged, and local farmers should ignore any trade boycott because it would lead to "the commencement of their ruin."[38]

The eighteen-year-old Hamilton took up the challenge and wrote two pamphlets against Seabury, "A Full Vindication of

Congress" and "The Farmer Refuted," in which he made the case for American rights. In "The Farmer Refuted," published on February 23, 1775, Hamilton argued that Parliament had "no right to govern us," because the colonists had the rights of Englishmen and could only be governed by their consent. "An authority is assumed over us, which we by no means assent to…we have no part in making the laws, that are to bind us." When Parliament violated the liberties of the colonists, they were reduced to a state of slavery.

Hamilton also argued that Americans had natural rights from God, which Britain was violating. Britain therefore was tyrannical, and the Americans had "no obligation to obedience." In an expression rivaling the eloquence of Jefferson's Declaration of Independence, Hamilton wrote, "The sacred rights of mankind are not to be rummaged for, among old parchments, or musty records. They are written, as with a sun beam, in the whole *volume* of human nature, by the hand of the divinity itself; and can never be erased or obscured by mortal power."[39]

Only days after minutemen battled redcoats at Lexington and Concord, New York patriots stormed into the streets "with drums beating and colors flying…inviting all mankind to take up arms in defense of the 'injured rights and liberties of America.'" They marched down to the arsenal and robbed it of over one thousand muskets and bayonets. Only a few weeks later, the menacing sixty-four-gun British warship, *Asia*, dropped anchor in the East River. New York was like a powder-keg.[40]

Hamilton actually risked life and limb to protect the rights of Tories who were set upon by angry mobs. Patriotic Americans constantly issued threats against Tories: "Fly for your lives or anticipate your doom by becoming your own executioners." During the night of May 10, 1775, a drunken, angry crowd stormed King's College to tar and feather its Tory president, Myles Cooper.

Hamilton chastised the mob for threatening Cooper. This impromptu lecture gave the president the time to escape bodily harm and make his way to a British ship for protection.[41]

Hamilton later wrote a letter to John Jay, who at that time was serving in the Second Continental Congress as a representative of New York, expressing alarm at those who were wantonly violating rights as much as the British were. He told Jay:

> While the passions of men are worked up to an uncommon pitch, there is a great danger of fatal extremes. The same state of the passions which fits the multitude, who have not a sufficient stock of reason and knowledge to guide them, for opposition to tyranny and oppression, very naturally leads them to a contempt and disregard for all authority...When the minds of these are loosened from their attachment to ancient establishments and courses, they seem to grow giddy and are apt more or less to run into anarchy.[42]

Hamilton stood for an ordered liberty in which Revolutionary freedom was tempered by virtue and natural principles of justice. He was shocked by the licentious mobs run amok.

That same night, the incompatible pair of Benedict Arnold and Ethan Allen captured Fort Ticonderoga, which stood between Lake Champlain and Lake George. At four o'clock in the morning, Allen commanded eighty-three men who stormed the decrepit fort and woke the sleeping British garrison with "three huzzas." Allen reported that he had found the captain at his bedroom door "with his breeches in his hand, when I ordered him to deliver to me the fort instantly." The British officer had little choice but to capitulate though he asked Allen under whose authority he was acting. Allen replied grandly, "In the name of the great Jehovah and the Continental Congress." Not satisfied by Allen's answer, the captain tried to speak again when Allen's "drawn sword over his head" shut him up and caused him to surrender the fort. With a garrison of only two officers and fifty men, who resided there with their wives and children, the British could not muster an effective defense, and the fort fell without a shot.

Allen and Arnold met while they were both moving on the fort for its desperately needed artillery and military stores. Ethan Allen led his Green Mountain Boys from their disputed territory between New York and New Hampshire in modern-day Vermont. They were backwoodsmen who were tough and handy with a rifle. Allen had threatened a British soldier with human sacrifice, warning "to offer a burnt sacrifice to the gods of the world."[43] Arnold labeled them as undisciplined, savage "wild men." Nevertheless, the Connecticut Committee of Safety authorized him to seize the fort.

Arnold was a wealthy New Haven merchant who was a graceful, charming commander. He persuaded the Massachusetts Committee of Safety to allow him to raise troops on the frontier and take the fort. When the two ambitious, headstrong men met before the attack, they squabbled over the command until they finally agreed to share it. They captured more than one hundred pieces of artillery but did not have the manpower to move it anywhere. They proceeded to gain control over two nearby forts. Their success was welcome news to the Second Continental Congress assembling in Philadelphia and enthusiastically cheered.[44]

During the summer and autumn of 1775, New Yorkers mobilized for war with their captured weapons and prepared for an assault while Boston was fighting the British army. Hamilton poured over military books and joined the Corsicans, a volunteer militia company that had revolutionary slogans of "Liberty or Death" stitched onto their clothing.[45] The following year, however, more than thirty-two thousand British troops would pour into New York and sweep the patriots out of the city like a fierce gale.

The Hurricane of Independence was heading north in the early morning hours of September 3. The Americans and British were both in the city, just as they were in Virginia. But, unlike the colony to the south, the Hurricane of Independence steered clear of this important site of violence. The reasons why the city was spared made understanding the ways of Providence even more difficult.

Chapter Thirteen

WHITHER THE HURRICANE OF INDEPENDENCE?

N ew York apparently was spared the effects of the Hurricane of Independence. After Philadelphia, the hurricane went quiet for a while, with few recordings of its effect until later in northern New England. Where it went during this time is uncertain. It might have spiraled toward the Atlantic since it had been hugging the coast during most of its journey across the colonies. However, David Ludlum, a meteorologist who wrote briefly about the hurricane in 1963, did not think so. Ludlum wrote that, "New England lay well to the east of the central track of the hurricane."[1] He thought that the storm hit the sparsely populated territory of upstate New York where wealthy merchants had great landholdings, rather than New York City.

If the hurricane hit New York, the weakening storm simply may not have been recognized as a hurricane by the mostly sleeping population. Many probably simply thought that a particularly bad series of thunderstorms were passing over. Because it rained along much of the Atlantic Seaboard during the previous week, this was not an unreasonable assumption. The winds were still gusting to maybe forty or fifty miles per hour in the quickly disorganizing tropical storm. It also was moving fast over land, much faster than the leisurely pace as it crossed warm waters of the equator. The people on land finally were being spared the wrath of the hurricane.

On the other hand, out at sea, ships were taking a beating in the Atlantic Ocean. A week later, on September 10, large swells became enormous waves. The rough seas threw around cargo of all sorts in the holds. Personal effects rolled across the decks when the boats rose and fell with every huge wave. The passengers were scared stiff. They were ordered off the decks as the sailors prepared for the approaching fury. A rapid succession of thuds could be heard above the screaming winds as the crewmen cut away the mainmasts before the storm tore them down and threatened the ships. Large items were tied down to prevent them from becoming dangerous projectiles. The captains took charge. Their lives and those of their crew (and any passengers on board the ships) were at stake. There was nowhere to run and no way to outrun the tempest. Soon, dark clouds enveloped them.

The sailors who braved the oceans were not surprised at the appearance of the storm. In addition to the inherent constant dangers of a life at sea (not all of them caused by nature), sailors understood what is known as "hurricane season." From the late summer until the winter, sailing in the Caribbean and Atlantic Oceans was an especially hazardous business. Men were washed overboard and killed in the violent thrashing of wind and waves.

All the ships were tempest-tossed when they encountered this destructive hurricane in the same general area of the Atlantic. The surviving ships' captains concurred that the storm was in the neighborhood of latitude 35° and longitude 70°, almost directly east of the

Outer Banks where the Hurricane of Independence made landfall. They all agreed that the hurricane had raised nature's fury against them on the same dates—September 10, 11, or 12, depending on their location. From the accounts provided in the press, it was a wonder any sailors made it out alive. In fact, many did not.

The most thorough and dramatic account of the hurricane was written down by Captain Robinson of the ironically named brig, *Fair Lady*. His logbook records the traumatic experience of the hurricane in the open sea:

> Sept 11th. Violent gale and high sea, scudded under bare poles, broached to, and was in a dangerous situation.

> Sept 12th. Half after one, the gale exceeding violent, cut away the maintopmast, shipped on a heavy sea which shifted the ballast and laid the vessel on her beam ends, cut away the mainmast, but she not righting, and we expecting the next sea would turn her keel upwards, cut away the foremast—when she righted a little—went to work below, and after some time, but throwing the ballast to windward, through God's blessing got her righted. The gale still increased till 6 o'clock—so violent that it was almost impossible for a man to stand the deck without being lashed. At 8 o'clock, the storm began to abate, but a very dangerous sea, continued till the afternoon. Saw a sail two leagues to windward, made a signal of distress, lost sight of her in the night, and saw her no more.[2]

Captain Cherdevoyne of the schooner, *Jenny*, had set out for Kingston, Jamaica, two weeks before. On September 10, in latitude 35°, longitude 69°50, the captain "met with a most violent gale of wind, in which he lost his mainmast, boom, quarter rails, etc., with all his stock off his decks." During the storm, Captain Cherdevoyne lost "three very fine horses" washed overboard "including one of which was the well-known coarser Auctioneer." With a great deal of difficulty, the crew managed to save seven other horses. The *Jenny* limped on the seas "with much of its cargo missing."[3]

On September 12, Cherdevoyne spoke with other captains who suffered a similar fate at sea. He reported that a Captain Harriot was also bound for Jamaica when the hurricane caused him to lose "everything off his decks, and stove his boat." A few days later, Cherdevoyne learned from another captain of a brig from Baltimore headed for Falmouth and a Captain Peterson from Philadelphia sailing for Jamaica that they were both blasted by the storm and somehow struggled to land back in New York.

A Captain George Stewart was sailing north in the sloop *Recovery* when he saw several dismasted ships floating aimlessly with the currents. At times, the ships were so damaged that they could not readily be identified. On September 11, "in latitude 34°13, longitude 75°30," Stewart saw the wreck of a vessel supposed to have been a single-decked sloop, loaded with wine, as the water to leeward was discolored. Her quarter deck was off, the mast and boom at her bows. It gave new meaning to Homer's "wine-dark sea."[4]

Other flotsam was seen in the wide waters of the Atlantic. One crew noticed a large quantity of onions floating in the waves. They also saw spermaceti candles (manufactured from the blubber of sperm whales) returned to the sea. Countless other objects that had not yet sunk—sails, casks of rum, an occasional drowned person—were hazarded upon by crews who sadly considered the fate of ships— including possibly their own someday—wrecked by hurricanes.[5]

One vessel, the *Snow Georgia*, later floated into New York Harbor after a harrowing transatlantic crossing of ten weeks topped off by the massive hurricane. The forty terrified passengers aboard went belowdecks to ride out the winds and waves that lashed her. For hours, they thought they would perish. Their horrible seasickness made them almost pray for a quick end. When the winds calmed, they were greatly fatigued from the encounter. The ship lost her mainmast, the sails were torn to shreds, and it was not seaworthy.[6]

Another ship, the *Nancy*, bearing passengers from Britain, fared much worse. The unfortunate souls on board were already tormented by thirst, starvation, scurvy, and other diseases after fourteen weeks at sea. Twenty of the ninety people on the ship already had died and had a sickly crew when the hurricane unmercifully grabbed it in its clutches. It was dismasted, further endangering the lives of all onboard. Finally, the *Rosamond* saw it drifting and supplied them with a much-needed seventy gallons of water and a barrel of bread, which they ravenously consumed.[7]

Seeing fellow sailors distressed at sea brought out the best of the brotherhood among sailors. At times, however, captains piloted ships that were too badly damaged and could not offer any assistance to anyone else. Sometimes the weather conditions prevented captains from helping another ship because they were too busy looking after their own. Just after the hurricane swirled off, on September 11, Captain Fenton from Coracoa reported that he "saw a ship in great distress" at latitude 36°30. The ship was in a bad way, having "lost her fore and main masts about half down, and the mizzen quite gone." Fenton would have offered help but "the sea ran so high he could afford her no assistance." He described the ship so that others who came across it would help if they did not otherwise notice the obvious destruction.[8]

Others were in fact able to take survivors aboard their ships, offering a means to avert an otherwise certain death. When the sloop *Catharine* was destroyed by the hurricane on September 10, Jamaican Captain Huntington took all of the crew onboard except the first-mate and cabin boy who were washed into steep seas and immediately drowned. On September 11, a Captain Winning and crew from Liverpool were forced to abandon ship because of the damage it sustained and were happily rescued by a Captain Cole who brought them safely to New York.[9]

On board the *Fair Lady*, the crew battled the elements for close to a month after being nearly overwhelmed by the meteorological leviathan. The ship barely survived though crewmembers were lost. They depended upon the selfless generosity of other captains during the struggle to return to port:

> 13th. Found we had lost great part of our water, came to allowance with the remainder—employed in securing our ballast and erecting a jury foremast, which was completed the 15th. On the 12th, from our jury mast head saw a sail to N. being short of bread and water, and the weather calm, hoisted out the yawl, with 4 hands who at 7 got on board her, found to be a schooner from Casco Bay bound to Barbados. On the 15th, they had seen one of the King's ships dismasted. They supplied us with 25 gallons of water and a small quantity of bisquit.

> 20th. Spoke with a sloop who had spoke with *Snow Aesop*, Captain John Forbes, from Eustatia, bound to Holland, who in Lat. 35°6 and Long. 64°22 had been in a severe gale of wind, which hove her on her beam ends, stove in his stern, washed the carpenter overboard, and almost killed the captain, whom they supplied with a small quantity of provisions.

23rd. Fresh gale and a high sea, John Garvan, mariner, fell overboard, threw over to save him a hen coop, and hoisted out the yawl, but she filled, and parting her painter, both man and boat were lost.

25th. Spoke with ship *Recovery*, Capt. Kyle, from Philadelphia for Cork. He supplied us with a cask of bread, a cask of water, and some small stores.

The weatherbeaten crew arrived in New York on October 9.[10] Theirs was a testament to the courage of the sailors of the day.

It was possible that some of the ship captains, merchants, and planters who lost goods aboard the ships were insured for their losses. Because of the insecurity of shipping items thousands of miles across the ocean, insurance protected against any unforeseen problems. Those who did not want to purchase insurance because of the cost had other alternatives to lessen the risk. They could avoid shipping during hurricane season, but this was not a real viable alternative while valuable perishable crops could be ruined. Goods also could be loaded on different ships to prevent having an entire load wiped out. Partial insurance also was available at a lower cost. Insurers, however, understood that hurricane season could wreck havoc with their profits from multiple losses and therefore doubled their rates.[11]

Hurricanes severely affected trade routes in the Atlantic. News of a late August hurricane traveled from Alexander Hamilton's sugar-producing island home of St. Croix, only a few hundred miles northwest of Dominica. This was the Hurricane of Independence. "We hear from St. Croix that a hurricane had happened in the West Indies," a published letter from New York reported, "which occasioned many vessels from that and the neighboring ports to put to sea." The ripple effect meant that commerce was disrupted throughout the Atlantic.[12]

Ships' masts had been chopped down or shattered by the elements and sails had been ripped asunder, rendering sailing impossible and leaving ships to the fortune of tides or the chance of coming across another ship. Sailors were lucky to arrive at a port for repairs after their ships took such massive damage. At their wharves, New Yorkers could witness the destruction leveled by this mysterious second hurricane.

As an important port in the Atlantic trade, the effects of a major hurricane were widely reported in New York among the captains, sailors, and merchants who took part in those trade networks. Haunted word passed quickly between passing ships or in the taverns of the harbor that a disastrous hurricane at sea had done significant damage to several boats and their cargo from several different ports of call.

Ships that departed from New York Harbor in the preceding days and weeks were forced to return after they barely survived the hurricane. Thomas Allen Jr. came back to New York when the heavy seas and strong winds ruined a pump onboard his vessel. He wrote to his father that, "A heavy gale of wind…obliged us to hoist our pump again."[13] The schooner *Jenny* reportedly "limped back into New York greatly damaged."[14]

This second hurricane, which was leveling destruction in the Atlantic off the coast of America a week after the Hurricane of Independence, maintained its awesome power by hovering over the Atlantic rather than going ashore. Therefore, it did not weaken in the same way as the Hurricane of Independence. The second hurricane might have lost some energy the farther north it went into slightly colder oceans, but it was still a formidable storm compared to the dwindling tropical storm coming upon New England. Ships' captains, crews, and hapless passengers caught in the stormy weather were not very interested in such speculation about which storm it was. People on land only saw whispers of the strength of this second hurricane as evidence in the form of demolished ships straggled back into port with desperate, half-dead survivors.

The second, massive monster of a hurricane was pounding its way up toward the Northeast in the wake of the Hurricane of Independence in the late summer of 1775. But, would it unleash its wrath against the British or Americans, or both warring parties facing each other off in Boston? As the hurricanes closed in on Boston, they threatened to hit the center of action against the British.

More than 4,000 people were fated to die.

Chapter Fourteen

WAR ERUPTS

Only a day after hitting North Carolina, the Hurricane of Independence left New York behind and raced into New England. As it thundered ahead, it converged upon the center of fighting that erupted between the redcoats and the colonists. After a decade of tumult, the Americans were ready to defend their liberties with arms. The British were equally determined to suppress the rebellion against its authority with force.

The hurricane first swept over Newport, Rhode Island, in the morning of September 3, 1775. Ezra Stiles, Puritan minister, amateur scientist, and future president of Yale University, recorded his meteorological observations in his weather diary that morning. Stiles wrote down that "the wind went around from northeast at 10:00." By 2:30, the wind came around from the southeast. "Plentiful rain" was dumped on the sleepy little college town of a few hundred homes.[1] Between the war and "it being a very rainy day," he had "not above half or two-thirds my usual congregation." He bemoaned that it was "a day of distress!" He prayed, "The good Lord direct all our ways and protect us."[2] The wind continued whipping around throughout the afternoon, but the sky soon cleared up revealing a deep blue view overhead.

Stiles was raised in New Haven, Connecticut, by a Yale-educated Puritan minister, Isaac Stiles. The sermons that young Stiles heard from the pulpit included his father's understanding that the beautiful universe was proof of God's creation. "The Earth (no less than the Heavens) with…its useful atmosphere and all its beautiful apparatus and rich furniture, the winged choristers which sing among the branches, every beast of the forest and the cattle upon a thousand hills…these all loudly proclaim the wisdom, the power, and the goodness of the munificent creator."[3]

The Stiles home and congregation was steeped in orthodox Puritanism. It stressed the doctrine of predestination—the idea that everyone was saved or damned before they were born and no amount of good works could alter that fact. In order to discover if one was a member of "the elect," each Puritan went through a rigorous self-examination and hoped for a religious conversion. No Puritan could be assured of salvation however, and many went to their deathbeds lamenting the state of their souls. When George Whitefield preached in New Haven during the Great Awakening, Isaac Stiles remained a steadfast "Old Light" even though he lost some members of his congregation.[4]

The emotional preaching of the Great Awakening may have presented a challenge to the New England Puritans, but science did not. Most Puritans thought that the new science of the Scientific Revolution was in perfect harmony with their religious doctrine. The natural law discoveries of Copernicus, Newton, and Kepler all were testimony that God created an orderly universe and was revealed in nature. Human reason provided the means by which nature could be studied, understood, and predicted through the experimental method.

Cotton Mather, for example, voraciously read all of the latest scientific tracts coming out of Europe. He was inducted into the Royal Society and conducted several scientific experiments. His father, Increase Mather, also was well-read in scientific ideas. John Winthrop Jr. studied chemistry and medicine, was a charter member of the Royal Society, and brought a telescope to Harvard.

That did not mean, however, that the Puritan scientists agreed with a purely materialist view of the universe. Nor did they see God as a "blind clockmaker" who created the universe and then left it alone. God's providence and intervention in human affairs was revealed in nature. God's wrath against sin was seen in punishments such as hurricanes, droughts, and epidemics. For example, comets had a natural explanation but were also a portent "that flaming vengeance is kindled and burning in Heaven against a sinful world." Beneficial events, conversely, were evidence of God's blessing upon the Puritans for being faithful. Sometimes events were seen as a revelation to simulate conversion. There also were many mysteries that science simply could not yet explain and were attributed to the mind of God.

On October 29, 1727, only weeks before Ezra Stiles was born, New England experienced a powerful earthquake that shook its foundations. Churches held days of fasting and prayer as congregations heard sermons that called for repentance. The earthquake was interpreted as a divine instrument to show the people their sins and remind them of their dependence upon God. When God seemed to speak so clearly through the earthquake, "Shall it not by all that have the faculties of reason in them rendering them capable of hearkening to it, be harkened to?"[5]

Stiles was both a minister (of the Newport Second Congregational Church) and an amateur scientist who represented the reconciliation of science and faith. He wrote that, "The universe is composed of two worlds—the natural and moral, both closely connected and conjoined by that almighty Power, on which they depend." Stiles waxed eloquent when he considered the majesty of the universe. With great advances in the sciences, "The sphere of action will probably be much enlarged…disclose new and surprising things among the starry worlds and their inhabitants—infinite perfection of the adorable Author of nature, in creation and moral government! How glorious, how expeditious these journeys of the mind, up and down, through the spacious, the boundless regions of immensity!"6

The earthquake that struck the Western world from New England to Lisbon on November 18, 1755, caused Stiles to reflect further on the relationship of science and religion. As a young man, Stiles began to agree with Harvard Professor John Winthrop that natural forces were at work. Stiles described a sermon to his father in which he expressed the view that "among other things I observed, that I didn't apprehend it a judgment in the moral government of God, as 'twas manifestly effected according to the laws of nature, as much as violent tempests, thunder, or comets, all of which I judged of beneficent influence in the universe." However, he continued to struggle with the issue, and when he later reread a copy of a letter he had written in 1771, he scribbled in the margins, "Herein I was mistaken."7

Stiles was up-to-date on the scientific literature but had few original thoughts of his own. He corresponded regularly with Benjamin Franklin, testing his ideas on electricity and hurricanes. When Stiles learned about Franklin's ideas about the path of hurricanes, he immediately began investigating the question to test its veracity. Franklin also shared his thoughts about temperature and the nature of heat and cold with Stiles. When Franklin returned from London, he brought a thermometer to Stiles. This stimulated Stiles's lifelong habit of recording the temperature at different times of the day, taking the wind direction, and writing down observations about atmospheric conditions. Franklin even secured Stiles an honorary doctorate from the University of Edinburgh, allowing his puffed-up ego to delight in being called "Dr. Stiles" henceforth.

Stiles proposed to Winthrop an American academy of arts and sciences with the purpose of promoting the investigation of many diverse topics including "celestial observations of eclipses of Jupiter's satellites...meteors or terrestrial comets, meteorological registers of the thermometer and barometer, effects of lightning and whatever may assist toward perfecting the theory of the electrical pointed rods; earthquakes and their species."[8]

Stiles was not merely interested in scientific matters. When the American Revolution started with the furor over the Stamp Act, Stiles was one of many Puritan ministers who preached sermons supporting American liberty. The ministers saw religious and civil liberty as a gift from God but also called on their congregations to live responsible, virtuous lives. They endorsed republican self-government and the constitutional liberties of the English tradition. They sermonized about preserving liberty against oppressive taxation and tyrannical government. Not many ordinary Americans read John Locke and other Enlightenment thinkers on these political principles but were imbued with them as they listened to erudite ministers preach on the Sabbath.[9] As one preacher stated, Puritans would not tamely "part with their natural and social rights, and slavishly bow their neck to any tyrant."[10] Massachusetts Governor Thomas Hutchinson recognized the power of the pulpit on American revolutionaries. After his home was ransacked by an angry Stamp Act mob, he blamed minister Jonathan Mayhew for exciting their passions and prompting their actions. Hutchinson reasoned they thought they were "doing God's service."[11]

Stiles repeated these themes from the pulpit Sunday after Sunday and in his correspondence for a decade. He thought that "no subjects be taxed but by themselves…Indeed a parliamentary taxation of America effectually strikes at the root of American liberty and rights and effectually reduces us to slavery." By the time that fighting erupted at Lexington and Concord in April 1775, Stiles was prodding men to "fight courageously and manfully and behave themselves bravely for liberty—commanding them to behave like men and not like cowards."[12]

Ezra Stiles encouraged the patriots to acquit themselves as courageous men. One such brave man was Paul Revere. On the night of April 18, 1775, the American spy network quickly spread the word that British light infantry and grenadiers were assembling and making ready to move out with the likely purpose of searching nearby towns for gunpowder. Revere heard the news from such diverse sources as a stable boy and Dr. Joseph Warren, who sent for Revere to come as quickly as possible. Revere raced across town to Warren's house between nine and ten o'clock at night. Warren dispatched the rider to "go to Lexington, and inform Mr. Samuel Adams and the Honorable John Hancock, esq. that there were a number of soldiers" on their way to arrest them and proceed to Concord "to destroy the colony stores."

Only a few days before, orders arrived aboard the HMS *Nautilus* from Lord Dartmouth to General Thomas Gage. Dartmouth instructed the general to put a halt to American actions that were tantamount to "actual revolt." Dartmouth warned that, "The King's dignity, and the honor and safety of the Empire, require, that, in such a situation, force should be repelled by force." Gage was told that the first order of duty was to "arrest and imprison the principal actors and abettors of the Provincial Congress whose proceedings appear in every light to be acts of treason and rebellion." Gage should act immediately, though with discretion, before the rebellion ripened further.[13]

Gage ordered the troops to march to Concord to seize the military stores that were stockpiled there as his network of spies informed him. The people of Concord had their own intelligence network, courtesy of Revere, who warned them the week before of an impending British foray into the town. One man from Concord wrote, "We daily expect a tumult…if they come I believe there will be bloody work." They immediately moved the military supplies to surrounding towns to escape capture.

Revere left Dr. Warren's house at the same time that the doctor dispatched at least one other rider, William Dawes. Revere sent word that two lanterns were lit in the steeple of the Old North Church as a warning beacon. Revere crossed the Charles River and got a horse in Charlestown. He wrote, "I set off, it was then about eleven o'clock, the moon shone bright."[14]

The fifteen hundred British troops departed, as Gage reported, "with as much secrecy as possible"—which was not much. Besides, they met interminable delays crossing such a large force across the Charles River. They disembarked in shallow water and then waded through some marshes. As they lost more time sitting around waiting for supplies to arrive for their forced march, they became wet, cold, and miserable. When they started marching at 2 a.m., they were tired as well. They were disheartened to hear bells pealing and gunshots ringing in the still nighttime air to warn of their approach; secrecy was completely lost as they marched through a hostile country of free people ready to defend their liberty.[15]

Revere had a head start on the British force but barely eluded capture by a horseback patrol. "I saw two officers on horseback, standing under the shade of a tree, in a narrow part of the road. I was near enough to see their holsters and cockades. One of them started his horse towards me, the other up the road, as I supposed, to head me should I escape the first. I turned my horse short about, and rode upon a full gallop for Mystic Road, he followed me about 300 yards, and finding he could not catch me, returned."16

Revere then rode hard to Lexington, where he joined up with Dawes and went immediately to warn Revolutionary leaders John Hancock and Samuel Adams of the British approach. Their horses were watered while the riders and radicals conferred with some members of the militia in the local tavern over some late-night refreshments. Concluding that the British were probably marching to seize the weapons in Concord, Revere and Dawes agreed to ride there and spread the alarm.17

The riders met Dr. William Prescott, a young Concord gentleman who that night was courting his fiancée who lived in Lexington. They invited Prescott to join their mission because he appeared to be a "high son of liberty" from Concord itself. He enthusiastically agreed. "The young doctor much approved of it, and said, he would stop with either of us, for the people between that [place] and Concord knew him, and would give the more credit to what we said."

The three spurred their horses on toward Concord, stopping at farmsteads along the way to spread the warning. About half way to Concord, Revere and Prescott were ensnared in a trap. Revere noticed two British officers under the cover of a tree when "in an instant, I saw four of them, who rode up to me, with their pistols in their hands, said 'God damn you, stop! If you go an inch further, you are a dead man.'" The Americans tried to escape but were surrounded. An officer warned that if they did not do as commanded, the soldiers "could blow our brains out." While moving out, Dr. Prescott saw his opportunity and escaped into the night after a brief chase. Revere, meanwhile, also tried to get away, but found his path blocked by six more British officers. He was now a captive to ten redcoats.

The British manhandled Revere and constantly threatened him. He stood up bravely under questioning even when an officer "clapped his pistol to my head…and if I did not tell the truth, he would blow my brains out." After an interrogation and more threats, they rode toward Lexington (taunting him with such insults as "rebel") and eventually took his horse and disappeared into the night. After walking back to Lexington and prompting Adams and Hancock to depart, Revere volunteered to go rescue a trunk containing Hancock's sensitive Revolutionary papers.[18]

While Revere trekked through the night back to Lexington, he heard a volley of muskets and the pealing of the bells coming from that direction. Captain John Parker, a solid farmer, was mustering the citizen-soldiers of the militia. Ordinary farmers and artisans pulled down their ancient weapons off their mantles and went to defend their liberty. As one man put it, "What we meant in going for those redcoats was this: we always had governed ourselves and we always meant to. They didn't mean we should."[19]

More than one hundred men stood around in the cold until it was clear that it was a false alarm. After an hour, they grumbled while they either went back to bed or repaired to Buckman's Tavern since they were up anyway. At 4:30 in the morning, the drums started beating again when a rider brought news that the British were coming. At the call, seventy bleary-eyed men formed up again on the green with their muskets. In a few moments, Royal Marine Major John Pitcairn marched his six companies of redcoats into sight and ordered them into battle formation. His men shouted huzzas excitedly.

Not a few of the militiamen were frightened senseless by the overwhelming show of force. One man started to back away, mumbling, "It is folly to stand here." Captain Parker warned that, "The first man who offers to run shall be shot down." He changed his tune when British officers rode up and commanded, "Lay down your arms, you damned rebels, and disperse." Parker ordered his men to comply and fall out. The free men were prudent enough to leave but would not surrender their right to bear their arms. Frustrated British officers were incensed at American intransigence. "Damn you! Why don't you lay down your arms?" Another oath was shouted, "Damn them! We will have them!"[20]

Shots suddenly pierced the night. No one was sure who fired first in the resulting confusion. Among the British ranks, the automatic response of countless hours of training took over. The redcoats "without any orders rushed in upon them, fired, and put them to flight." The cacophony of bullets reached a crescendo as the British fired their weapons. With balls flying through the air, the colonists returned fire. One of them promised, "I'll give them the guts of my gun."

With great precision, the British rapidly reloaded their weapons and sent another volley crashing into the militia who were either on the line or walking away. Clouds of smoke obscured vision while the acrid smell of sulfur choked lungs. In the melee, eight colonists lay dead and several screamed in agony from horrible wounds. Shocked colonists watched speechless while the British officers finally gained control and formed ranks to continue their march. The redcoats fired off a victory round and gave a cheer while their drummers played their marching tune. Moments later they were gone.[21]

Patriots and Tories took different views of the violence in the heated aftermath. John Dickinson thought that the "most unnatural and inexpressibly cruel war began with the butchery of the unarmed Americans at Lexington." Loyalist Peter Oliver for his part argued that the "armed rabble" fired first at the innocent British soldiers who merely defended themselves.[22]

At Mount Vernon, George Washington was saddened by the news that the British Empire was fracturing. He much preferred, as he would later say, to sit "under the shadow of my own vine and my own fig-tree," but he would not sit idly by while American liberties were taken away.[23] "Unhappy it is, though, to reflect that a brother's sword has been sheathed in a brother's breast and that the once-happy and peaceful plains of America are either to be drenched with blood or inhabited by a race of slaves. Sad alternative! But can a virtuous man hesitate in the choice?"[24]

As first light dawned in the New England sky, the storm that had been brewing for a decade finally broke. The weary British column marched to Concord, hearing gunshots and church bells announcing their approach. The element of surprise was completely lost. They may have been dispirited, but the professional soldiers maintained their discipline and were an impressive spectacle. More importantly, they were ready for action.

In Concord, militiamen from surrounding towns who heard the call swelled the ranks of the local minutemen to more than one thousand fighters. They initially took positions on a hill but pulled back into town near a liberty pole. They were spoiling for a fight—even the minister yelled, "Let us stand our ground. If we die, let us die here!" Nevertheless, they wisely crossed the North Bridge and took the high ground, waiting to see what happened.

The people of Concord silently glared at the British who began their warrantless search of homes and public buildings. Very little contraband—only a few cannon and lead bullets—was found. The stockpile of weapons had been moved out of town because of the anticipated raid. Lead bullets were thrown into a pond but fished out the next day. The British burned wooden gun carriages and accidentally caught a nearby building on fire. Soldiers helped civilians douse the flames.

The militia on the surrounding hills immediately noticed the smoke rising from the center of town. One young man asked, "Will you let them burn the town down?" They did not need to be asked.

Weapons were loaded and swords were unsheathed. The militia marched to defend their property and families from such seemingly naked British aggression.[25]

The American ranks converged on the bridge in step to the sound of the fife and drums. The British were positioned in battle formation, ready to meet the charge. From less than one hundred yards, the two sides started pouring lead balls into the opposing ranks. Ironically, the British were deployed poorly and soon were a confused mess. The British lost several officers in the exchange because the colonists concentrated their fire on the reddest redcoats. The colonists, on the other hand, kept their cool and were able to deliver constant fire. The jumbled British formation collapsed under the withering American fire. The British beat an ignominious and hasty retreat back to Concord. The exhausted soldiers began another forced march under constant attack twenty miles back to Boston.[26]

The men of Massachusetts continued to arrive to reinforce the militia as it chased the British. The fabled American Revolutionary militiaman fighting from behind rocks and trees was a reality for this battle. General Gage reported that there was "a continual skirmish for the space of fifteen miles, receiving fire from every hill, fence, house, and barn."[27] The frustrated British soldiers were harassed and killed constantly but "had very few opportunities of getting good shots at the Rebels, as they hardly ever fired but under cover of a stone wall, from behind a tree, or out of a house."[28]

The farmers knew the terrain and used it to every advantage. They used horses to gallop ahead of the British and get into hidden positions. "Numbers of them were mounted, and when they had fastened their horses at some little distance from the road, they crept down near enough to have a shot; as soon as the column had passed, they mounted again, and rode round until they got ahead of the column, and found some convenient place from whence they might fire again. These fellows were generally good marksmen, and many of them used long guns made for duck-shooting."29

The militia hit the British from every conceivable angle, especially their flanks and rear. The British were caught in deadly crossfire and in several ambushes. Along the road, some small pockets of American resistance assembled into a formation that the British could charge, only to be repulsed time and again. "A number of Americans behind a pile of rails raised their guns and fired with deadly effect. The officer fell and the horse took fright." The colonists taunted the British, yelling, "King Hancock forever," and other such jibes. The Americans suffered losses as they were rooted out and killed in farmhouses and other structures that were assaulted or torched. The redcoats were so furious that they gave the Americans no quarter.

"We began to run rather than retreat in order," one British officer reported. "The whole behaved with amazing bravery but little order. We attempted to stop the men and form them two deep, but to no purpose. The confusion increased rather than lessened." They were dead tired, thirsty, out of ammunition, and almost unable to act. Just as they were ready to despair ever getting back to Boston, the British were finally rescued by reinforcements with artillery close to Lexington, where the citizens were eager for revenge. Even more vicious fighting occurred when they marched, but the redcoats finally shook off their pursuers and limped into Boston.30

America and Britain were now at war. General Gage started to build his defenses in Boston. Americans assembled into militia units and began to pour into Boston to break the siege.

At dawn on May 25, 1775, British Generals William Howe, Henry Clinton, and John Burgoyne sailed into Boston Harbor aboard the *Cerberus* to assume command from the bungling Gage and quickly crush the rebellion. The ship had been tossed about the treacherous Atlantic by gales that ripped off some of its sails and made the generals seasick. The generals agreed with the view that the Americans were "the most absolute cowards on the face of the earth," and a "rabble in arms." Clinton pressed Gage for an attack to take the high ground at Charlestown and Dorchester Heights— a council of war agreed to the plan and set the date of attack for June 18.[31]

The American commanders—Artemas Ward, Joseph Warren, Nathanael Greene, William Prescott, and Israel Putnam—were a mixed lot representing the democratic character of the American army lumped together from different militia units. Some had experience in the French and Indian Wars; others read books on military science from bookseller-soldier Henry Knox. Some, like Putnam, were decisive and courageous; others, like Ward, were hesitant and cautious. They were farmers, politicians, physicians, and merchants rather than professional soldiers. When they learned of the British plans, the Massachusetts Provincial Congress ordered Ward to take Bunker Hill. Prescott was given one thousand men for the task.[32]

In the fading light of the evening of June 16, the ragtag regiments of American militia mustered quietly without uniforms but with a burning desire to guard their liberties against the enemy. They were encouraged with a prayer and marched off with their entrenching tools to Breed's Hill next to Bunker Hill. In the dark, they moved silently to avoid British detection and immediately started digging fortifications to the measured specifications. They had until dawn to accomplish their mission.

When the sun rose, the British were shocked to stare at a redoubt that was 6 feet high and 330 feet across. General Clinton and British sentries had heard the Americans but did not take any action. That was about to change.

The British ship *Lively* swung into position and lived up to its name, firing a deafening salvo in the early morning hour at the exhausted Americans. Other ships joined the *Lively* but were largely ineffective against the patriots, except for one American who was decapitated and the American supply of water when the hogsheads were shattered. Several green, frightened American troops began to desert under the bombardment, so Prescott mounted the redoubt and shouted encouragement to his troops.[33]

The British quickly organized an attack to drive the Americans off the hill. It took several hours for the British to make the necessary preparations. They were further hampered by low tide and had to wait until it rose so that the transports could sail. This barely gave the Americans time to extend their lines down to the shore of the Mystic River to cover their flank. They hastily rolled down large stones and tore down fence rails for a slapdash fortification. The militiamen did not have the time to spend looking at the impressive redcoats with their equipment glittering in the sun, obscured only by the smoke hovering from the ships' cannon fire. The British were more nonchalant, though, stopping for an afternoon dinner when they landed unopposed.

The attack soon came. The British formed up and moved out slowly and methodically, marching bravely toward the enemy shoulder-to-shoulder. The Americans forgot their hunger and thirst and targeted the approaching redcoats. On the small beach and up Breed's Hill, the British advanced closer with each passing moment. Officers whispered commands to their soldiers about holding their fire and shooting low.

When the British came into range, the American lines let loose a devastating volley that ripped into the enemy ranks. Several redcoats and their officers were knocked down, clutching mortal wounds. Screams were heard through the pandemonium. The

British tried to maintain discipline, closing gaping holes in the ranks and returning fire. But the Americans would not let up. They continued to fire into the British line. Within minutes, dozens of elite British infantrymen lay dead on the beach or in the long grass on the hill. The redcoats tried to stand up to the punishment but soon broke ranks and ran. Almost in disbelief, the inexperienced Americans started "huzzaing, supposing, at the time, that we had driven the enemy."[34]

The British were far from done, however. Howe re-formed his lines, organizing them for another attack. Despite the pounding they had just taken—and having just seen their friends killed—the British soldiers marched out again. From behind their defenses, the colonists once more took deadly aim at the British. One British officer remembered, "As we approached, an incessant stream of fire poured from the rebel lines; it seemed a continued sheet of fire for nearly thirty minutes." The Americans even brought some artillery to bear against the advancing enemy. The British were again repulsed, taking staggering losses and retreating to safety.[35]

Although Prescott strictly ordered his men to conserve their ammunition and powder, the second assault used up most of their supplies. They awaited yet a third attack by the British, which began thirty minutes after the last. Covered by artillery and freshened by reinforcements, the British stormed up the hill. They lost some officers and infantrymen but charged the redoubt with bayonets affixed. Meanwhile, the American ammunition supply was completely spent. The Americans picked up shovels and clubs but could not withstand the onslaught. Many who stood their ground were bayoneted after fighting "more like devils than men," but most others realized the futility of a stand and followed the order to retreat.[36]

The colonial inexperience showed with their poorly planned, chaotic retreat. Under a withering fire "where balls flew like hailstones, and cannons roared like thunder," most of the fighters escaped safely, however, and regained order before they started digging in again. The British were exhausted and gave up the pursuit.[37]

The Battle of Bunker Hill was a pyrrhic victory for the British. The Americans took fewer losses and proved that they could stand up to a major military power. The Tory Peter Oliver thought that the "memorable day…crowned British valor with laurels of unfading honor," whereas the cowardly Americans had a "savage way of fighting, not in open field, but by aiming at their objects from houses and behind walls and hedges."[38] Not all on the British side, however, felt that way. General Howe was shocked by the carnage when he inspected the battlefield. The colonists won the grudging respect of British officers who cursed, "Damn the rebels— that they would not flinch." One officer thought that the Americans fought bravely "far beyond any idea I could ever have formed of them."[39]

The Americans had fought their way to a stalemate that would last several months. Soon after the Battle of Bunker Hill, the newly appointed commander, George Washington, would arrive. What he found there would not please him. Rather than fighting the British, the Virginian found himself struggling against the ingrained democratic liberties of a free people to build a disciplined army and battling the elements that would bring sickness and disease to encampments.

Chapter Fifteen

GENERAL WASHINGTON BATTLES THE BRITISH AND THE WEATHER

Before the Hurricane of Independence hit Boston in September 1775, General George Washington had two months to shape his army into a real fighting force. He knew that an army of militia hiding behind rocks could not stand up to the British for very long. When he accepted his command, he probably had not realized that one of the main sources of his storm of troubles would be his own men.

On June 23, Washington left Philadelphia for Boston to assume command of the army. In New York, Washington received an address from the Provincial Congress expressing a hope that he would "cheerfully resign the important deposit committed into your hands, and reassume the character of our worthiest citizen." The fear of a large standing army ran deep among a free people, but the Continental Congress had chosen the right man as commander-in-chief. Washington promised the state assembly that when American liberty had been firmly established, he would return to his "private station in the bosom of a free, peaceful, and happy country." He already was sensitive to setting a proper precedent for military deference to the civilian government. It was a sacred promise to protect republican government from the ambition of a Caesar. Eight years later, he kept his pledge.[1]

Washington even expressed his republican sympathies to his adversary General Gage: "I cannot conceive any more honorable, than that which flows from the uncorrupted choice of a brave and free people—the purest source and original fountain of all power."[2] Washington deferred to civilian authority even when it damaged the war-making abilities of the army.

General Washington rode into Boston on July 2, 1775. Abigail Adams told her husband that Washington's appointment was met with "universal satisfaction." She also related to her jealous husband just how smitten she was with the general: "I was struck with General Washington. You had prepared me to entertain a favorable opinion of him, but I thought the half was not told me. Dignity with ease and complacency, the gentleman and soldier, look agreeably blended in him. Modesty marks every line and feature of his face." She even quoted poetry to explain her swooning admiration:

> Mark his majestic fabric; he's a temple
> Sacred by birth, and built by hands divine;
> His soul's the deity that lodges there;
> Nor is the pile unworthy of the god.[3]

Even Tories admitted Washington's greatness and charisma. Peter Oliver wrote that Washington "had the greatest reputation as a soldier among the Southern colonies. He was polite, humane, and popular."[4]

On July 3, the Massachusetts Assembly sent Washington a message, cautioning him that the army's discipline was a work in progress. Washington realized that the "course of human affairs forbids an expectation that troops formed under such circumstances should at once possess the order, regularity, and discipline of veterans." However, when he took command of the army, he saw that the assembly's concern was, if anything, understated. The general's "great concern" was to establish discipline in the army or "general confusion must infallibly ensue."[5] And it would be difficult to establish discipline in an army while facing the enemy only a mile away.

Much of the discipline problem, in Washington's view, stemmed from the democratic spirit of the people of Massachusetts. The citizen-soldiers of the militias had a strong streak of independence. They democratically elected their officers from among the soldiers. Washington put an end to this practice because it tended to make the officers "curry favor with the men" rather than strictly enforce orders. It did not help that states also had a great deal of control over the appointment of officers, which Washington begged Congress to change.

In letters home, Washington candidly expressed his low opinion of New Englanders. "The people of this government have obtained a character which they are by no means deserved—their officers generally are the most indifferent kind of people I ever saw...They are an exceeding dirty and nasty people."[6]

By November, a kind of malaise grew in Washington's mind. He thought there was "a dearth of public spirit and want of virtue," and noted that a "dirty, mercenary spirit pervades the whole." These problems led him to regret his decision to lead the army: "No consideration upon Earth should have induced me to accept this command."[7]

Washington exhorted his officers to increase discipline. He issued orders in which he reminded his officers of their responsibility to model discipline for their soldiers:

> When officers set good examples, it may be expected that
> the men will with zeal and alacrity follow them, but it
> would be a mere phenomenon in nature, to find a well

disciplined soldiery, where officers are relaxed and tardy in their duty; nor can they with any kind of propriety, or good conscience, sit in judgment upon a soldier for disobeying an order, which they themselves are every day breaking.[8]

Washington issued various orders to the army, instructing officers to enforce discipline. To that end, he urged them to attend religious services "to implore the blessings of heaven upon the means used for our safety and defense."[9] He called on his officers and soldiers to "endeavor to live and act as becomes a Christian soldier, defending the dearest rights and liberties of his country."[10] He forbade cursing and drunkenness, and even issued orders for his men to cease skinny-dipping in front of ladies. He inculcated the need for cleanliness in order to prevent outbreaks of sickness in camp. The Continental Army became a disciplined, moral army under Washington's command.

Washington had many other problems to solve while establishing his army. He begged Congress and nearby states to supply his army with adequate weapons, gunpowder, food, and clothing. He had to contend with smallpox and other illnesses that plagued his army and reduced its strength. In addition, his army lost thousands of men who simply walked home when their short enlistments expired.

Perhaps the greatest concern on Washington's mind was creating a truly Continental Army. The soldiers considered themselves citizens of the states from which they hailed. He had to foster a devotion to the common cause and create a national allegiance. As he told John Hancock, Washington wanted to find a means of abolishing "those provincial distinctions which lead to jealousy and dissatisfaction."[11] He commanded his army to join Boston in a day of thanksgiving and prayer for liberty and to "strengthen the harmony of the United Colonies."[12] On August 5, 1775, Washington informed the army that,

"The regiments of the several provinces that form the Continental Army, are to be considered no longer in a separate and distinct point of view, but as parts of the whole army of the United provinces."[13]

While he was instituting reforms into the army, General Washington and his troops had to struggle with the elements. The harsh weather in New England and to the north presented the army with a series of challenges to overcome—sometimes they were able to conquer them against great odds, at other times they succumbed. Perhaps divine Providence was testing the mettle of the American forces early in the war before favoring the American cause.

As a planter and general, Washington was profoundly interested in the weather. He recorded his weather observations in a diary throughout his life. The weather was his ally during several key incidents during the war. A providential fog allowed his army to escape Long Island before the British cut off its retreat in 1776 during the Battle of New York. Also that year, Washington led the daring Christmas-night attack on Trenton across the Delaware River under the cover of a nor'easter. In 1781, another storm hampered General Charles Cornwallis's escape at the Battle of Yorktown, which led to the British defeat.

Washington was no stranger to hurricanes that struck the East Coast. In the middle of the debate over the ratification of the Constitution, he kept track of a hurricane that passed right over his plantation—it has come to be known as the "Mount Vernon hurricane." On Thursday, July 24, 1788, the planter saw the eye of a hurricane strike overhead:

> A very high northeast wind all night, which, this morning, being accompanied with rain, became a hurricane— driving the miniature ship Federalist from her moorings,

and sinking her—loosening the roots, and forcing many others to yield and dismantling most, in a greater or lesser degree of their bows, and doing other and great mischief to the grain, grass, etc., and not a little to my mill race. In a word, it was violent and severe—more so than has happened for many years. About noon the wind suddenly shifted from northeast to southwest and blew the remaining part of the day as violently from that quarter. The tide about this time rose near or quite four feet higher than it was ever known to before—and must it is to be apprehended have done infinite damage on their wharves at Alexandria—Norfolk—Baltimore, etc. At home all day.[14]

Washington dutifully kept a diary until 1775, but he stopped writing his private thoughts to a diary for the duration of the Revolutionary War. With endless details to attend to and decisions to make regarding the war, the general did not have the leisure to record meteorological observations or personal observations.

The Hurricane of Independence does not seem to have hampered military operations or significantly affected the army, which was staring only at the enemy, daily exchanging artillery fire. If the army had been in Yorktown during the hurricane, as it was later in the war, it might have been a very different story indeed. Washington and his army, however, certainly felt the hurricane's presence and learned of its effects at sea.

On September 5, 1775, Jonathan Trumbull Sr. wrote a letter to Washington explaining recent British naval operations along the coast. "Our coasts are kept in continual alarm," Trumbull reported as New England towns prepared for naval bombardments and invasions. He explained that on the "Lord's day morning, constrained by the weather, came into the harbor at New London, a schooner taken

by the *Rose*. Captain Wallace at Stonington four hands on board."
Trumbull's description of the ship was similar to those of Virginia
that washed ashore with escaped slaves because of the Hurricane of
Independence. "One, a white man sent to Windham jail, the other,
three Negroes, two belonging to Governor Cook, and one to
Newport—ordered to be returned to their masters—and the
schooner to her owner." No one publicly thanked Providence this
time for the return of the slaves.[15]

Boston shipping was affected by the hurricane in Virginia when
sailing in the south along the coast in early September. A letter from
Cambridge read, "The ship *Minerva*, Captain Ewing, from this port
for Maryland, and the ship *Hibernia*, from Ireland for this port,
were both drove ashore in the late gale at the capes of Virginia; the
people saved, but the vessels lost."[16]

Although General Washington did not note the weather in a
diary during the war, at least one of his soldiers did and briefly
described the hurricane. Caleb Haskell of Newburyport was a sailor
and cabinetmaker. Haskell also was a fifer who patriotically joined
the war with his town's regiment two weeks after the battles of
Lexington and Concord. He attested to the democratic nature of the
New England militias. One day after he enlisted, the company
mustered and "chose our sergeants and corporals." Naturally, that
afternoon they heard a "suitable discourse" from the preacher
Mr. Parsons on Judges, Chapter 7 and Chapter 20.[17] They heard
more prayers the following day while parading and making preparations to march to Cambridge, which they promptly did.

In mid-June, Haskell and his company "were ordered to Bunker's
Hill in Charlestown to entrenching." He surveyed the course of the
battle, noting that the Americans "stood the fire some time" before
having to retreat. Over the next two months, Haskell attended several
prayer meetings on different days of the week, carefully writing down

the chapter and verse numbers used by the ministers. He wrote in his diary nearly every day and frequently included meteorological observations. When it rained, he joined the forty thousand troops on both sides in thinking that it was "uncomfortable weather for us in our tents."[18]

On Tuesday, August 29, Haskell and the other members sat in their tents and awaited the passing of the weather: "It being rainy we did no work." A few cannonballs dropped near them but did no damage. The poor weather that plagued the East Coast continued the next day. "This morning is thick weather and rainy. The storm continued all day."[19] It rained for two more days while he (and tens of thousands of soldiers from both sides) sat miserably in his tent. Finally, it cleared up Friday morning, September 1. The blue skies betrayed the approach of the Hurricane of Independence.

On Sunday morning, September 3, Haskell wrote, "There was a storm of rain"—the Hurricane of Independence. The rainy weather continued through the next morning when there was another "storm of rain." Finally, it "clears off pleasant in the afternoon." It had rained so much in the week leading up to the hurricane that his notation for the following day was "Good weather!" It was about time. On September 9, Haskell received orders to join Benedict Arnold's expedition into Canada.[20]

Others also recorded evidence that a hurricane struck New England. In Salem, Massachusetts, a scientist noted that there was a lot of rain and moist air. Further north, in Bedford, New Hampshire, Matthew Patten documented the weather late on September 3. He logged rudimentary observations about the wind and precipitation. "The wind high at about ENE and in the afternoon it rained considerably," he wrote.[21]

People blamed the stormy weather for their poor health. James Warren wrote John Adams that he would have contacted sooner about the Second Continental Congress that was meeting in Philadelphia, but he was sick in bed with a terrible cold. "I should have wrote you before if I had been well, but from a cold I took in the long storm we had here, have been much indisposed since you left us...Am now better," Warren assured Adams.[22]

As the Hurricane of Independence inundated Boston with wind and rain, Colonel Benedict Arnold assembled troops and supplies for a planned invasion of Quebec. Washington accepted Arnold's proposal because he feared that the British would storm the colonies from Canada and cut them in two at the Hudson River. But the plan had several flaws—inaccurate maps and poor understanding of local terrain and weather—that doomed the military expedition before it even began.[23] He attempted to find succor for their trip when they went to the grave of preacher George Whitefield at Newburyport, Massachusetts. After opening his five-year-old coffin, the men removed the clerical collar and wristbands. The chaplain cut them into pieces and distributed them among the soldiers for protection.[24]

On September 18, the troops embarked from Newburyport and immediately encountered inclement weather. A fog rolled in and dangerously reduced visibility. Heavy rain pounded sailors who were on-deck. A gale tossed the eleven-ship fleet about on the Atlantic. The rough seas led one soldier to write, "During this short voyage I became very seasick and such a sickness, making me feel so lifeless, so indifferent whether I lived or died! It seemed to me that had I been thrown into the sea I should hardly have made an effort to have saved myself." Only eight out of the eleven ships arrived at the mouth of the Kennebec River the next morning.[25]

One thousand men under Arnold's command set out in small boats called *bateaux* with tons of supplies between them. The men started to drive through mountainous gorges in the wilderness dotted with swamps and ponds. Heavy rain plagued the soldiers, swelling rivers and ponds several feet and churning up deep mud. On October 20, a major thunderstorm knocked down trees and carried supplies away. The small teams were forced to divert around rapids several times and to carry their four-hundred-pound canoes laden with provisions.[26]

The poorly constructed bateaux were made of green wood and leaked interminably—and did not take kindly to the hidden rocks that gouged big holes in their bottoms. The rain and water ruined the food and supplies—barrels of dried cod, flour, pork, and peas that they carried quickly became spoiled and inedible. Nor did the countryside supplement their diets in the right way: The trout they caught and moose they shot were loaded with protein but not enough calories for the arduous trek.[27]

The soldiers' suffering was compounded by their inadequate clothing. Their clothes ripped apart, and their shoes were soon cut up, forcing men to go barefoot. A few days later, a snowstorm and plunging temperatures revealed how inadequate their clothing was. Many men sickened, and some were beginning to die along the trail. As the food gave out, they were forced to eat their pet dogs. The men grew disgruntled and frightened: After a council of war, more than three hundred men and their officers quit and went back home.[28]

Although the expedition was far behind schedule and was continuing to lose its members to death and desertion, more than six hundred of Arnold's weak, haggard men finally struggled to within sight of their objective: the fortress at Quebec. Yet another storm prevented their crossing of the formidable St. Lawrence River. By December 31, reinforced and gratefully resupplied by General Richard Montgomery's forces (after they took Montreal), Arnold was ready to make his assault.

It was a suicidal attack. Arnold waited for a snowstorm to

provide cover for his troops. The weather had slowed the entire journey, and it did not fail to hinder the attack. The eighteen hundred British troops expected an attack and slept in their clothes for a week. They easily repulsed the American attack. In the fighting, Montgomery was shot in the head and killed. Arnold was wounded in the leg and carried from the scene bleeding badly. Virginia rifleman Daniel Morgan took command and captured some British soldiers. Nevertheless, the Americans came under heavy fire and were surrounded. Several were killed and hundreds were taken prisoner. They suffered terribly at the hands of the British. The invasion of Canada had failed.[29]

Another journey to Canada was undertaken by the esteemed Benjamin Franklin, Samuel Chase, and (in an obvious ploy) Catholic Charles Carroll to persuade Canada to join the American patriotic cause against British tyranny. Carroll, who had been discriminated against for his religion until only recently, convinced his cousin, priest John Carroll, to join the mission.

In June 1774, Parliament had passed the Quebec Act, which extended Canada's boundary, denied trial by jury in civil cases, and allowed the Crown to levy most taxes. The colonists labeled it one of the "Intolerable Acts" that punished the colonies for the Boston Tea Party. Most objectionable of all, it granted religious freedom to Roman Catholics, whipping up a frenzy of opposition among the mostly Protestant Americans who hysterically feared "Popery is established."[30]

The precocious Alexander Hamilton joined this chorus of concerned voices. He wrote that the Act created an absolute monarchy in which the king governed according "to the dictates of his own will" rather than the traditional constitutional limits of England. Even more frightening to Hamilton was his belief that the Act established Catholicism as the official religion. He predicted that, "We may see another inquisition erected in Canada and priestly tyranny."

Hamilton argued that religious freedom was one of the most cherished liberties. "No Protestant Englishman would consent to let the free exercise of religion depend upon the mere pleasure of any man, however great or exalted. The privilege of worshipping the deity in the manner his conscience dictates…is one of the dearest he enjoys," wrote Hamilton. As a result, he suspected "the disposition of the Canadians…is averse to the present regulation of Parliament."[31]

Members of Congress agreed with Hamilton's assessment. Congress sent a letter to "the oppressed Inhabitants of Canada" expressing sympathy that the fellow-subjects of the British Empire were "fellow-sufferers" and "slaves" to British tyranny. On June 1, 1775, Congress demonstrated its good will by forbidding an American invasion of Canada. Less than a month later, it reversed itself and authorized Philip Schuyler to invade north.[32]

General Washington encouraged the Canadians to support the American cause. "My brethren," he wrote,

> unite with us in an indissoluble Union. Let us run together to the same goal. We have taken up arms in defense of our liberty, our property, our wives, and our children. We are determined to preserve them or die. We look forward with pleasure to that day not far remote (we hope) when the inhabitants of [North] America shall have one sentiment and the full enjoyment of the blessings of a free government.[33]

Although it authorized the invasion, Congress was eager to recruit Canada to the American side. It could not, however, send the aged Benjamin Franklin (who was pushing seventy years old) on the difficult journey that autumn or winter. Winter weather forced Congress to wait until the following spring. Congress instructed the commissioners that they should emphasize that America would help Canada resist "designs of the British court against our common liberties." They should convince the Canadians of the "mutual interests of the two countries...that the people of Canada may set up such a form of government as will be most likely, in their judgment to produce their happiness." America also would help to secure the "sacred rights of conscience" from the threat of popery.[34]

In early March 1776, Charles Carroll and Father John faced harsh weather before they even reached Philadelphia to receive their instructions. "We crossed the bay in two hours and a half...there was a very high swell in the bay and we were both very sick."[35] They had to wait a month before they left the city. Once on the road to Canada, however, Franklin kept his companions entertained since he was a "most engaging and entertaining companion...full of facetious stories."[36]

They set out for Canada on March 26. Franklin informed friends at home that, "I am here on my way to Canada, detained by the present state of the lakes, in which the unthawed ice obstructs navigation." Charles Carroll reported that they were continuously delayed by "the obstructions of the weather, carriages, winds, and climate."[37] Franklin feared that he had undertaken a fatiguing journey "that at my time of life may prove too much for me." Franklin sat down to write to a few friends "by way of farewell" thinking he might not survive the trip.[38]

Along the way, Franklin purchased the iconic fur cap that would endear him to the French as an American backwoodsman. He wore it at the time for warmth rather than symbolic value, though. The trip was painful for Franklin, who suffered a number of large boils, swollen legs, and terrible gout as he struggled home. "I find I grow daily more feeble," he wrote. Carroll missed his wife and children, telling his father, "I beg she will write frequently to me and let me know how she and the children are—I wish I could hear a little of two shoe's prattle."[39] Moreover, the commissioners were no more successful than Benedict Arnold and utterly failed to win over the Canadians. The Americans were on their own.[40]

On July 5, 1775, only a few days after arriving in Boston to assume command of the army, General Washington met Henry Knox who was a large, affable Boston bookseller (who like many of Washington's staff learned about military science in books). Knox was taken by Washington's presence: "General Washington fills his place with vast ease and dignity," Knox wrote.[41]

Knox drilled in the militia artillery company while redcoats paraded through the streets of Boston. His bookshop was affected by the Stamp Act taxes, and he was present at several key events leading up to the Revolution—the Boston Massacre, the Boston Tea Party, and the Battle of Bunker Hill. He saw intimately how the Revolution divided Tories and patriots when his new wife was estranged from her Tory family (which eventually sailed to England).[42]

Knox had the fierce courage and determination to accomplish a daring enterprise. He proposed to travel to Fort Ticonderoga, which Arnold and Allen had daringly captured, to recover its abandoned artillery, which lay there dormant while the Continental Army desperately needed guns to relieve the siege of Boston. Washington eagerly agreed to the plan, and Knox set off in mid-November in the hopes of somehow dragging the massive guns three hundred miles back to Boston.[43]

Covering forty miles per day (which was no mean feat itself) with his brother, Knox arrived at the dormant fort and selected the guns that local militia and hired hands would attempt to move across the wilderness. The twelve-, eighteen-, and twenty-four-pound cannons individually weighed a ton or more. Knox and his men did not dawdle, though, loading the guns aboard boats for the first leg of the journey rowing across Lake George, which was still mostly unfrozen. One boat actually sank, but it was recovered and made seaworthy again. The men rowed through ice chunks and entered into a titanic struggle against headwinds, praying to God for them to die down so they could make progress. Knox's brother wrote that they were "beating all the way against the wind…God send us a fair wind."

Providence seemed to answer their prayers, allowing the men to reach Fort George. Yet, they had to pray more because they needed the Hudson River to freeze so that they could cross over thick ice with their massive loads pulled on sleds by oxen. A Christmas gift of three feet of snow and chilly temperatures obliged them, but a trick was played on them when a thaw followed and impeded their progress. Knox realized how dependent he was on nature. He wrote his wife, "Without snow my very important charge cannot get along."

When the temperatures dropped again, the men crazily drove the sleds over sheets of ice that hid bone-chilling rushing water underneath. As the sleds carefully slid across the frozen surface, tiny, unseen fissures dangerously weakened the ice. Finally, a sled with an eighteen-pounder plunged into the ice and sank to the bottom of the river. With incredible ingenuity and a great deal of sweat, the men (aided by patriotic locals) actually raised the gun from the watery depths and continued their trek.

After crossing Berkshire Mountains with all of the guns intact, Knox shocked the commander-in-chief by triumphantly entering Boston and offering his prize. Washington immediately rewarded Knox with command of the artillery. Knox's perseverance had changed the entire course of events in Boston.[44]

With Knox's artillery in hand, Washington wanted to attack, but his council of war disagreed. Washington and his officers agreed to seize Dorchester Heights to employ the new guns against British lines and ships in the harbor. Because the frozen ground precluded digging-in, however, they developed a plan for fortifications to prevent the British from driving them off the hill.

In a repeat of the daring move at Bunker Hill, thousands of American soldiers climbed up at night with barrels, chandeliers, and bales of hay to erect a wooden barrier above ground. They worked quietly through the night and again surprised the British the next morning.

General Howe had planned to evacuate Boston but now decided on an immediate attack to remove the Americans that night. He still had his doubts because of the slaughter at Bunker Hill. A storm blew in, however, and allowed him to save face when large waves and wind scattered his fleet and prevented the attack. The Continental Army had been protected by the stormy weather.

Washington and Howe struck a gentlemen's deal. Howe would embark and depart without being molested. In exchange, Howe promised not to burn down Boston.

The British Army departed for Halifax with many Tories who feared for their lives. "[We left] with women and children, civil officers, followers of the army, and many of the principal inhabitants of Boston (who if they did not accompany us) would be either hung or sent to the mines."45 The destination of the British army in the spring was anyone's guess. But a combination of American pluck and the vagaries of the weather altered the outcome of the war in 1775. The Americans survived the first year of war. Whether they would be able to fight off the next wave of war remained to be seen.

The Hurricane of Independence swept across more than six hundred miles of the American colonies in about thirty-six hours at the beginning of the American Revolution. It passed through several important capitals where the ideas of liberty and resistance to the British were spreading. The hurricane caused the greatest destruction near the coasts of the mid-Atlantic before weakening over land.

Because it affected both sides in the war, the ways of Providence remained inscrutable. The hurricane did not suddenly turn the entire course of the Revolutionary War, but it did affect all of the actors, great and small, in the great drama. Moreover, it provided a window through which to understand the people and thought of the time, not the least of which was the American concept of liberty and their relationship to the divine.

The Hurricane of Independence traveled another thousand miles on to Newfoundland, where it—or possibly the unnamed second hurricane silently shooting up the coast—unleashed its greatest fury against thousands of English and Irish fishermen who did not very much care what was going on in the colonies. There were also French Catholic fishermen on two small islands who had even less of an interest in the outcome of the war. They only wanted to catch fish.

Chapter Sixteen

FISHING FOR COD DURING THE SUMMER IN NEWFOUNDLAND

In the late winter of 1775, the West Country ports of Bristol and Dartmouth were buzzing with activity. The masts of fishing vessels in the harbor looked like a forest of trees gently bobbing in the harbor. They were loaded with fishing equipment, barrels of salt from Spain, and provisions for the transatlantic journey. Nets were mended and brought aboard along with thousands of hooks and miles of line. As they loaded crates in the cold, damp weather, experienced fishermen loudly joked with each other or teased "green" young men preparing for their first voyage. Curious on-lookers came to gawk at the fishermen, and loved ones tearfully said good-bye.

The crews generally were sturdy young men between the ages of sixteen and thirty who were local farm labor or aspiring artisans. Many had experience fishing since they lived in coastal towns. Many had been to Newfoundland for a few seasons before. With precious little land available and depressed wages, recruiters convinced them over strong beer or cider at a tavern or in a local advertisement that they could earn a great deal more money fishing in Newfoundland.

With dreams of saving enough money to buy some land so that they could get married or become independent, they agreed to spend the summer in a distant land catching fish. It also appealed to their sense of adventure.[1]

The young men who were going for the first time probably all harbored secret regrets about agreeing to cross the Atlantic to fish. They were raised on stories recounting the village members and relatives who were lost at sea. Young men like themselves had set out for Newfoundland and never returned. As they drank to numb their fears or quietly sobbed alone, they thought about all of the perilous dangers they would face. Fishermen suffered freezing cold, lost limbs and digits to fishing line accidents, and were thrown overboard and drowned. With good reason, most of the fishermen who set out usually did not sign up for more than a handful of these dangerous trips.

A British parliamentary committee estimated that the "annual loss of life, occasioned by the wreck or foundering of British vessels at sea, may, on the same grounds—the boisterous nature of the weather and the badness of the ship—be fairly estimated at not less than one thousand persons in each year." The story was not any different for Newfoundlanders, New England Gloucestermen, or any other fishermen. It was a dangerous job.[2]

One mitigating factor in favor of going was that they would only be gone a few months. The Newfoundland fishing season lasted from the spring until the fall. The seasonal nature of the fishing season meant that the young men were landlubbers for half the year and had saltwater in their veins for the other half. One person thought that "their lives may be compared to the otter, which is spent half on land, and half in sea."[3]

The most appealing draw however was the pay. The fishermen earned money according to their skill: Experienced men who dared the seas daily garnered higher wages than young boys who cleaned the fish. The mostly illiterate fishermen signed a written contract with an "X" to prevent their escape to the New England colonies where there was an abundance of land. They were paid in the time-honored way of receiving a "share" or portion of the catch. Individual initiative and hard work were rewarded. If they caught a lot of fish, they would do well.

Merchants oversaw the preparations and made sure that every last detail was attended to by his crew. They had made a large investment and hoped to reap a tidy profit with the third most valuable commodity from the New World behind sugar and tobacco. During the 1760s and 1770s, Newfoundland exported a whopping annual average of £453,000 worth of fish (mostly cod).[4]

The merchants usually owned only one or two boats and set up small, generally temporary operations on-shore in Newfoundland. One captain noted, "Few of the colony keep above three boats."[5] They were individual entrepreneurs who were just as subject to the tides of fortune as were the fishermen they hired. They could be ruined by a bad year, raiding pirates, or stormy weather. They also could reap a handsome reward for their risk by trading rum, tobacco, olive oil, and slaves across the Atlantic. There were no government subsidies and little affordable insurance to protect them, only their strenuous effort and willingness to take a risk.

Occasionally, a family could be seen loading their worldly belongings on board the ships. Although Europeans fished for cod in Newfoundland for centuries, few of them joined permanent settlements. The terrain and climate forbade it. The rocky landscape contained spruce forests and intermittent bogs but not much else. There were not many species of animals for subsistence. Agriculture was next to impossible in the brutal and lengthy winter climate. Many attempts at settlement failed miserably and by the 1770s few Europeans inhabited the island permanently. The local population, however, swelled by thousands for the duration of every summer. The families who made Newfoundland their home had their work cut out for them.[6]

The women who boarded usually were married, though some hired themselves out as servants. The mostly male population of the island happily welcomed the women. If the women were single, they could have their pick of eligible bachelors.

Many young boys joined the ships' crews. They performed menial tasks onboard the ships during the voyage and on the shores of Newfoundland. They worked hard and learned practical lessons about life while serving informal apprenticeships in fishing—as well as drinking, cursing, and fighting. They did not attend school and could expect to spend most of their lives poor and illiterate. The boys received very low wages but faced many of the same dangers as the well-paid, experienced men.

The annual ritual included thousands of people who were migrating to Newfoundland to catch the prized codfish. Because everything was ready, there was nothing further left to do but to shove off and begin what they hoped would be a five- or six-week journey across the Atlantic.

The boats slowly rolled out of port and out onto the Atlantic as they began their long, hazardous trip, which was fraught with many dangers. Storms rolled up from nowhere and tossed the boats about like toy ships. Fog caused boats to lose their way, while still winds left ships slowly adrift for days. Disease quickly spread in the narrow confines of the boats and wiped out ship populations. It was a watery graveyard.[7]

The merchants and their fishermen were following the well-trodden sailing paths that had been traveled for centuries by Europeans seeking the succulent flaky white fish. The Vikings, the

Basques, the Portuguese, and the French all sailed for Newfoundland for cod. The British were relative latecomers to the valuable trade.

Along with other Renaissance monarchs, Henry VII patronized voyages to the New World to exploit its riches. The Italian with the Anglicized name, John Cabot, did not find the riches of India or gold flowing from the hills when he sailed along the northern American coast. He did, however, report back of forests dense with wood for shipbuilding and cod so plentiful that they practically jumped into the boats. Milan's envoy to London reported to his duke about Cabot's voyage:

> The sea there is swarming with fish which can be taken not only with the net but in baskets let down with a stone, so that it sinks in the water. I have heard this Messer Zoane state so much. These same English, his companions, say that they could bring so many fish that this kingdom would have no further need of Iceland, from which there comes a very great quantity of the fish called stockfish.[8]

Word from another discoverer in New England confirmed the account from Cabot's expedition. Whoever sailed Newfoundland waters agreed on an obvious truth—there were lots and lots of cod to be caught:

> In the months of March, April, and May, there is upon this coast better fishing, and in as great plenty as in Newfoundland...And besides the places were but in seven fathoms water and within less than a league of the shore, where in Newfoundland they fish in forty or fifty fathoms water and far off.[9]

By the time they spotted land, the passengers were tired of the ship's maggoty fare and foul water. They may have been suffering the painful effects of scurvy—swollen legs, hemorrhaging in muscles, bleeding gums—because their diets lacked vitamin C. They were eager to finish their voyage and start making money catching fish. As they stood on the deck, they were probably more than a little disappointed to be staring at the desolate land coming into sight.

They were lucky to be in Newfoundland because sailing was not always a precise science. Only two years before, an English clockmaker named John Harrison collected a large monetary prize from Parliament for inventing a virtually frictionless clock that sailors could use to figure out longitude in their voyages. Only about a month before the Hurricane of Independence struck Newfoundland, Captain James Cook returned from the South Pacific to England with great praise for Harrison's invention.[10]

Indeed, in the wake of the French and Indian War, it had been Cook who had been appointed the "King's Surveyor" and assigned the task of charting the island. The British had firmly wrested control of most of Newfoundland after the peace of 1763 had been signed and wasted no time in dispatching the young mariner. He had left in April and was in Newfoundland for the summer catch.

Cook completed his work expertly (with his maps enduring for well over a century), returning annually for the summer with the fishermen and wintering in England. After his daring three-year voyage of discovery aboard the *Endeavour*, the heroic Cook turned around and went right back to circumnavigating the globe on the HMS *Resolution*. He departed on his second voyage a few days after the Americans voted for the Declaration of Independence and again plunged into the southernmost part of the planet in his elusive search for Antarctica. On his third voyage, he explored the northwest coast of America in an even more fruitless search for the fabled

Northwest Passage (with William Bligh). Cook died in a dramatic way, slaughtered on a beach in the islands he discovered, Hawaii.[11]

The British ships probably saw the large oceanside town of St. John's first. They sailed into the many bays—Placentia, St. Mary's, Conception, and Bonavista—that were carved in and around the easternmost part of the Newfoundland peninsula. Even though Britain now owned Newfoundland, the British made only slow inroads into settling around the coast of the island. Moreover, the French retained rights to the tiny islands of Saint-Pierre and Miquelon to the south.

Newfoundland was segregated by ethnicity. Irish ships went to St. John's and St. Mary's and Placentia Bays. The English dominated the other bays. The French were restricted to their islands. They also worshipped God according to different faiths, but shared the superstitions of seamen around the world.[12]

In 1775, Newfoundland was a bit like the Wild West. The fishermen experienced a high degree of autonomy and self-government. They generally had to work out their own problems; sometimes violence erupted. Angry competitors stole the boats and vandalized the fishing platforms of their neighbors. The Royal Navy supplied a sparse government administration to settle disputes that were not resolved by a fistfight.[13]

It was April or early May when the boats packed the waters around Newfoundland. The pack ice had cleared away, permitting fishermen to sink their lines and pull up the valued cod from the bottoms. The transient life of the fishermen and seasonal nature of their jobs was a centuries-long tradition:

> Five hundred sail great and small do from England yearly sail
> to this coast…and, arriving there about the middle of April,

unrig their ships, set up booths, and cabins on the shore in
diverse creeks and harbors, and there, with fishing provisions
and salt, begin their fishing in shallops and boats.[14]

When they entered one of several settled bays around
Newfoundland, they sailed among much smaller fishing boats up to
the permanent wharves that were built by 1775. The drying areas
and storehouses filled the rocky shoreline with dwellings further
back. Some of the structures were meant to last and were made of
sawn lumber. Some livestock might be visible in the distance. Still,
Newfoundland was sparsely settled, with only 12,000 residents who
lived in the coves along the shore.

Because most of the fishermen who came were planning to leave
in the fall, they immediately disembarked and got down to business.
They unloaded the boats and constructed temporary fishing stations
to process the tons and tons of cod that were caught daily. They built
tiny, one-room cabins by annually raiding the nearby spruce forests
for their lumber. The rough-hewn wood was caulked with mud and
insulated with moss. The roofs were made of bark or sod, with a hole
poked through for the fireplace built into the floor. The shelters
were simply torn at the end of the season or left to be quickly
destroyed by the unmerciful winter elements. They would repeat the
building process the following spring (with the result that the forests
were slowly denuded).[15]

The provisions and equipment were carried to the proper locations. Men started going out onto the water to catch herring for
baitfish that the cod enjoyed. Once they were done with all the
necessary preparations, they started doing what they had come to
do—fish.

In time-honored tradition, the fishermen arose with the dawn.
They wasted little time getting dressed in their little ramshackle

huts. They took a few bites of a simple breakfast and stepped outside into the chill air, shells, small rocks, and fish bones crunching under their feet. They unconsciously scanned the skies and made a quick mental weather forecast.

The men who derived their livelihood from the sea were probably among the most expert meteorologists around. They did not need a thermometer or barometer to tell them what to expect in terms of the weather and their probable catch for the day. They handed down their weather lore to each new young stripling. They were a superstitious lot, reading the heavens for omens like the Greeks. They were a rather pessimistic lot, so almost all of it predicted stormy weather. They looked at the heavens and examined the sun, the moon, the clouds, and the winds when making their forecast:

> A red dawn is a sign of rain and storm.
> Brilliant Northern Lights foretell a fine day and then a storm.
> Hoar frost in autumn is a sign of south wind and rain.
> When distant hills appear near, rainy weather is coming.
> When the wind shift against the sun, trust it not for back 'twill run.
> When the wind is in the east, 'tis neither good for man nor beast.
> Mackerel sky and mares' tails make the sailor furl his sails.
> Watch the new moon. If you can hang a powder horn on the lower rim of the crescent, it is a sign of stormy weather.

They not only scanned the sky, but watched the movement of animals. The strange behavior of creatures before a hurricane or earthquake (or even just rain) provided useful warning signs:

When gulls fly high, stormy weather may be expected.
When goats come home from the hills expect rain soon.
The following are common signs of rain: soot falling to the
ground, dogs sleeping through the day, spiders very active.
When cats are very playful, they are said to "gale up the
weather."

The fishermen not only needed to watch the activity of animals but also the visions of dreams about them: "To dream of horses is a sign with sailormen that storms will come." They could not ignore the old, grizzled sailor who experienced pains in his knees and other joints as another common sign of rain: "Rheumatic pains with elderly people."[16]

With so many different signs of impending storms, it was surprising that the men sailed at all. Nevertheless, seeing no indication of foul weather, they decided to set out. Speaking in hushed tones or not at all to their boatmates, they loaded the bait, fishing lines, and a few provisions. The three-man team untied their lines and climbed aboard their boat. They were going to work.

The boats were small, maneuverable boats called *shallops* with one, perhaps two, masts. They were open boats, resembling the whale boats of the next century. Expeditions to the Grand Banks were accomplished with larger sloops (in the thirty-ton range) or with schooners (one hundred tons or more). But daily off-shore fishing was done mostly in the three-man shallops.[17]

The boat crew was not alone in the early morning tides. Scores of boats set out each day from the different bays and jockeyed for position. By 1775, thousands of fishermen worked in almost one thousand boats off of Newfoundland. It was getting a little crowded but there were plenty of fish to catch.

The fishermen used the ancient hardlining technique of catching fish. Each man had three weighted lines to fish and deftly baited the hooks with the herring. They sank their lines to the shallow ocean bottom where the cod lived. The fishermen looped the line around his hand and waited for a tug when he yanked to set the hook in the fish's mouth. Simultaneously, he pulled it up swiftly, moving his two index fingers in broad, circular motions. Cod were no sport fish and did not struggle when hooked. When he hauled in his prize, the fisherman unhooked it, baited his line, and set it out again in an action that quickly became repetitive.[18] The sun rose in the sky and the boat began to fill with cod. The men enjoyed each other's company as they spent a pleasant day on the water. They shouted ribald jokes to each other and spied their neighbors' catches with envious eyes.

In summer, the cod were intercepted swimming to warmer, shallow waters to spawn and feed. Catching them sometimes was easier than tugging on a line; oftentimes they simply could be scooped up in nets without a fight. In September, when many boats had left already for Europe with full hulls, the remaining fishermen followed the cod when they returned to colder, deeper shoals.[19]

The Newfoundland cod that they brought in usually weighed between eight and thirty pounds apiece. Oversized cod up to two hundred pounds and several feet in length sometimes were hauled up. They had amber leopard spots on an olive green back, a white belly, and a long white stripe separating the two. This unsuspecting bottom-dweller was the most highly-prized fish in the Atlantic. Many men died trying to catch it, and British merchant ships laden with fish often received a naval escort home for this fish.[20]

As Sir Walter Scott wrote in *The Antiquary* (1816), "It's no fish ye're buying: it's men's lives. (A fishmonger to a customer haggling over the price of a haddock.)"[21]

Over the course of the day, the boats were weighted down by the large catch. The three-man crew caught an average of several hundreds of pounds of fish between them. The fishermen worked at a steady pace without much of a break because they were not going to get a higher share for loafing. After all, as one observer noted, "Their daily food comes out of the sea." Indeed, the cod was both their dinner and their source of income. In the late afternoon, they started to make their way to shore to clean their catch.[22]

As they approached the rocky shore, seagulls circled overhead, waiting for their chance to feed off the scraps or steal a small fish or two. The young boys who did much of the work preparing the cod waited on shore for the arrival of the shallops. They also prepared dinner for the famished fishermen.

Because Newfoundland was so barren, the meals consisted primarily of the same fish that the fishermen caught thrown into a stew with a few vegetables from the gardens. They might have followed a variation of the following recipe (if they had the ingredients, which they probably did not):

> Beat it soundly with a mallet for half an hour or more and lay it three days a soaking, then boil it on a simmering fire about an hour, with as much water as will cover it till it be soft, then take it up, and put in butter, eggs, and mustard champed together, otherwise take 6 potatoes, boil them very tender, and then skin them. Chop them, and beat up the butter thick with them, and put it on the fish and serve them up. Some use parsnips.

The mouth-watering thick white flakes in cod meat were rich in protein for the hard-working fishermen. The cod had eighteen percent protein, which increased to eighty percent when dried, and almost no fat. The fishermen enjoyed a nutritious, delicious dinner while they told stories. There was no need to lie about the "one that got away" since cod almost never did escape their clutches.[23]

Their work was done for the day but there was almost nothing else to do on Newfoundland except fish. As a result, almost all of the houses doubled as a tavern, plying liquor and tobacco to the fishermen. Many were deeply in debt to the merchants for the provisions and alcohol that they consumed.

One frowning observer noted that the "keeping of tipling houses and selling of brandy and other strong waters, wine, beer, and tobacco, debased the fishermen sent thither in fishing voyages and thereby hinder them and detain them from their employments to the great loss in the voyages...and cause them to expend and waste a great part of their wages."

The young men were not as worried. They kept up a highly demanding regime of physical labor. They fished every day except for the Sabbath for months on end. They happily drank a lot and enjoyed every minute of it.[24]

After several drinks, the fishermen broke into song. They sang the same tunes over and over, never tiring of them. Their songs symbolized the hard life they—the "Jack Tars"—lived. The fishermen's songs may have sounded something like the following:

> Now 'twas twenty-five or thirty years since Jack first saw
> the light.
> He came into this world of woe one dark and stormy night...
> When Jack grew up to be a man, he went to the Labrador.
> He fished in Indian Harbor, where his father fished before.
> On his returning in the fog, he met a heavy gale.
> And Jack was swept into the sea and swallowed by a whale.[25]

Most songs were significantly more off-color and became louder with every drink. Raucous laughter erupted from the rickety taverns into the night.

Unsurprisingly, the Newfoundland men were seen with a jaundiced eye by moralists as a "rude, profane, and atheistic" group. They were described as "some loose sort of people and ill-governed men" as a result of "the barrenness of that island (it affords neither food nor clothing) and the inhabitants for the most part are poor and debauched, that their poverty and debauchery puts them upon committing of all vice and mischiefs."[26]

While the fishermen ate and drank, the young boys processed the catch. They had a language all their own. On the covered wharf called the fishing "stage," they unloaded the fish using pitchforks and began performing their different tasks. The "header" dexterously beheaded the fish and passed them on. The "splitter" sliced the fish open, gutting them and saving the valuable livers that were dumped into a vat for cod-liver oil. The roe also was collected and was sure to fetch a high price in Europe. The "salter" then preserved the pile of fish and laid them out on platforms called "flakes" to dry. "A salter is a skillful officer," one writer described, "for too much salt burns the fish and makes it break, and wet, too little makes it redshanks, that is, look red when dried, and so is not merchantable."

The fish cured best on shore in temperate, windy conditions in about ten days. To complicate the boys' lives, the weather liked to conspire against them. Fog and rain caused the boys to work quickly to turn the fish skin side up or cover them for protection. This could take quite a long time since the hundreds of tons of fish on the flakes often covered several acres along the shores of Newfoundland.[27] The fish were piled into large stacks and covered with an old sail cloth weighted down to remove any moisture. The dried fish then were moved to a store until it was shipped to market in late summer or early fall.[28]

The fish was headed for different markets in the Atlantic trade depending upon its quality. Regardless of where it went, it was a source of cheap, high-quality nutrition for those who could not afford to eat meat. It rarely spoiled when dried and salted because of its low fat content. When it was restored with water, it had an excellent flavor even surpassing the fresh-caught cod the fishermen ate.[29]

"Dumb fish" was ironically dubbed since it was the best quality cod that was sold in Mediterranean markets, particularly to satiate Spanish and Portuguese appetites for the fish. It commanded the highest price for the season's catch. "Middling" cod was bound for Portuguese Atlantic islands and the prosperous English colony of Jamaica. Finally, the remainder of the catch was poor quality "refuse fish" that was sold to the Caribbean sugar islands and fed to the African slaves with the necessary protein and salt for the murderous work in the tropics.[30]

Not every day was as profitable. Rainy, stormy weather kept fishermen in their cabins, performing small repairs on their equipment or having a drink or two. On other days, they were simply unlucky or chose the wrong spot. One observer stated, "It happens that some months are better fish and more than in another; for none knows when it will be a good or a bad year until the time be quite over, and being in different bays they know not where it is good, where bad." Nonetheless, the crew could expect to catch more than twenty thousand fish weighing more than ten tons during the course of a few months in Newfoundland.[31]

When the fishing season was over in late July or August, initial preparations were made to pack up the trade ships for the return to homes in Great Britain. The last catches were dried, equipment collected, and the ship readied. Return trips were made at the height of hurricane season when the swirling storms threatened shipping lanes in the Caribbean and North Atlantic even when they did not strike North America:

> [The fishermen stayed] until September…and this fishing
> ended and the cold beginning, they leave their stations and

booths and repairing aboard their ships, laid their fish and, rigging their vessels, return to their native homes, where these fishermen winter and then become husbandmen.[32]

Ships were headed to the Caribbean to drop off the refuse fish and purchase rum, molasses, and sugar to satisfy the European sweet tooth. Merchants brought the most valuable part of the cargo to the Mediterranean where they sold the best cod for French wine, salt, olive oil, and gold. Merchants then completed their several months journey selling those goods in England and counted up their profits, figuring out if another voyage the following year was worth it. It generally was—unless a major hurricane struck.[33]

Chapter Seventeen

THE HURRICANE

On September 4 or 5, 1775, before they saw the clouds appear off in the distance, the codfishermen felt the ocean become angry. Experienced fishermen saw the rough seas indicating an approaching storm and prepared for it. They looked at their catch and might have frowned but fishing was a dangerous business, full of risk. Those who ran at the sight of every squall were poor fishermen indeed, and not just because of their empty purses.

A long season of fishing still had not cured the new men of their seasickness when their boats rode the crest of each wave and then crashed down, only to rise and fall again and again. The old salts smiled and issued firm orders that restored the confidence of the frightened young men.

The winds picked up and the rain came, stinging their faces and drenching them. Crashing waves soaked them until they were chilled to the bone. The ocean became dangerously high. Sails were taken in, and men clung tightly to the boat. They generally lost sight of other boats. They were alone except for the two other men in the boat. Their lives were in each other's hands. They trusted each other and would willingly give their own lives for each other.

The waves grew, and the storm worsened. The Hurricane of Independence had arrived. Men went into the water, and if they were lucky, stretched out their arms and were pulled back in to safety. A couple of men might have been drowned that day, killed by the storm. Their names were screamed out by their boat mates, echoing out over the waves, but their voices quickly drowned out by the ferocity of nature. It was a dangerous business. Long lists of names of sailors lost every year did not even begin to capture the essence of their story, yet told volumes. They were remembered by the brotherhood of the sea.

Eventually, the storm abated. It was a rapidly moving tropical storm headed for its demise. The hurricane had lost a lot of steam, and although it was still a treacherous storm for those who made their living fishing for cod, it did not have the power left to kill hundreds of people as it did in North Carolina and Virginia. Still, it had the respect of fishermen who understood the peril.

The Hurricane of Independence was the topic of conversation that night. The deaths (if indeed there were a couple) led to some grim toasts for their friends. The storms at the end of the fishing season were no laughing matter. The fishermen looked forward to going home soon.

They had weathered another storm. They had done so before, and would do so again.

Or, so they thought.

A few days later, the remaining fishermen on the island must have seen the telltale signs of a major storm brewing from the south. The sky turned eerie colors and the breakers began methodically pounding the shores of the bays. The hurricane appeared as an ominous wall of thunderclouds and rain on the entire breadth of the horizon. Gusts of wind blew their shallops through the choppy waves.

As conditions worsened and fishing became impossible, many disappointed fishermen began hauling in their lines and nets. They headed back in and hoped for better luck the next day. On the shore, the young boys tried to weigh down the flakes and make sure that the drying cod would be protected from the impending tempest as the wind grew and the waves crashed closer. They scurried about and helped the crews back to the wharves, quickly obeying shouted commands. Residents on shore, including men, women, and children, did what they could to prepare for a storm. Little did they know that it was all for naught.

The hurricane was releasing the naked, raw power of nature upon the poor young fishermen. The hurricane targeted the bays of the eastern end of Newfoundland, hitting almost all of the major settlements—Placentia, Conception, Trinity, Bonavista Bays, the French Islands, and St. John's. Thousands of permanent and lingering temporary settlers were about to experience North America's second deadliest hurricane.

The hurricane advanced rapidly. The waves became larger and larger. Nervous, frightened fishermen stopped joking and used all of their skill to maneuver their boats home. The wind picked up and started to howl furiously. A steady downpour soon became an unstopping torrent from the thick thunderclouds that descended upon Newfoundland in swirling bands. As it became apparent that this was a hurricane rather than a common thunderstorm, everyone became terrified and did the best they could to find shelter.

Many of the structures they hid in for shelter, however, were close to shore and held together with mud, moss, and tree bark. It did not take long for a few large waves and steady winds to rip them apart or blow them down. The gale sent loose pieces shooting through the air, creating a hail of debris. People ran hysterically and helped each other to sturdier permanent structures in the hope of finding safety.

They fared better than the fishermen who were still at sea and could not get in. Sails ripped and were carried aloft. Masts broke. Waves grew in height to unimaginable heights of ten, twenty, thirty feet—maybe higher. Boats filled with water or were overturned. Fishermen reached out their hands or jumped in the water to save their friends without thinking of their own safety. Soon, there was no one left to help.

The boats that were moored down did not fare any better. Waves battered and smashed them against wharves. Many were torn loose and thrown on the rocky shore to be shattered. Others were carried further inland as the sea steadily rose. The wind lifted small boats at first and then larger ones through the air until they struck buildings, spruce trees, or fleeing people.

The terrible symphony of screeching winds, rumbling thunder, crashing waves, and sickening crunch of boats drowned out the awful human screams. Visibility was reduced to darkness at noon when the dark thunderclouds passed overhead. The growing deluge of rain dropped at the rate of several inches per hour as the clouds wrung the moisture carried from the Caribbean and Atlantic.

The Newfoundlanders were too busy thinking about their own safety to worry any longer about the valuable cod that was being destroyed by the storm. The waves washed over and broke the flakes where the fish were drying. The drying cod seemed almost alive as the wind flopped them on the rocky shore. Thousands of fish with their white innards exposed were floating in the waves. The sea was reclaiming its own.

Because storm-watchers at the time believed that hurricanes were divided into two storms at the eye and were only beginning to understand the direction of hurricanes, they did not know that the right quadrant was the mightiest part of the storm. This narrow part of the hurricane with the highest winds caused the ocean to rise to unbelievable heights with waves of several stories and release incredible amounts of energy. Throughout history, they have reduced seaside communities to rubble. In minutes, the landscape of the bays resembled the surface of the moon. It was one of the most powerful furies that nature could unleash.

Although the winds of hurricanes destroy a lot of property and take human lives, meteorologists now know that the surges of ocean water they produce are what actually do the most damage. Storm surges cause three quarters of all deaths by drowning and much of the property destruction associated with hurricanes.

The hurricane soon obliged, loosing a colossal storm surge against the helpless fishermen. The royal governor of Newfoundland, Admiral Robert Duff, resided in St. John's that summer and fall. He filed a report with the British Colonial Office describing the rising sea. He said, "The waters, which then rose to a height scarcely ever known before, committed great devastation." Another annual report mentioned the storm surge. "At St. John's, and other places, in Newfoundland, there arose a tempest of a most particular kind," it read, estimating that, "The sea rose on a sudden 30 feet."[1]

There is no reason to doubt the veracity of this claim. Even if the estimate was slightly off, the destruction was all the proof needed. The experience of it could only be imagined in the worst of nightmares. The ruin it caused was complete.

The huge wall of water came instantly as wave upon wave piled on top of each other. It inundated the shore and swept away hundreds of people and structures without discrimination regarding national background or religion. The people had very little time to react as the inexorable waves rose several feet in a matter of minutes.

Those who were not drowned immediately clung desperately to anything to stay above the water breaking down on them. Choking on seawater and bruised by debris, they reached out for loved ones who only moments before they had held tightly. They tried to get a hold of a piece of wood from a boat or cabin. A stray fishing net in the water could be grabbed for or as often ensnared a foot and dragged victims under.

The eye passed overhead, probably in the vicinity (most likely slightly to the west) of St. John's. It brought a temporary reprieve, including a peculiar calm and sunshine. Few Newfoundlanders at ground zero probably experienced this calm because so many were already dead and the destruction so complete from the first wave of the storm. Nevertheless, the eye quickly passed and brought a redoubled fury as the worst of the storm followed. It may not have seemed possible, but the winds blew faster and the surge rose higher. The relentless "gust" continued for what seemed like another eternity. As the surge approached its zenith, anyone who had somehow managed to stay alive in the water was pounced off of the tops of trees and houses.

Permanent settlers who lived in a house built to last for more than the usual three months had better chances of survival. They tried to climb to higher levels of their houses. If they, or any neighbors, could reach the roofs of their houses, they surveyed the dreadful scene around them, which lasted for what seemed an eternity. They said prayers with tears in their voices, fooling themselves that the water would not rise above roof levels or that the waves would not claim their houses very soon.

The massive height of the storm surge has led to some speculation that it could only have been a tsunami. Surely, some have thought, a hurricane could not be powerful enough in the North

Atlantic to perform such a feat. The theory is that an underwater earthquake, probably off Cabot Trench, generated a wave that sped at five hundred miles an hour or more as a disturbance that lifted the sea only a few inches higher. When it reached land, it swelled to the recorded height of thirty feet and swarmed over the land with great destruction.

The scholars who developed this idea in the 1930s seem to have been influenced by a 1929 earthquake that measured 7.2 on the Richter Scale and tragically did, indeed, cause a tsunami to strike a part of Newfoundland just as surely as the Stock Market crashed that year in New York wiping out billions of dollars.

The idea is intriguing but wrong. Duff, the royal governor, reported two months after the event that:

> I herewith transmit to you, my lord, accounts of the ordnance and ordnance stores in the garrisons of St. John's and Placentia within my government, as also schemes of the English and French fisheries at Newfoundland; and I am sorry to inform your lordship, that these fisheries, as well as the trade of the island of Newfoundland, in the month of September last, received a very severe stroke from *the violence of a storm of wind*, which almost swept everything before it.

Duff clearly stated that "a storm of wind," not an earthquake (which was felt nowhere else across the Atlantic), was responsible for the terrible event. Seismologists who have investigated the question have conclusively proven that there was no earthquake and tsunami but rather a devastating hurricane.[2]

All evidence about the date of the storm indicates that it was a giant hurricane that tracked up the Atlantic and skirted the colonies like a silent killer. We have overwhelming evidence that there was a much more powerful hurricane at sea than the Hurricane of Independence, and its timeframe for striking Newfoundland is much closer than its predecessor. The second hurricane pounded shipping lanes, destroying numerous ships almost due east of Norfolk around the tenth, eleventh, and twelfth of September 1775, and sped up to fifteen to twenty miles per hour, hitting Newfoundland a few days later.

This killer storm, which hit Newfoundland and caused the second most deaths from a hurricane in North American history, was probably not the Hurricane of Independence. Rather it was a completely anonymous and never-before-described hurricane. The Hurricane of Independence was greatly weakened by its journey over the eastern seaboard. It had passed by Newfoundland at least a week before the catastrophic event occurred.

One scholar who has briefly written about the hurricane concedes: "It is not at all clear whether we are dealing with one or more storms, since the Newfoundland reports came six to eight days after the cyclone was recorded inland over the Carolinas." Actually, the difference between the time that the Hurricane of Independence struck North Carolina and the date a hurricane hit Newfoundland could stretch out to at least ten days, rendering it highly improbable that the Hurricane of Independence was the killer tempest. Meteorologist David Ludlum confessed that, "It is also quite logical to believe that it was a second storm."[3]

Although several different dates were given by contemporary observers, none was before September 9, and most were at least a couple of days later. Our main piece of evidence simply mentions that the hurricane happened "in the month of September." One young man noted the number of dismasted ships that occurred sometime after September 10 but before September 21. This frustratingly imprecise and conflicting timeline of the storm leads to a puzzling enigma. History is full of ultimately unanswerable questions, but the task of the historian is to assess the evidence and draw probable conclusions.[4]

However, due to the overwhelming evidence I have seen, I am concluding that the hurricane that suddenly unleashed its fury upon Newfoundland was a hurricane no historian has ever correctly attributed, for they have wrongly assumed it to be the Hurricane of Independence. Just as the Hurricane of Independence was appropriately named because of the tumultuous Revolutionary events occurring in September 1775, the unnamed hurricane deserves to be named after the courageous young men who braved the elements each summer in a hostile environment. I am calling it the "Codfishermen's Hurricane," because the incredible death toll was comprised of the thousands of fishermen who were killed by the storm.

The tempest eventually waned as it plunged further into the depths of the North Atlantic where the cold waters consumed its power. Only the nature that spawned them could conquer the might of hurricanes. The scope of the damage became clear in the waning minutes of light that evening and in the days and weeks to follow. The aftermath revealed an almost unprecedented human toll.

Duff's report to England conservatively estimated "the number of people who perished not under three hundred." This was a wildly low number as a subsequent report testified. Hundreds of shallops were at sea with crews of three or more fishermen apiece (and more for larger schooners). As the annual report stated, "Above seven hundred boats, with all the people belonging thereto, were lost, as also eleven ships with most of their crew."[5]

According to the governor of the French islands of Saint-Pierre et Miquelon, dozens of French boats were sunk, with larger crews than the English shallops. He estimated that at least four hundred people died.[6]

In addition, hundreds of people were killed in the various bays when they could not escape the destruction when the storm surge deluged the shore. "Even on shore they severely felt its effect, by the destruction of numbers of people." More testimony agreed, "Nor was the mischief much less on the land, the waves overpassing all mounds, and sweeping everything before them." With considerable understatement, one of the reports stated that, "The shores presented a shocking spectacle for some time after."7

For centuries, European fishermen had pulled up thousands of tons of cod, which offered no struggle once caught up in the nets. The cod fishermen were caught up in these very same nets that earned their daily bread. They struggled frantically but ultimately really could offer no more resistance in the nets than did the cod. The morose irony of the scene was not lost on observers who noted simply, "The fishing nets were hauled up loaded with human bodies." Similarly, another report stated, "For some days after, in drawing the nets ashore, they often found twenty or thirty bodies in them." The bloated, disfigured bodies were truly a "shocking spectacle."8

With thousands of men lost at sea, the coves were filled with dead bodies. The young and the old, male and female, Protestant and Catholic, Frenchman and Briton, planter and indentured servant lay on the beaches while the waters gently lapped against them in the cool, sunny weather in the days following the hurricane. Hundreds of corpses were found hidden in the debris field hundreds of yards inland. The mangled bodies struck strange poses crushed by the weight of the wreckage. In the days and weeks to come, hundreds of unidentifiable, battered corpses washed up on the shore. On the other hand, the sea claimed hundreds, the bodies washed out to sea and were never recovered. It was said that the bones of the dead were found on the beaches for years to come.

The tormented survivors climbed down from their houses and from out of their shelters. They were bruised and cut; some had broken bones. They wandered aimlessly through the heart-wrenching, macabre scene in shock. When they came to their senses, they wordlessly and tearfully buried countless friends, boat mates, and neighbors. The grisly task of burying the dead and cleaning up the mess took an interminable amount of time. They may have said a few words of prayer over those who perished. They surely never forgot the day this hurricane assaulted the fishing villages of Newfoundland. Englishmen and Irishmen who had already sailed for the Mediterranean to sell their catch later heard word of the storm and counted their blessings. Some may have decided never to sail to the island again and settle for a simple life of farming.

One touching story of survival is still commemorated by a small marker by a mass gravesite near a camping area in Northern Bay Sands Provincial Park. A small boy nimbly climbed a tree and watched with terror as the growing waves crashed around him. The wind blew him and pelted him with debris as he clutched the limbs with all of his might. Miraculously, he lived through the ordeal. Thomas English, an Irish planter who lived nearby and also survived, immediately adopted the boy—the only inhabitant of the beach who lived to tell the tale.[9]

In total, it is probable that upward of four thousand or more Newfoundlanders perished as a result of the Codfisherman's Hurricane. As a Pennsylvania paper later reported:

> A person lately from Halifax to Cape Cod, reports that he saw at Halifax, a particular account of the loss of several harbors of Newfoundland, in a violent storm on the 9th of September, amounting in the whole to more than four thousand men.[10]

This figure is still accepted today and ranks the Codfisherman's Hurricane as the second deadliest storm to hit North America (behind the Galveston, Texas, hurricane of 1900). The death toll may have been even higher: we just do not know.

Despite the catastrophic nature of the disaster, virtually no one has heard about Codfisherman's Hurricane (or the Hurricane of Independence, for that matter). The pair of storms has been largely lost to history. Moreover, the Hurricane of Independence has probably been wrongly blamed for thousands of deaths that were caused by the even more obscure Codfishermen's Hurricane.

Beyond the human cost, the hurricane laid waste to the cod fishing industry in Newfoundland for 1775. Boats were sunk in their bays as well as lifted up by the winds and deposited in unusual locations and amazing distances inland with irreparable damage. Duff stated:

> A considerable number of boats, with their crews, have been totally lost, several vessels wrecked on the shores, and a number of those lying in the harbors were forced from their anchors and sustained much damage. The fishing works in those places mostly exposed, were in a great measure defaced.[11]

In addition to the hundreds of small commercial boats that were destroyed, larger naval vessels could also not withstand the indomitable storm. Duff reported:

> Two of His Majesty's armed schooners belonging to the squadron under my command, one of which was stationed at the time on the Banks, and the other on the northeast coast of Newfoundland, were unfortunately wrecked, but

happily by this accident, only two persons belonging to the crews of these vessels have been lost.[12]

The traveler from Halifax to New England surveyed the damage that the storm did to the fishing industry and fleet. He reported widespread destruction:

> Nearly all the shallops employed in that fishery, as well other vessels, were wholly lost; and those that rode out the gale, were chiefly dismasted, and otherwise much damaged, that many houses, etc., were blown down, and that it would take the chief part of the spring to repair the flakes, they having received almost incredible damage.[13]

Salted cod normally were reconstituted in water as they were prepared for their stews and other dishes on European dinner tables. The taste of the dried fish was usually even better than the fresh cod that the Newfoundland fishermen ate on the shores.[14] However, the salt water that bloated the drying fish on the day of the hurricane only ruined the cod when it was washed from their flakes. Tons of white, flaky fish floated on top of the water rather than their usual spot on the bottom of the ocean when alive. They rotted on the beaches, adding to the awful stench of the dead.

Contemporary estimates of the cost of the storm reached staggering proportions. Governor Duff tried to make an initial approximation of the cost of the hurricane though he admitted that, "I cannot give your lordship a very correct estimate of the damages sustained by this storm." He surmised from different accounts "that the amount of it in shipping, boats, fishing works, etc., cannot be less than £30,000."[15] He was more specific in his report about what was lost: "In a violent gale of wind, 12th September, three vessels wrecked, in which were lost 9,400 quintals fish [1 quintal equaled 50 kg.] and thirty tons of oil: many boats destroyed, and considerable damage done to fishing works, etc."[16] The known destruction of only three ships led to the costly loss of two hundred thousand pounds of cod. That was only the tip of the iceberg.

Another person had a higher estimate, putting the damage at £140,000 for "the loss in ships, fish, oil, and merchandise of various kinds." The French Minister of Marine and Colonies was shocked to receive an estimate of the damages made by the royal governor of the French islands to be 155,978 livres.[17]

The financial ruin was borne mostly by individuals, particularly merchants who had invested their money in the codfisheries. Because there were no international relief agencies or swollen government agencies with expert bureaucrats who could assess damages and cut the appropriate check, an accurate final accounting of the actual cost of the storm will never be known. It did not matter much because people did not need some statistics to tell them they lost everything (nor to tell them how lucky they were to survive the storm).

The idea of government assistance was exceptional even for a disaster of this magnitude. A few years later, in the Great Hurricane of 1780, which killed twenty-two thousand people in the Caribbean, the British government sent disaster relief to Barbados. The total damages there, including the death of slaves and cattle, the loss of the sugar crop, and destruction of the infrastructure for manufacturing were a whopping £1,320,564. The government provided £120,000 to the islands but only to pay for provisions and supplies to avert mass starvation, not to help the planters rebuild. Wealthy Britons sent a generous, if inadequate, £30,000 in private voluntary donations. Churches and communities generally took care of their own. Merchants, for their part, were at the mercy of nature and on their own in a self-reliant age.[18]

In the September 1775 Newfoundland hurricane, the French Minister of Marine and Colonies procured the less than princely sum of 8,000 livres to relieve their distress. He assured the Newfoundlanders that he was sorry for their suffering but looked rather askance at their request for three months worth of provisions for the whole colony. He apologized but pleaded that the figure was the best that he could do given the financial situation of his department. In addition, the French crown was deeply in debt from a series of European wars, and it would soon increase by the aid sent to the Americans for their revolution. The debt would lead to the storming of the Bastille and France's own revolution a little more than a decade hence.[19]

The merchants were not indemnified against the losses that they suffered because of the hurricane. Indeed, their financial independence was probably in some cases destroyed. Sometimes, they could call in their credit from friends as honorable gentlemen. However, "If he be not well friended, he can never entertain a hope of rising again."[20] Their entire worth was poured into the vessels and the labor that caught fish. They had no choice other than to start over again and make modest gains until they could achieve success. They may have been reduced to do the very same labor that they had hired others to do before the storm. In other words, they might be thrust into poverty. Such were the vagaries of fortune. Few would listen to complaints—after all, life was tough for most people, not just fishermen.

A British report the year after still discussed the great natural disaster, but with some hindsight looked beyond all of the compilation of statistics to a more philosophical understanding of the hurricane. It tied the hurricane to the American fight over parliamentary measures as a judgment of God. Some judged God to be on the side of the colonists and their British allies in Parliament. In short, the British fishermen were receiving God's punishment for the mother country's tyranny. "Those who were averse to the American measures, considered the calamities which fell on the British fishery as a sort of judgment from heaven, against those who made laws to deprive mankind of the benefits of nature. To the same cause they were ready to attribute a dreadful tempest, the fury of which was chiefly discharged on the shores of Newfoundland."[21]

Perhaps they believed this in part because in the summer of 1775, Parliament passed the Restraining Act in retribution for the American boycott of British imports. Parliament thereby restricted New England trade to the ports of England. It also barred New England fishermen from the Grand Banks. Providence was wreaking its vengeance upon the apparently innocent Newfoundland fishermen for this act.[22]

The Hurricane of Independence and Codfishermen's Hurricane seemed to the people at the time as one more tangible piece of evidence that God was on the side of America. Those storms began a chain of providential events affecting the weather that brought a miraculous victory to a bunch of provincials against the mighty British Empire: the storm that prevented a British assault on Dorchester Heights; the fog that covered Washington's retreat from Long Island; the nor'easter that blew on the fateful night over the Delaware; and the strong gale that prevented Cornwallis's escape from Yorktown. There were countless other examples of benevolent Providence. General Washington had ridden ahead of his men into battle, and just as when he was a young colonel of the militia, seemingly impenetrable as the bullets whizzed harmlessly by him.

THE PROVIDENTIAL AMERICAN VICTORY

The Hurricane of Independence struck the colonies at the very start of the American Revolution. If there was providential agency in the storm, it was difficult most of the time to discern exactly who was being punished. The Americans thought God on their side, but so did their enemy. Each side believed it was fighting for the just cause. Whether God was on one side or the other, which side was receiving divine punishment in the two hurricanes—these questions were best relegated to faith rather than fact. Throughout, Americans certainly saw providential support for their war for independence.

At the successful conclusion to the war, eight years after the Hurricane of Independence, General Washington said farewell to his troops. He asked them to reflect on their wartime experience: "Who has before seen a disciplined army formed at once from such raw materials? Who, that was not a witness could imagine that the most violent local prejudices would cease so soon, and that men who came from the different parts of the continent, strongly disposed, by the habits of education to despise and quarrel with each other would instantly become one patriotic band of brothers?" Washington credited "the singular interpositions of Providence in our feeble condition" for the victory over the British that "was little short of a standing miracle."[1]

God was on America's side, so many Americans believed. As a blessed nation, they received covenantal blessings and duties. God seemed to be working through human agency (of Americans) to prepare the world for the expansion of liberty. They had to prove themselves worthy to the task by being constant in their piety and devotion to Revolutionary ideals of justice, virtue, and liberty. More than two centuries have seen many countries around the world emulate the American model and embrace liberty and self-government. As John Adams gave a concise summary of America's role in being a city upon a hill as a beacon for liberty for all peoples around the globe. "I always consider the settlement of America with reverence and wonder, as the opening of a grand scheme and design in Providence for the illumination of the ignorant, and the emancipation of the slavish part of mankind all over the earth."[2]

More than anyone, George Washington embodied these ideals and fleshed them out for the American people, reminding them of their exceptionalism. When Washington gave his First Inaugural Address upon his election as President after the successful creation and ratification of a "more perfect Union," he prayed that God's "benediction may consecrate to the liberties and happiness of the people of the United States, a government instituted by themselves for these essential purposes." Washington thought that, "No people can be bound to acknowledge and adore the invisible hand which conducts the affairs of men more than the people of the United States. Every step by which they have advanced to the character of an independent nation seems to have been distinguished by some token of providential agency."[3]

Washington believed that the "preservation of the sacred fire of liberty, and the destiny of the republican model of government, are justly considered as deeply, perhaps as finally, staked on the experiment entrusted to the hands of the American people."[4]

ENDNOTES

AUTHOR TO READER

1. GW, "Thanksgiving Proclamation," October 3, 1789, in William B. Allen, ed., *George Washington: A Collection* (Indianapolis: Liberty Fund, 1988), 534.

2. John Witherspoon, "The Dominion of Providence over the Passions of Men," in Ellis Sandoz, ed., *Political Sermons of the American Founding Era, 1730–1805*, vol. I, 2nd ed. (Indianapolis: Liberty Fund, 1998), 534–35.

3. Samuel Langdon, "The Republic of the Israelites an Example to the American States," in Sandoz, *Political Sermons of the American Founding Era*, I: 958.

4. Steven Waldman, *Founding Faith: Providence, Politics, and the Birth of Religious Freedom in America* (New York: Random House, 2008), 41.

PROLOGUE

1. GW to Bryan Fairfax, July 20, 1774, *PGW, Colonial Series*, 10:129.

2. Mark Puls, *Samuel Adams: Father of the American Revolution* (New York: Palgrave Macmillan, 2006), 140–47.

3. Robert Middlekauf, *The Glorious Cause: The American Revolution, 1763–1789* (New York: Oxford University Press, 1982), 225–32.

4. Frank Lambert, *The Founding Fathers and the Place of Religion in America* (Princeton: Princeton University Press, 2003), 216–17.

CHAPTER 1

1. Philip D. Curtain, *The Atlantic Slave Trade: A Census* (Madison: University of Wisconsin Press, 1969); and Marcus Rediker, *The Slave Ship: A Human History* (New York: Viking, 2007).

2. *New York Gazette and Weekly Mercury*, September 25, 1775.

3. David Ludlum, *Early American Hurricanes, 1492–1870* (Boston: American Meteorological Society, 1963), 26.

4. Kerry Emanuel, *Divine Wind: The History and Science of Hurricanes* (New York: Oxford University Press, 2005), 18–20, 26–7, 35–6, 98–9, 140.

5. Michael Novak and Jana Novak, *Washington's God: Religion, Liberty, and the Father of Our Country* (New York: Basic Books, 2006), 178–81.

6. John Witherspoon, "The Dominion of Providence over the Passions of Men," in Sandoz, *Political Sermons of the American Founding Era,* I: 533–58.

CHAPTER 2

1. William S. Powell, *North Carolina through Four Centuries* (Chapel Hill: University of North Carolina Press, 1989), 113–34.

2. Carl J. Richard, *The Founders and the Classics: Greece, Rome, and the American Enlightenment* (Cambridge: Harvard University Press, 1994), 10.

3. Middlekauf, *The Glorious Cause*, 248.

4. H.G. Jones, *North Carolina Illustrated, 1524–1984* (Chapel Hill: University of North Carolina Press, 1983), 113.

5. Harry L. Watson, "An Independent People: North Carolina, 1770–1820," in Joe A. Mobley, ed., *The Way We Lived in North Carolina* (Chapel Hill: University of North Carolina Press, 2003), 184.

6. "Extract from New Bern," *Pennsylvania Gazette*, September 27, 1775.

7. Elizabeth A. Fenn and Peter H. Wood, "Natives and Newcomers: North Carolina before 1770," in Mobley, *The Way We Lived in North Carolina*, 93.

8. Watson, "An Independent People: North Carolina, 1770–1820," in Mobley, *The Way We Lived in North Carolina*, 184–6.

9. Ibid., 184.

10. Fenn and Wood, "Natives and Newcomers: North Carolina before 1770," in Mobley, *The Way We Lived in North Carolina*, 96–8.

11. Powell, *North Carolina through Four Centuries*, 162–4.

12. *Ibid.*, 108–9; and Milton Ready, *The Tar Heel State: A History of North Carolina* (Chapel Hill: University of North Carolina Press, 2005), 109–11.

13. Marcus Rediker, *Between the Devil and the Deep Blue Sea: Merchant Seamen, Pirates, and the Anglo-American Maritime World, 1700–1750* (Cambridge: Cambridge University Press, 1987), 11–2.

14. Paul A. Gilje, *Liberty on the Waterfront: American Maritime Culture in the Age of Revolution* (Philadelphia: University of Pennsylvania Press, 2004), 11, 34–6.

15. Watson, "An Independent People: North Carolina, 1770–1820," in Mobley, *The Way We Lived in North Carolina*, 184, 192–3.

16. Middlekauf, *The Glorious Cause*, 249.

17. Gilje, *Liberty on the Waterfront*, 14, 28–32.

18. Jones, *North Carolina Illustrated*, 93.

19. *Ibid.*, 111.

20. Linda K. Kerber, *Women of the Republic: Intellect and Ideology in Revolutionary America* (Chapel Hill: University of North Carolina Press, 1980), 38.

21. Mary Beth Norton, *Liberty's Daughters: The Revolutionary Experience of American Women, 1750–1800* (Boston: Little, Brown and Company 1980), 160–2.

22. Norton, *Liberty's Daughters*, 160–9.

23. Ready, *The Tar Heel State*, 109; and Jones, *North Carolina Illustrated*, 112.

24. Simon Schama, *Rough Crossings: Britain, the Slaves, and the American Revolution* (New York: Harper, Collins, 2006), 65–9; and Ready, *The Tar Heel State*, 107–11.

25. Ready, *The Tar Heel State*, 107–11.

CHAPTER 3

1. "Extract from New Bern," *Pennsylvania Gazette*, September 27, 1775.

2. *Ibid.*

3. Rediker, *Between the Devil and the Deep Blue Sea*, 1–4.

4. "Extract from New Bern," *Pennsylvania Gazette*, September 27, 1775.

5. *Ibid.*

6. *Ibid.*

7. Gilje, *Liberty on the Waterfront*, 12.

8. "Extract of a letter from New Bern," *Virginia Gazette*, October 21, 1775.

9. Powell, *North Carolina through Four Centuries*, 119–27.

10. Jay Barnes, *North Carolina's Hurricane History*, 3rd ed. (Chapel Hill: University of North Carolina Press, 2001), 36.

11. Barnes, *North Carolina's Hurricane History*, 36.

12. David Longshore, *Encyclopedia of Hurricanes, Typhoons, and Cyclones* (New York: Facts on File, 1998), 227.

13. Ludlum, *Early American Hurricanes*, 26.

14. Ready, *The Tar Heel State*, 108–10.

15. "Extract from New Bern," *Pennsylvania Gazette*, September 27, 1775.

16. *Ibid.*

17. *Ibid.*

CHAPTER 4

1. Allan Kulikoff, *Tobacco and Slaves: The Development of Southern Cultures in the Chesapeake, 1680–1800* (Chapel Hill: University of North Carolina Press, 1986), 109.

2. Paul K. Longmore, *The Invention of George Washington* (Charlottesville: University Press of Virginia, 1999), 76–85.

3. Thomas C. Paramore, *Norfolk: The First Four Centuries* (Charlottesville: University Press of Virginia, 1994), 72.

4. Paramore, *Norfolk*, 70–1, 75.

5. *Ibid.*, 71–9.

6. *Virginia Gazette, or Norfolk Intelligencer*, September 6, 1775.

7. *Virginia Gazette*, September 7, 1775.

8. John Witherspoon, "The Dominion of Providence over the Passions of Men," in Sandoz, *Political Sermons of the American Founding Era*, I: 540.

9. *Virginia Gazette, or Norfolk Intelligencer*, September 6, 1775.

10. *Virginia Gazette*, September 7, 1775.

11. *Virginia Gazette*, September 8, 1775.

12. *Virginia Gazette, or Norfolk Intelligencer*, September 6, 1775.

13. *Ibid.*

14. *Ibid.*

15. *Ibid.*

16. "Continental Congress: Resolution Regarding Inspections," in Robert L. Scribner and William J. Van Schreeven, eds., *Revolutionary Virginia: The Road to Independence* (Charlottesville: University of Virginia Press, 1973), IV: 106.

17. "Caroline County Committee: Loads of Tobacco and Officers for the Militia," and, "Further Resolution in the Case of Captain James Dunlop's Tobacco," in Scribner, *Revolutionary Virginia*, IV: 109, 152.

18. *Virginia Gazette*, September 8, 1775.

19. "Norfolk County Committee: Summons for Mr. Andrew Sprowle," in Scribner, *Revolutionary Virginia* III: 411.

20. "Norfolk County Committee: Andrew Spowle to Gentlemen of the County Committee Residing in the Borough of Norfolk," in Scribner, *Revolutionary Virginia*, III: 433.

21. "Norfolk County Committee: Remissness and Most Unfriendly Disposition," in Scribner, *Revolutionary Virginia*, III: 452.

22. "Norfolk Borough Committee: Retirement of the Little General," in *Scribner, Revolutionary Virginia*, III: 420.

23. "Norfolk Borough Committee: Sincere Repentance and Determined Resolution of John Schaw," in Scribner, *Revolutionary Virginia*, III: 414–5.

24. "Introductory Note," in Scribner, *Revolutionary Virginia*, III: 225.

25. *Virginia Gazette, or Norfolk Intelligencer*, September 6, 1775.

26. *Ibid.* (Emphasis in original.)

27. *Virginia Gazette*, September 8, 1775.

28. "Introductory Note," in Scribner, *Revolutionary Virginia*, IV: 4.

29. *Virginia Gazette*, September 8, 1775.

30. "Norfolk County Committee: Remissness and Most Unfriendly Disposition," in Scribner, *Revolutionary Virginia*, III: 452–3.

31. "The Capital: Municipal Common Hall to Governor Dunmore, An Humble Address," in Scribner, *Revolutionary Virginia*, III: 54–5.

32. "Governor Dunmore to the Municipal Common Hall, An Oral Reply," in Scribner, *Revolutionary Virginia*, III: 55.

33. Burke Davis, *A Williamsburg Galaxy* (Williamsburg: Colonial Williamsburg Foundation, 1968), 106.

34. *Virginia Gazette*, September 8, 1775.

35. "Spotsylvania Council: Pledge of Readiness at a Moment's Warning," in Scribner, *Revolutionary Virginia*, III: 71.

36. *Virginia Gazette*, September 8, 1775.

37. "Elizabeth City County: Wilson Miles Cary to Alexander Purdie, An Open Letter, with Enclosures," in Scribner, *Revolutionary Virginia*, IV: 69–71.

38. *Ibid.*

39. Novak and Novak, *Washington's God*, 112–6, 192.

40. Henry Wiencek, *An Imperfect God: George Washington, His Slaves, and the Creation of America* (New York: Farrar, Straus, and Giroux, 2003), 247–51; and Thomas Fleming, *The Perils of Peace: America's Struggle for Survival After Yorktown* (New York: Smithsonian Books, 2007), 19–20.

41. "Royal Chief Magistracy: A Most Disagreeable but Absolutely Necessary Step, By His Excellency the Right Honorable John Earl of Dunmore, His Majesty's Lieutenant and Governor General of the Colony and Dominion of Virginia, and Vice Admiral of the same, A Proclamation," in Scribner, *Revolutionary Virginia*, IV: 334.

42. Benjamin Quarles, *The Negro in the American Revolution* (New York: Norton, 1961), 21.

43. Schama, *Rough Crossings,* 79.

44. *Ibid.,* 70–83.

45. Quarles, *The Negro in the American Revolution,* 20, 31; and Schama, *Rough Crossings,* 70–83.

46. Rhys Isaac, *Landon Carter's Uneasy Kingdom: Revolution and Rebellion on a Virginia Plantation* (Oxford: Oxford University Press, 2004), 8–10.

47. *Virginia Gazette,* September 7, 1775.

48. "Introductory Note," in Scribner, *Revolutionary Virginia,* IV: 4–5.

49. *Virginia Gazette,* September 7, 1775.

50. *Ibid.*

51. *Virginia Gazette,* September 8, 1775.

52. *Virginia Gazette, or Norfolk Intelligencer,* September 6, 1775.

53. *Ibid.*

54. *Virginia Gazette, or Norfolk Intelligencer,* September 13, 1775.

55. *Ibid.*

56. "Norfolk Borough: John Hunter Holt's Further Notice of the Generosity of Captain Matthew Squire," in Scribner, *Revolutionary Virginia,* IV: 134.

57. "Royal Chief Magistry: Address of the Common Hall of the Borough of Norfolk to His Excellency Lord Dunmore," in Scribner, *Revolutionary Virginia,* IV: 153.

58. "Royal Chief Magistry: Lord Dunmore to the Common Hall of the Borough of Norfolk," in Scribner, *Revolutionary Virginia,* IV: 161. (Emphasis in original.)

59. "Virginia Committee of Safety: Edmund Pendleton to the Honorable the Delegates from Virginia to the Congress at Philadelphia," in Scribner, *Revolutionary Virginia,* IV: 294.

60. "Virginia Committee of Safety: Virginia Delegates in Congress to the Committee of Safety at Williamsburg," in Scribner, *Revolutionary Virginia,* IV: 169–70.

61. "Elizabeth City County–Hampton Town Committee: Captain Matthew Squire to the Gentlemen of the Committee," in Scribner, *Revolutionary Virginia,* IV: 92–3.

62. "Elizabeth City County–Hampton Town Committee: To Matthew Squire, Esq; Commander of His Majesty's Ship *Otter*, Lying in Hampton Road" in Scribner, *Revolutionary Virginia*, IV: 119–20.

63. "Elizabeth City County–Hampton Town Committee: To Matthew Squire, Esq; Commander of His Majesty's Ship *Otter*, Lying in Hampton Road" in Scribner, *Revolutionary Virginia*, IV: 119–20.

64. "Royal Chief Magistracy: A Most Disagreeable but Absolutely Necessary Step, By His Excellency the Right Honorable John Earl of Dunmore, His Majesty's Lieutenant and Governor General of the Colony and Dominion of Virginia, and Vice Admiral of the same, A Proclamation," in Scribner, *Revolutionary Virginia*, IV: 334.

65. Paramore, *Norfolk*, 94–6.

66. Burke, *Williamsburg Galaxy*, 109, and Ludlum, *Early American Hurricanes*, 69–72.

CHAPTER 5

1. Thomas Bolling, owner, *1775 Virginia Almanack*, Rockefeller Library, Colonial Williamsburg Foundation.

2. John Page Roswell, owner, *1776 Virginia Almanack*, Rockefeller Library, Colonial Williamsburg Foundation.

3. *Ibid.*

4. *Ibid.*

5. *Virginia Gazette*, September 7, 1775.

6. *Virginia Gazette*, September 8, 1775.

7. *Ibid.*

8. Rhys Isaac, *The Transformation of Virginia, 1740–1790* (New York: Norton, 1982).

9. Davis, *Williamsburg Galaxy*, 8–15, and Carl Bridenbaugh, *Seat of Empire: The Political Role of Eighteenth Century Williamsburg* (Williamsburg: Colonial Williamsburg Foundation, 1950), 24–9.

10. Davis, *Williamsburg Galaxy*, 104–5.

11. *Ibid.*, 105.

12. "Introductory Note," in Scribner, *Revolutionary Virginia*, III: 6.

13. "Spotsylvania Council: Pledge of Readiness at a Moment's Warning," in Scribner, *Revolutionary Virginia*, III: 70–1.

14. Davis, *Williamsburg Galaxy*, 106.

15. Richard R. Beeman, *Patrick Henry: A Biography* (New York: McGraw–Hill, 1974), 70–1.

16. Beeman, *Patrick Henry,* 37–8.

17. Davis, *Williamsburg Galaxy*, 189, and Beeman, *Patrick Henry*, 39.

18. "Resolutions Offered by Patrick Henry in Condemnation of the Stamp Act, 29–30 May 1765," in Scribner, *Revolutionary Virginia,* I: 15–18

19. J. Kent McGaughy, *Richard Henry Lee of Virginia: A Portrait of an American Revolutionary* (Lanham, MD: Rowman & Littlefield, 2004), 76–8.

20. Davis, *Williamsburg Galaxy*, 189.

21. Beeman, *Patrick Henry*, 59.

22. William Safire, ed., *Lend Me Your Ears: Great Speeches in History*, rev. ed. (New York: Norton, 2004), 96–101.

23. Safire, *Lend Me Your Ears,* 96–101.

24. Beeman, *Patrick Henry*, 63–8.

25. *Ibid.*, 71.

CHAPTER 6

1. Jack P. Greene, *Landon Carter: An Inquiry into the Personal Values and Social Imperatives of the Eighteenth–Century Virginia Gentry* (Charlottesville: University Press of Virginia, 1967), 1–6.

2. T. H. Breen, *Tobacco Culture: The Mentality of the Great Tidewater Planters on the Eve of the Revolution* (Princeton: Princeton University Press, 1985), 64, 68.

3. Greene, *Landon Carter*, 50–4.

4. "Address, Memorial, and Remonstrance of the General Assembly to King, Lords, and Commons respectively in Opposition to a Proposed Stamp

Tax," December 18, 1764, in Scribner, *Revolutionary Virginia*, I: 9–14.

5. Scribner, *Revolutionary Virginia*, I: 10.

6. Greene, *Landon Carter*, 59.

7. *Ibid.*, 53–61.

8. Isaac, *Landon Carter's Uneasy Kingdom*, xvii–xviii, 54–84.

9. *Ibid.*, 92–8.

10. Greene, *Landon Carter*, 11–13, 36–49.

11. Jack P. Greene, ed., *The Diary of Colonel Landon Carter of Sabine Hall, 1752–1778*, vol. II (Charlottesville: University Press of Virginia, 1965), 932–48.

12. Greene, *The Diary of Colonel Landon Carter*, II: 932–48.

13. *Ibid.*

14. Breen, *Tobacco Culture*, 45–55.

15. *Ibid.*, 59–61.

16. Joseph Ellis, *His Excellency: George Washington* (New York: Knopf, 2004), 49.

17. Breen, *Tobacco Culture*, 106–203.

18. John Norton & Sons Papers, 1750–1902: 1775, September—December. Folder 127. Rockefeller Library, Colonial Williamsburg Foundation.

19. *Virginia Gazette*, September 7, 1775.

20. *Virginia Gazette*, September 8, 1775.

21. John Witherspoon, "The Dominion of Providence over the Passions of Men," in Sandoz, *Political Sermons of the American Founding Era*, I: 540.

22. Greene, *The Diary of Colonel Landon Carter*, II: 932–48.

23. *Ibid.*

24. *Ibid.*

25. Merrill D. Peterson, ed., *Writings of Thomas Jefferson* (New York: Library of America, 1984), 290.

26. *Virginia Gazette*, September 8, 1775.

27. Greene, *The Diary of Colonel Landon Carter*, II: 932–48.

28. *Ibid.*

29. Greene, *Landon Carter*, 20–30.

30. *Ibid.*, 61.

CHAPTER 7

1. Richard L. Bushman, *The Refinement of America: Persons, Houses, Cities* (New York: Knopf, 1992), 151–2.

2. Lisa Jardine, *On a Grander Scale: The Outstanding Life and Tumultuous Times of Sir Christopher Wren* (New York: Harper, Collins, 2003), 238.

3. Jardine, *On a Grander Scale*, 109–11, 185, 274.

4. *Ibid.*, 248–50.

5. *Ibid.*, 52, 239–47.

6. *Ibid.*, 262–3, 291–2.

7. *Ibid.*, 411–28.

8. Ronald Hoffman, *Princes of Ireland, Planters of Maryland: A Carroll Saga, 1500–1782* (Chapel Hill: University of North Carolina Press, 2000), 186.

9. Dorothy Twohig, ed., *George Washington's Diaries: An Abridgement* (Charlottesville: University Press of Virginia, 1999), 163–5, 175.

10. Jane McWilliams and Morris L. Radoff, "Annapolis Meets the Crisis," in Ernest McNeill, ed., *Chesapeake Bay in the American Revolution* (Centreville, MD: Tidewater Publishers, 1981), 403–6.

11. Hoffman, *Princes of Ireland*, 283, 301.

12. *Ibid.*, 295–6.

13. McNeil, *Chesapeake Bay*, 407–8.

14. *Ibid.*, 407–8.

15. *Ibid.*, 407–8.

16. Larry Witham, *A City Upon a Hill: How Sermons Changed the Course of American History* (New York: Harper Collins, 2007), 64–6.

17. Hoffman, *Princes of Ireland*, 286–90.

18. Novak and Novak, *Washington's God*, 112–6.

19. James H. Hutson, *Religion and the Founding of the American Republic* (Washington, D.C.: Library of Congress, 1998), 65.

20. Allen, *George Washington*, 521.

21. *Maryland Gazette*, September 7, 1775.

22. *Ibid.*

23. Ronald Hoffman, ed., *Dear Papa, Dear Charley: The Papers of Charles Carroll of Carrollton, 1748–1782*, vol. II (Chapel Hill: University of North Carolina Press, 2001), 843.

24. Hoffman, *Dear Papa, Dear Charley*, 842–3.

25. *Maryland Gazette*, September 7, 1775.

26. *Ibid.*

27. Charles Wallace to Daniel of St. Thomas Jenifer, ca. November, 1784, in, "Protecting the State House from Lightning: The Franklin Lightning Rod." www.mdarchives.state.md.us.

CHAPTER 8

1. Chapter 32, Acts of 1773, quoted in, "Protecting the State House from Lightning: The Franklin Lightning Rod." www.mdarchives.state.md.us.

2. Thomas E. Woods, Jr., *How the Catholic Church Built Western Civilization* (Washington, D.C.: Regnery, 2005), 93.

3. See the several essays in David C. Lindberg and Ronald L. Numbers, eds., *God and Nature: Historical Essays on the Encounter between Christianity and Science* (Berkeley: University of California Press, 1986); and David C. Lindberg and Ronald L. Numbers, eds., *When Science and Christianity Meet* (Chicago: University of Chicago Press, 2003).

4. James Gleick, *Isaac Newton* (New York: Pantheon, 2003), 32, 104–5.

5. John Page Roswell, owner, *1776 Virginia Almanack*, Rockefeller Library, Colonial Williamsburg Foundation.

6. BF, "A Proposal for Promoting Useful Knowledge among the British Plantations in America," May 14, 1743, *PBF*, 2:380–3.

7. Gordon Wood, *The Americanization of Benjamin Franklin* (New York: Penguin, 2004), 53–6.

8. BF to Cadwallader Colden, September 29, 1748, *PBF*, 3:318.

9. Philip Dray, *Stealing God's Thunder: Benjamin Franklin's Lightning Rod and the Invention of America* (New York: Random House, 2005), xvi.

10. BF to Jared Eliot, *PBF*, February 13, 1750, 3:463–5.

11. BF to Jared Eliot, *PBF*, February 13, 1750, 3:463–5.

12. BF to Jared Eliot, *PBF*, February 13, 1750, 3:463–5.

13. Ludlum, *Early American Hurricanes*, 22.

14. Dray, *Stealing God's Thunder*, 103.

15. Walter Isaacson, *Benjamin Franklin: An American Life* (New York: Simon and Schuster, 2003), 85–8.

16. BF to Cadwallader Colden, April 12, 1753, *PBF*, 4:463.

17. Lambert, *The Founding Fathers and the Place of Religion in America*, 167–9.

18. Benjamin Franklin, June 28, 1787, in James Madison, *Notes of Debates in the Federal Convention of 1787* (New York: Norton, 1987), 209–10.

19. Dray, *Stealing God's Thunder*, 69–70, 111.

20. Lambert, *The Founding Fathers and the Place of Religion in America*, 167.

21. BF to John Winthrop, July 2, 1768, *PBF*, 15:168–9.

22. "Gazette Extracts, 1732," *PBF*, 1:272–5.

23. BF to Richard Dawson, May 29, 1772, *PBF*, 19:153.

24. BF, "Opinions and Conjectures," July 29, 1750, *PBF*, 4:19.

25. Dray, *Stealing God's Thunder*, 47–51.

26. BF to Peter Collinson, March 28, 1747, *PBF*, 3:118–9.

27. BF to John Franklin, December 25, 1750, *PBF*, 4:82–3.

28. Dray, *Stealing God's Thunder*, 83–5.

29. *Ibid.*, 103–5.

30. *Ibid.*, 128.

31. "Purfleet Committee to the Royal Society," December 10, 1772, *PBF*, 19:427–8.

32. BF to John Winthrop, July 2, 1768, *PBF*, 15:169.

33. BF to Peter Collinson, September, 1753, *PBF*, 5:69–70.

34. Jerry Weinberger, *Benjamin Franklin Unmasked: On the Unity of His*

Moral, Religious, and Political Thought (Lawrence: University Press of Kansas, 2005), 124.

35. GW to John Augustine Washington, June 15, 1783, in Allen, *George Washington,* 255–6.

36. "Address to Congress on Resigning His Commission," December 23, 1783, in Allen, *Washington,* 272–3.

37. Stanley Weintraub, *General Washington's Christmas Farewell: A Mount Vernon Homecoming* (New York: Free Press, 2003), 93–170.

38. Garry Wills, *Cincinnatus: George Washington and the Enlightenment: Images of Power in Early America* (New York: Doubleday, 1984), 13.

CHAPTER 9

1. Jack N. Rakove, *The Beginnings of National Politics: An Interpretive History of the Continental Congress* (New York: Knopf, 1979), 22–7.

2. Gary B. Nash, *The Urban Crucible: The Northern Seaports and the Origins of the American Revolution* (Cambridge: Harvard University Press, 1986), 162, 179, 194–6, 202, 240–2.

3. Jeffry H. Morrison, *John Witherspoon and the Founding of the American Republic* (South Bend: University of Notre Dame Press, 2005), 1–2, 72.

4. AA to JA, September 2, 1774, in Frank Shuffelton, ed., *Letters of John and Abigail Adams* (New York: Penguin, 2004), 28.

5. JA to AA, August 28, 1774, in Shuffelton, *Letters of John and Abigail Adams,* 25.

6. L.H. Butterfield, ed., *Diary and Autobiography of John Adams* (Cambridge: Harvard University Press, 1961), 100.

7. JA to AA, July 6, 1774, in Shuffelton, *Letters of John and Abigail Adams,* 18.

8. JA to AA, August 28, 1774, in Shuffelton, *Letters of John and Abigail Adams,* 25.

9. JA to AA, June 30, 1774, in Shuffelton, *Letters of John and Abigail Adams,* 6.

10. Butterfield, *Diary of John Adams,* 114.

11. Bushman, *The Refinement of America,* 173–4.

12. *Ibid.*, 162–3.

13. Butterfield, *Diary of John Adams*, 114.

14. *Ibid.*, 116.

15. *Ibid.*

16. Middlekauf, *The Glorious Cause*, 241.

17. Butterfield, *Diary of John Adams*, 119–20.

18. JA to AA, September 14, 1775, in Shuffelton, *Letters of John and Abigail Adams*, 30.

19. Rakove, *The Beginnings of National Politics*, 45.

20. Butterfield, *Diary of John Adams*, 121.

21. Twohig, *George Washington's Diaries*, 191.

22. GW to Bryan Fairfax, August 24, 1774, in Allen, *George Washington*, 38–9.

23. Middlekauf, *The Glorious Cause*, 241.

24. Butterfield, *Diary of John Adams*, 117.

25. *Ibid.*, 121.

26. *Ibid.*, 123.

27. Davis, *Williamsburg Galaxy*, 125–6.

28. *Ibid.*, 131.

29. *Ibid.*

30. Peterson, *Thomas Jefferson*, 105.

31. JA to AA, September 8, 1774, in Shuffelton, *Letters of John and Abigail Adams*, 29.

32. JA to AA, October 9, 1774, in Shuffelton, *Letters of John and Abigail Adams*, 42–3.

33. JA to AA, September 25, 1774, in Shuffelton, *Letters of John and Abigail Adams*, 39.

34. JA to AA, September 16, 1774, in Shuffelton, *Letters of John and Abigail Adams*, 34–5.

35. Witham, *A City Upon a Hill*, 71.

36. Hutson, *Religion and the Founding of the American Republic*, 51.

37. JA to AA, October 9, 1774, in Shuffelton, *Letters of John and Abigail Adams*, 43–4.

38. Butterfield, *Diary of John Adams*, 128–9.

39. "Declaration and Resolves of the First Congress," in Henry Steele Commager and Richard B. Morris, eds., *The Spirit of 'Seventy–Six: The Story of the American Revolution as told by Participants* (New York: Da Capo, 1995), 57–8.

40. "The Suffolk Resolves," in Commager and Morris, *The Spirit of 'Seventy–Six*, 53–4.

41. "The Continental Congress Endorses the Suffolk Resolves," in Commager and Morris, *The Spirit of 'Seventy–Six*, 54–5.

42. Butterfield, *Diary of John Adams*, 135.

43. Rakove, *Beginnings of National Politics*, 48.

44. Butterfield, *Diary of John Adams*, 139.

45. Middlekauf, *The Glorious Cause*, 249.

46. Butterfield, *Diary of John Adams*, 127.

47. JA to AA, September 29, 1774, in Shuffelton, *Letters of John and Abigail Adams*, 40.

48. Twohig, *George Washington's Diaries*, 325.

CHAPTER 10

1. King to Lord North, November 18, 1774, in Commager and Morris, *The Spirit of 'Seventy–Six*, 61.

2. "Burke Pleads for Conciliation with the Colonies," in Commager and Morris, *The Spirit of 'Seventy–Six*, 233–8.

3. Scribner, *Revolutionary Virginia*, III: 166.

4. Burke, *Williamsburg Galaxy*, 132.

5. "Williamsburg: The Gentlemen Volunteers of the Independent Company to Peyton Randolph, An Open Letter," and, "Peyton Randolph to the Gentlemen Volunteers of the Independent Company, An Open Letter," in Scribner, *Revolutionary Virginia*, III: 178.

6. JA to AA, May 8, 1775, in Shuffelton, *Letters of John and Abigail Adams*, 51.

7. Rakove, *Beginnings of National Politics*, 70–1.

8. Butterfield, *Diary of John Adams*, 161.

9. Middlekauf, *The Glorious Cause*, 277–8.

10. Ellis, *His Excellency*, 66, 68.

11. JA to AA, June 10, 1775, in Shuffelton, *Letters of John and Abigail Adams*, 58.

12. JA to AA, May 29, 1775, in Shuffelton, *Letters of John and Abigail Adams*, 56.

13. Rakove, *Beginnings of National Politics*, 71–2.

14. Middlekauf, *The Glorious Cause*, 278–9.

15. Ellis, *His Excellency*, 68–9, and Richard Brookhiser, *Founding Father: Rediscovering George Washington* (New York: Free Press, 1996), 20–2.

16. "Editorial Note," in *PGW, Revolutionary Series*, 1–3.

17. "Commission from the Continental Congress," *PGW, Revolutionary Series*, 1:7.

18. GW to the President of the Second Continental Congress, June 16, 1775, in Allen, *George Washington*, 40.

19. "Editorial Note," in *PGW, Revolutionary Series*, 1:3.

20. "Editorial Note," in *PGW, Revolutionary Series*, 1:2.

21. Daniel Palm, ed., *On Faith and Free Government* (Lanham, MD: Rowman & Littlefield, 1997), 29.

22. GW to Martha Washington, June 18, 1775, in Allen, *George Washington*, 40–2, and Middlekauf, *The Glorious Cause*, 293–6.

23. GW to Burwell Bassett, June 19, 1775, in John Rhodehamel, ed., *George Washington: Writings* (New York: Library of America, 1997), 169–70.

24. GW to Burwell Bassett, June 19, 1775, and GW to John Augustine Washington, June 20, 1775, in Rhodehamel, *George Washington*, 169–71.

25. JA to AA, June 17, 1775, in Shuffelton, *Letters of John and Abigail Adams*, 64.

26. JA to AA, June 23, 1775, in Shuffelton, *Letters of John and Abigail Adams*, 68.

27. GW to Martha Washington, June 18, 1775, in Allen, *George Washington*, 40–2.

28. "Declaration of the Causes and Necessity of Taking up Arms," in Commager and Morris, *The Spirit of 'Seventy-Six*, 278–79.

29. "Congress Sends an Olive Branch Petition," in Commager and Morris, *The Spirit of 'Seventy–Six*, 279–80.

30. Gordon S. Wood, *Revolutionary Characters: What Made the Founders Different* (New York: Penguin, 2006), 84.

31. Hutson, *Religion and the Founding of the American Republic*, 51–53.

32. "The King's Speech on Opening the Session of Parliament, October 26, 1775," in Commager and Morris, *The Spirit of 'Seventy–Six,* 253–4.

33. Scribner, *Revolutionary Virginia*, IV: 75–6.

CHAPTER 11

1. *Pennsylvania Gazette*, September 6, 1775.

2. Ludlum, *Early American Hurricanes*, 26–7.

3. *Pennsylvania Gazette*, September 6, 1775.

4. *Ibid.*

5. *Ibid.*

CHAPTER 12

1. Richard Brookhiser, *Alexander Hamilton, American* (New York: Touchstone, 1999), 26.

2. "Report from New York," *Virginia Gazette*, September 9, 1775.

3. AH to Edward Stevens, November 11, 1769, in Joanne B. Freeman, ed., *Alexander Hamilton: Writings* (New York: Library of America, 2001), 3.

4. Brookhiser, *Alexander Hamilton,* 13–20.

5. AH to Nicholas Cruger, February 24, 1772, in Freeman, *Alexander Hamilton*, 4–5.

6. AH to Tileman Cruger, February 1, 1772, *PAH*, 1:13.

7. AH to Walton and Cruger, February 24, 1772, *PAH*, 1:30.

8. Forrest McDonald, *Alexander Hamilton: A Biography* (New York: Norton, 1979), 10–1.

9. AH, "To the *Royal Danish American Gazette*," September 6, 1772, in Freeman, *Alexander Hamilton*, 6–9.

10. Hugh Knox to AH, July 28, 1784, *PAH*, 3:474–5.

11. David McCullough, *John Adams* (New York: Simon and Schuster, 2001), 25.

12. Richard M. Ketchum, *Divided Loyalties: How the American Revolution came to New York* (New York: Henry Holt, 2002), 90.

13. Ketchum, *Divided Loyalties*, 5–22; and Edward Countryman, *A People in Revolution: The American Revolution and Political Society in New York, 1760–1790* (New York: Norton, 1989), 3–13.

14. Ketchum, *Divided Loyalties*, 97–8, 128.

15. *Ibid.*, 105, 148.

16. Samuel Eliot Morison, ed., *Sources and Documents Illustrating the American Revolution 1764–1788 and the Formation of the Federal Constitution* (Oxford: Oxford University Press, 1965), 33.

17. Ketchum, *Divided Loyalties*, 109–32.

18. *Ibid.*, 117–8.

19. Countryman, *A People in Revolution*, 37–8.

20. *Ibid.*, 38.

21. Ketchum, *Divided Loyalties*, 142.

22. Countryman, *A People in Revolution*, 38–9.

23. *Ibid.*, 37.

24. Countryman, *A People in Revolution*, 12–3, 37, 65.

25. Ketchum, *Divided Loyalties*, 175–85.

26. Countryman, *A People in Revolution*, 41.

27. Ketchum, *Divided Loyalties*, 188–9, 208.

28. *Ibid.*, 226.

29. *Ibid.*, 224–9.

30. Ketchum, *Divided Loyalties*, 216, 219–23, and Countryman, *A People in Revolution*, 91.

31. Ketchum, *Divided Loyalties*, 151–2.

32. *Ibid.*, 243.

33. Ron Chernow, *Alexander Hamilton* (New York: Penguin, 2004), 54, and Countryman, *A People in Revolution*, 45.

34. Ketchum, *Divided Loyalties*, 272.

35. *Ibid.*, 282.

36. *Ibid.*, 296, 300, 330.

37. Chernow, *Alexander Hamilton*, 55.

38. *Ibid.*, 57–8.

39. "A Full Vindication of Congress, December 15, 1774," and "The Farmer Refuted," February 23, 1775, *PAH*, 1:45–79; 81–165.

40. Chernow, *Alexander Hamilton*, 62; and Ketchum, *Divided Loyalties*, 327.

41. Chernow, *Alexander Hamilton*, 63–4.

42. AH to John Jay, November 26, 1775, *PAH*, 1:177.

43. Countryman, *A People in Revolution*, 43.

44. Robert Middlekauf, *The Glorious Cause*, 276–7; and "Accounts of Fort Ticonderoga," in Commager and Morris, *The Spirit of 'Seventy–Six*, 97–105.

45. Chernow, *Alexander Hamilton*, 62–3.

Chapter 13

1. Ludlum, *Early American Hurricanes*, 27.

2. *New York Gazette and Weekly Mercury*, October 16, 1775.

3. *New York Gazette and Weekly Mercury*, September 25, 1775.

4. *Ibid.*

5. *New York Gazette and Weekly Mercury*, October 2, 1775.

6. *Ibid.*

7. *Ibid.*

8. "Letter from New York, September 25," *Maryland Gazette*, October 5, 1775.

9. *New York Gazette and Weekly Mercury*, October 2, 1775.

10. *New York Gazette and Weekly Mercury*, October 16, 1775.

11. Matthew Mulcahy, "Weathering the Storms: Hurricanes and Risk in the British Greater Caribbean," *Business History Review*, 78 (Winter 2004): 635–63.

12. "Letter from New York, August 28," *Virginia Gazette*, September 9, 1775.

13. Alan Ruffman, "The Multidisciplinary Rediscovery and Tracking of 'The Great Newfoundland and Saint–Pierre et Miquelon Hurricane of September 1775,'" *The Northern Mariner*, VI, no. 3 (July 1996): 18.

14. *New York Gazette and Weekly Mercury*, September 25, 1775.

CHAPTER 14

1. Ludlum, *Early American Hurricanes*, 27.

2. September 3, 1775, in Franklin Bowditch Dexter, ed., *The Literary Diary of Ezra Stiles*, vol. I (New York: Charles Scribner's Sons, 1901), 610–11.

3. Edmund S. Morgan, *The Gentle Puritan: A Life of Ezra Stiles, 1727–1795* (New Haven: Yale University Press, 1962), 7.

4. Morgan, *The Gentle Puritan*, 12–41.

5. Morgan, *Gentle Puritan*, 52–5, and Perry Miller, *The New England Mind: From Colony to Province* (Cambridge: Harvard University Press, 1953), 437–46.

6. Morgan, *Gentle Puritan*, 73–6.

7. *Ibid.*, 170.

8. *Ibid.*, 91, 135–6, 158–61.

9. Paul A. Rahe, *Inventions of Prudence: Constituting the American Regime*, vol. III (Chapel Hill: University of North Carolina Press, 1994), 10.

10. Sandoz, *Political Sermons of the American Founding Era*, I: xiii–xx.

11. Witham, *A City Upon a Hill*, 59–62.

12. Morgan, *Gentle Puritan*, 224, 273–4.

13. David Hackett Fischer, *Paul Revere's Ride* (New York: Oxford University Press, 1994), 75–7.

14. Paul Revere, "Memorandum on Events of April 18, 1775," in John Rhodehamel, ed., *The American Revolution: Writings from the War of Independence* (New York: Library of America, 2001), 1.

15. Thomas Gage to the Earl of Dartmouth, April 1775, in Rhodehamel, *The American Revolution*, 19.

16. Paul Revere, "Memorandum on Events of April 18, 1775," in Rhodehamel, *The American Revolution*, 1.

17. Fischer, *Paul Revere's Ride*, 108–12.

18. Paul Revere, "Memorandum on Events of April 18, 1775," in Rhode-hamel, *The American Revolution*, 2–3.

19. Fischer, *Paul Revere's Ride*, 149–64.

20. Middlekauf, *The Glorious Cause*, 269–70.

21. Fischer, *Paul Revere's Ride*, 193–201.

22. John Dickinson to Arthur Lee, April 29, 1775; and Peter Oliver, *The Origin and Progress of the American Rebellion*, in Rhodehamel, *The American Revolution*, 21, 25.

23. GW to Marquis de LaFayette, February 1, 1784, in Allen, *George Washington*, 280–2.

24. GW to George William Fairfax, May 31, 1775, in Rhodehamel, *George Washington*, 164.

25. Fischer, *Paul Revere's Ride*, 202–9.

26. Middlekauf, *The Glorious Cause*, 271–2.

27. Thomas Gage to the Earl of Dartmouth, April 1775, in Rhodehamel, *The American Revolution*, 20.

28. Frederick MacKenzie: Diary, April 18–21, 1775, in Rhodehamel, *The American Revolution*, 9.

29. Frederick MacKenzie: Diary, April 18–21, 1775, in Rhodehamel, *The American Revolution*, 15.

30. Fischer, *Paul Revere's Ride*, 218–32.

31. Richard Ketchum, *Decisive Day: The Battle for Bunker Hill* (New York: Henry Holt, 1962), 25.

32. Ketchum, *Decisive Day*, 54–72.

33. Middlekauf, *The Glorious Cause*, 284–6.

34. Ketchum, *Decisive Day*, 160.

35. *Ibid.*, 161.

36. Middlekauf, *The Glorious Cause*, 291–2.

37. Bruce Chadwick, *The First American Army: The Untold Story of George Washington and the Men behind America's First Fight for Freedom* (Naperville, IL: Sourcebooks, 2005), 4–5.

38. Peter Oliver, *The Origin and Progress of the American Rebellion*, in Rhode-hamel, *The American Revolution*, 44.

39. Ketchum, *Decisive Day*, 191.

CHAPTER 15

1. "Address to the New York Provincial Congress," June 26, 1775, in Rhode-hamel, *George Washington,* 174.

2. GW to Thomas Gage, August 19, 1775, in Rhodehamel, *George Washington*, 182.

3. AA to JA, July 16, 1775, in Schuffelton, *The Letters of John and Abigail Adams,* 77.

4. Peter Oliver, "The Origins and Progress of the American Revolution," in Rhodehamel, *The American Revolution*, 51.

5. GW to John Hancock, July 21, 1775, *PGW, Revolutionary Series*, 1:138.

6. GW to Lund Washington, August 20, 1775, in Rhodehamel, *George Washington*, 184.

7. GW to Joseph Reed, November 28, 1775, *PGW, Revolutionary Series*, 2:449.

8. "General Orders," August 22, 1775, *PGW, Revolutionary Series*, 1:347.

9. "General Orders," July 4, 1775, in Rhodehamel, *George Washington*, 174–6.

10. Waldman, *Founding Faith*, 69.

11. GW to John Hancock, July 10, 1775, *PGW, Revolutionary Series*, 1:88.

12. "General Orders," November 18, 1775, *PGW, Revolutionary Series*, 1:393.

13. "General Orders," August 5, 1775, *PGW, Revolutionary Series*, 1:245.

14. Twohig, *George Washington's Diaries*, 330–1.

15. Jonathan Trumbull, Sr. to GW, September 5, 1775, *PGW, Revolutionary Series*, 1:416–8.

16. "Extract of a Letter from Cambridge, September 10," *Maryland Gazette*, September 28, 1775.

17. "Caleb Haskell's Diary," in Kenneth Roberts, ed., *March to Quebec: Jour-*

nals of the Members of Arnold's Expedition (Garden City: Doubleday, 1942), 457–72.

18. "Caleb Haskell's Diary," in Roberts, *March to Quebec,* 457–72.

19. *Ibid.*

20. *Ibid.*

21. Ludlum, *Early American Hurricanes,* 27.

22. James Warren to John Adams, September 11, 1775, *PJA,* 3:75–6.

23. Chadwick, *The First American Army,* 62–3.

24. Waldman, *Founding Faith,* 27.

25. Thomas A. Desjardin, *Through a Howling Wilderness: Benedict Arnold's March to Quebec, 1775* (New York: St. Martin's Press, 2005), 21.

26. Chadwick, *The First American Army,* 65–6.

27. Desjardin, *Through a Howling Wilderness,* 36–44.

28. Chadwick, *The First American Army,* 65–8.

29. Middlekauf, *The Glorious Cause,* 307–8.

30. *Ibid.,* 239.

31. AH, "Remarks on the Quebec Bill," June 15, 1775, *PAH,* I:165–75.

32. Middlekauf, *The Glorious Cause,* 280.

33. GW, "To the Inhabitants of Canada," September 15, 1775, in Allen, ed., *George Washington,* 46–8.

34. "Instructions and Commission from Congress to Franklin, Charles Carroll, and Samuel Chase for the Canadian Mission," March 20, 1776, *PBF,* 22:381–6.

35. CCC to CCA, March 4, 1776, in Hoffman, *Dear Papa, Dear Charley,* II:860–1.

36. CCC to CCA, March 29, 1776, in Hoffman, *Dear Papa, Dear Charley,* II: 888.

37. CCC to CCA, April 28, 1776, in Hoffman, *Dear Papa, Dear Charley,* II: 900.

38. BF to Josiah Quincy, Sr., April 15, 1776, *PBF,* 22:400.

39. CCA to CCC, March 30, 1776, in Hoffman, *Dear Papa, Dear Charley,* II: 890.

40. Isaacson, *Benjamin Franklin*, 305–7.

41. David McCullough, *1776* (New York: Simon and Schuster, 2005), 59.

42. Mark Puls, *Henry Knox: Visionary General of the American Revolution* (New York: Palgrave Macmillan, 2008), 6–30.

43. Middlekauf, *The Glorious Cause*, 308.

44. McCullough, *1776*, 82–5.

45. John Bowater to the Earl of Denbigh, March 25, 1776, in Rhodehamel, *The American Revolution*, 113–14.

CHAPTER 16

1. Stephen J. Hornsby, *British Atlantic, American Frontier: Spaces of Power in Early Modern British America* (Hanover: University Press of New England, 2005), 32–3.

2. Alan Ruffman, "The Multidisciplinary Rediscovery and Tracking of the 'Great Newfoundland and Saint–Pierre et Miquelon Hurricane of September 1775,'" *The Northern Mariner*, vol. VI, no. 3 (July, 1996): 19.

3. Peter E. Pope, *Fish into Wine: The Newfoundland Plantation in the Seventeenth Century* (Chapel Hill: University of North Carolina Press, 2004), 250.

4. Hornsby, *British Atlantic, American Frontier*, 27.

5. Pope, *Fish into Wine*, 41.

6. Hornsby, *British Atlantic, American Frontier*, 24–36.

7. Mark Kurlansky, *Cod: A Biography of the Fish That Changed the World* (New York: Penguin, 1997), 111–6.

8. Pope, *Fish into Wine*, 11–2.

9. Kurlansky, *Cod*, 65.

10. Dava Sobel, *Longitude: The True Story of a Lone Genius Who Solved the Greatest Scientific Problem of His Time* (New York: Penguin, 1995), 1–32, 149–50.

11. Martin Dugard, *Farther Than Any Man: The Rise and Fall of Captain James Cook* (New York: Washington Square Press, 2001), 39–41, 48–51.

12. Hornsby, *British Atlantic, American Frontier*, 36.

13. Pope, *Fish into Wine*, 9–10, 65, 257–8.

14. *Ibid.*, 234.

15. Hornsby, *British Atlantic, American Frontier*, 34–5.

16. Pamphlet, Tourism Branch of the Department of Development for the Province of Newfoundland and Labrador (Historic Newfoundland and Labrador, 1955), 38.

17. Robert G. Albion, William A. Baker, and Benjamin W. Labaree, *New England and the Sea* (Middletown, CT: The Marine Historical Association and Wesleyan University Press, 1972), 23–9.

18. Kurlansky, *Cod*, 6–7.

19. *Ibid.*, 6–7, 42.

20. *Ibid.*, 9.

21. *Ibid.*, 175.

22. Pope, *Fish into Wine*, 169.

23. Kurlansky, *Cod*, 11–34, 61.

24. Pope, *Fish into Wine*, 346–50.

25. Pamphlet, Tourism Branch of the Department of Development for the Province of Newfoundland and Labrador (Historic Newfoundland and Labrador, 1955), 63.

26. Pope, *Fish into Wine*, 2.

27. *Ibid.*, 24–8.

28. Hornsby, *British Atlantic, American Frontier*, 35.

29. Kurlansky, *Cod*, 22, 24.

30. Albion, *New England and the Sea*, 27.

31. Pope, *Fish into Wine*, 23, 35.

32. *Ibid.*, 234.

33. Albion, *New England and the Sea*, 33–9.

CHAPTER 17

1. Alan Ruffman, "The Multidisciplinary Rediscovery and Tracking of 'The

Great Newfoundland and Saint–Pierre et Miquelon Hurricane of September 1775,'" *The Northern Mariner*, vol. VI, no. 3 (July 1996): 15–6.

2. Anne E. Stevens and Michael Staveley, "The Great Newfoundland Storm of 12 September 1775," *Bulletin of the Seismological Society of America*, vol. 81, no. 4 (August 1991): 1398–402. (Emphasis in original.)

3. Alan Ruffman, "The Multidisciplinary Rediscovery and Tracking of 'The Great Newfoundland and Saint–Pierre et Miquelon Hurricane of September 1775,'" *The Northern Mariner*, vol. VI, no. 3 (July 1996): 12.

4. Alan Ruffman, "The Multidisciplinary Rediscovery and Tracking of 'The Great Newfoundland and Saint–Pierre et Miquelon Hurricane of September 1775,'" *The Northern Mariner*, vol. VI, no. 3 (July 1996): 11–23.

5. Alan Ruffman, "The Multidisciplinary Rediscovery and Tracking of 'The Great Newfoundland and Saint–Pierre et Miquelon Hurricane of September 1775,'" *The Northern Mariner*, vol. VI, no. 3 (July 1996): 15–6.

6. Alan Ruffman, "The Multidisciplinary Rediscovery and Tracking of 'The Great Newfoundland and Saint–Pierre et Miquelon Hurricane of September 1775,'" *The Northern Mariner*, vol. VI, no. 3 (July 1996): 17–8.

7. Alan Ruffman, "The Multidisciplinary Rediscovery and Tracking of 'The Great Newfoundland and Saint–Pierre et Miquelon Hurricane of September 1775,'" *The Northern Mariner*, vol. VI, no. 3 (July 1996): 16.

8. *Ibid.*

9. Alan Ruffman, "The Multidisciplinary Rediscovery and Tracking of 'The Great Newfoundland and Saint–Pierre et Miquelon Hurricane of September 1775,'" *The Northern Mariner*, vol. VI, no. 3 (July 1996): 14.

10. Alan Ruffman, "The Multidisciplinary Rediscovery and Tracking of 'The Great Newfoundland and Saint–Pierre et Miquelon Hurricane of September 1775,'" *The Northern Mariner*, vol. VI, no. 3 (July 1996): 17.

11. Alan Ruffman, "The Multidisciplinary Rediscovery and Tracking of 'The Great Newfoundland and Saint–Pierre et Miquelon Hurricane of

September 1775,'" *The Northern Mariner*, vol. VI, no. 3 (July 1996): 15.

12. *Ibid.*

13. Alan Ruffman, "The Multidisciplinary Rediscovery and Tracking of 'The Great Newfoundland and Saint–Pierre et Miquelon Hurricane of September 1775,'" *The Northern Mariner*, vol. VI, no. 3 (July 1996): 17.

14. Kurlansky, *Cod*, 23.

15. Alan Ruffman, "The Multidisciplinary Rediscovery and Tracking of 'The Great Newfoundland and Saint–Pierre et Miquelon Hurricane of September 1775,'" *The Northern Mariner*, vol. VI, no. 3 (July 1996): 11–23.

16. Anne E. Stevens and Michael Staveley, "The Great Newfoundland Storm of 12 September 1775," *Bulletin of the Seismological Society of America*, vol. 81, no. 4 (August 1991): 1398–402.

17. Alan Ruffman, "The Multidisciplinary Rediscovery and Tracking of 'The Great Newfoundland and Saint–Pierre et Miquelon Hurricane of September 1775,'" *The Northern Mariner*, vol. VI, no. 3 (July 1996): 17.

18. Matthew Mulcahy, "Weathering the Storms: Hurricanes and Risk in the British Greater Caribbean," *Business History Review*, 78 (Winter 2004): 635–63.

19. Alan Ruffman, "The Multidisciplinary Rediscovery and Tracking of 'The Great Newfoundland and Saint–Pierre et Miquelon Hurricane of September 1775,'" *The Northern Mariner*, vol. VI, no. 3 (July 1996): 18.

20. Matthew Mulcahy, "Weathering the Storms: Hurricanes and Risk in the British Greater Caribbean," *Business History Review*, 78 (Winter 2004): 635–63.

21. Alan Ruffman, "The Multidisciplinary Rediscovery and Tracking of 'The Great Newfoundland and Saint–Pierre et Miquelon Hurricane of September 1775,'" *The Northern Mariner*, vol. VI, no. 3 (July 1996):11–23.

22. Albion, *New England and the Sea*, 67.

Epilogue

1. Allen, *George Washington*, 267–8.

2. Michael Novak, *On Two Wings: Humble Faith and Common Sense at the American Founding* (San Francisco: Encounter Books, 2002).

3. Allen, *George Washington*, 460–62.

4. *Ibid.*

BIBLIOGRAPHY

PRIMARY SOURCES

Newspapers

Boston Gazette

Maryland Gazette

New York Gazette and Weekly Mercury

Pennsylvania Gazette

Rivington's New York Gazetteer

Virginia Gazette

Virginia Gazette, or *Norfolk Intelligencer*

Manuscript Collections

Rockefeller Library, Colonial Williamsburg

Thomas Bolling, *Virginia Almanack*, 1775

John Norton & Sons Papers, 1750–1902

John Page Roswell, *Virginia Almanack*, 1776

Published Sources

Abbot, W. W., et al., eds. *The Papers of George Washington: Confederation Series.* Charlottesville: University Press of Virginia, 1992.

Adair, Douglass, and John A. Schutz, eds. *Peter Oliver's Origin and Progress of the American Rebellion.* Stanford: Stanford University Press, 1961.

Allen, William B., ed. *George Washington: A Collection.* Indianapolis: Liberty Fund, 1988.

Boyd, Julian P., et al., eds. *The Papers of Thomas Jefferson.* Princeton: Princeton University Press, 1950.

Butterfield, L. H., ed. *Diary and Autobiography of John Adams.* Cambridge: Harvard University Press, 1961.

Chase, Philander, et al., eds. *The Papers of George Washington: Revolutionary War Series.* Charlottesville: University Press of Virginia, 1985.

Commager, Henry Steele, and Richard B. Morris, eds. *The Spirit of 'Seventy-Six: The Story of the American Revolution as Told by Participants.* New York: Da Capo, 1958.

Dexter, Franklin Bowditch, ed. *The Literary Diary of Ezra Stiles.* Vol. I. New York: Charles Scribner's Sons, 1901.

Fitzpatrick, John C., ed. *Writings of George Washington.* Washington, D.C.: U.S. Government Printing Office, 1931–9.

Freeman, Joanne B., ed. *Alexander Hamilton: Writings.* New York: Library of America, 2001.

Greene, Jack P., ed. *The Diary of Colonel Landon Carter of Sabine Hall, 1752–1778.* Vol. II. Charlottesville: University Press of Virginia, 1965.

Hoffman, Ronald, et al., ed. *Dear Papa, Dear Charley: The Papers of Charles Carroll of Carrollton, 1748–1782*, vol. II. Chapel Hill: University of North Carolina Press, 2001.

Isaacson, Walter, ed. *A Benjamin Franklin Reader.* New York: Simon and Schuster, 2003.

Kurland, Philip B., and Ralph Lerner, eds. *The Founders' Constitution.* Vol. 1. Chicago: University of Chicago Press, 1987.

Labaree, Leonard, et al., eds. *The Papers of Benjamin Franklin.* New Haven: Yale University Press, 1959.

Lemay, J. A. Leo, ed. *Benjamin Franklin: Autobiography, Poor Richard, and Later Writings*. New York: Library of America, 1987.

Lemay, J. A. Leo, and P. M. Zall, eds. *Benjamin Franklin's Autobiography*. New York: Norton, 1986.

Morison, Samuel Eliot, ed. *Sources and Documents Illustrating the American Revolution 1764–1788 and the Formation of the Federal Constitution*. Oxford: Oxford University Press, 1965.

Peterson, Merrill D. *Thomas Jefferson: Writings*. New York: Library of America, 1984.

Rhodehamel, John, ed. *The American Revolution: Writings from the War of Independence*. New York: Library of America, 2001.

————, ed. *George Washington: Writings*. New York: Library of America, 1997.

Roberts, Kenneth, ed. *March to Quebec: Journals of the Members of Arnold's Expedition*. Garden City: Doubleday, 1942.

Safire, William, ed. *Lend Me Your Ears: Great Speeches in History*, rev. ed. New York: Norton, 2004.

Sandoz, Ellis, ed. *Political Sermons of the American Founding Era, 1730–1805*. Indianapolis: Liberty Fund, 1998.

Scribner, Robert L., and William J. Van Schreeven, eds. *Revolutionary Virginia: The Road to Independence*. Vols. I–V. Charlottesville: University Press of Virginia, 1973.

Schuffelton, Frank, ed. *The Letters of John and Abigail Adams*. New York: Penguin, 2004.

Sparks, Jared. *The Works of Benjamin Franklin*. Boston: Tappan, Whittemore and Mason, 1840.

Syrett, Harold, ed. *The Papers of Alexander Hamilton*. New York, 1974–92.

Taylor, Robert J., et al., eds. *Papers of John Adams*. Cambridge: Harvard University Press, 1977.

Twohig, Dorothy, ed. *George Washington's Diaries: An Abridgement*. Charlottesville: University Press of Virginia, 1999.

Twohig, Dorothy, et al., eds. *The Papers of George Washington: Presidential Series*. Charlottesville: University Press of Virginia, 1987.

————. *The Papers of George Washington: Retirement Series*. Charlottesville: University Press of Virginia, 1997.

SECONDARY SOURCES

Articles

Mulcahy, Matthew. "Weathering the Storms: Hurricanes and Risk in the British Greater Caribbean." *Business History Review* 78 (Winter 2004): 635–63.

Ruffman, Alan. "The Multidisciplinary Rediscovery and Tracking of 'The Great Newfoundland and Saint-Pierre et Miquelon Hurricane of September 1775.'" *The Northern Mariner* VI, no. 3 (July 1996): 11–23.

Stevens, Anne E., and Michael Staveley. "The Great Newfoundland Storm of 12 September 1775." *Bulletin of the Seismological Society of America* 81, no. 4 (August, 1991): 1398–1402.

Books

Albion, Robert, William A. Baker, and Benjamin W. Labaree. *New England and the Sea*. Middletown, CT: The Marine Historical Association and Wesleyan University Press, 1972.

Alexander, John K. *Samuel Adams: America's Revolutionary Politician*. Lanham, MD: Rowman & Littlefield, 2002.

Bailyn, Bernard. *The Ideological Origins of the American Revolution*. Cambridge: Harvard University Press, 1967.

_____. *The Ordeal of Thomas Hutchinson*. Cambridge: Harvard University Press, 1974.

Barnes, Jay. *North Carolina's Hurricane History*, 3rd ed. Chapel Hill: University of North Carolina Press, 2001.

Beeman, Richard R. *Patrick Henry: A Biography*. New York: McGraw-Hill, 1974.

Bowen, Catherine Drinker. *Miracle at Philadelphia: The Story of the Constitutional Convention May to September 1787*. Boston: Little, Brown and Company 1966.

Brands, H. W. *The First American: The Life and Times of Benjamin Franklin*. New York: Anchor, 2000.

Breen, T. H. *The Marketplace of Revolution: How Consumer Politics Shaped American Independence*. Oxford: Oxford University Press, 2004.

_____. *Tobacco Culture: The Mentality of the Great Tidewater Planters on the Eve of the Revolution*. Princeton: Princeton University Press, 1985.

Bridenbaugh, Carl. *Seat of Empire: The Political Role of Eighteenth-Century Williamsburg*. Williamsburg: Colonial Williamsburg Foundation, 1950.

Brookhiser, Richard. *Alexander Hamilton, American*. New York: Touchstone, 1999.

_____. *Founding Father: Rediscovering George Washington*. New York: Free Press, 1996.

Bushman, Richard L. *The Refinement of America: Persons, Houses, Cities*. New York: Knopf, 1992.

Chadwick, Bruce. *The First American Army: The Untold Story of George Washington and the Men behind America's First Fight for Freedom*. Naperville, IL: Sourcebooks, 2005.

_____. *The General and Mrs. Washington: The Untold Story of a Marriage and a Revolution*. Naperville, IL: Sourcebooks, 2006.

_____. *George Washington's War: The Forging of A Revolutionary Leader and the American Presidency*. Naperville, IL: Sourcebooks, 2005.

Chernow, Ron. *Alexander Hamilton: A Life*. New York: Penguin, 2004.

Countryman, Edward. *A People in Revolution: The American Revolution and Political Society in New York, 1760–1790*. New York: Norton, 1989.

Cunningham, Noble E., Jr. *In Pursuit of Reason: The Life of Thomas Jefferson*. Baton Rouge: Louisiana State University, 1987.

Davis, Burke. *A Williamsburg Galaxy*. Williamsburg: Colonial Williamsburg Foundation, 1968.

Desjardin, Thomas A. *Through a Howling Wilderness: Benedict Arnold's March to Quebec, 1775*. New York: St. Martin's Press, 2005.

Dray, Philip. *Stealing God's Thunder: Benjamin Franklin's Lightning Rod and the Invention of America*. New York: Random House, 2005.

Dreisbach, Daniel L., Mark D. Hall, and Jeffry H. Morrison, eds. *The Founders on God and Government*. Lanham, MD: Rowman & Littlefield, 2004.

Dugard, Martin. *Farther Than Any Man: The Rise and Fall of Captain James Cook*. New York: Washington Square Press, 2001.

Ellis, Joseph J. *American Sphinx: The Character of Thomas Jefferson*. New York: Knopf, 1998.

_____. *Founding Brothers: The Revolutionary Generation*. New York: Knopf, 2000.

_____. *His Excellency: George Washington*. New York: Knopf, 2004.

_____. *Passionate Sage: The Character and Legacy of John Adams*. New York: Norton, 1993.

Emanuel, Kerry. *Divine Wind: The History and Science of Hurricanes*. New York: Oxford University Press, 2005.

Fagan, Brian. *The Little Ice Age: How Climate Made History, 1300–1850*. New York: Basic Books, 2000.

Ferling, John. *Almost a Miracle: The American Victory in the War of Independence*. Oxford: Oxford University Press, 2007.

_____. *A Leap in the Dark: The Struggle to Create the American Republic*. Oxford: Oxford University Press, 2003.

_____. *Setting the World Ablaze: Washington, Adams, Jefferson, and the American Revolution*. Oxford: Oxford University Press, 2000.

Fischer, David Hackett. *Paul Revere's Ride*. New York: Oxford University Press, 1994.

_____. *Washington's Crossing*. Oxford: Oxford University Press, 2004.

Fleming, Thomas. *The Perils of Peace: America's Struggle for Survival After Yorktown*. New York: Smithsonian Books, 2007.

Frey, Sylvia R. *Water from the Rock: Black Resistance in a Revolutionary Age*. Princeton: Princeton University Press, 1991.

Gilje, Paul A. *Liberty on the Waterfront: American Maritime Culture in the Age of Revolution*. Philadelphia: University of Pennsylvania Press, 2004.

Gleick, James. *Isaac Newton*. New York: Pantheon, 2003.

Golway, Terry. *Washington's General: Nathanael Greene and the Triumph of the American Revolution*. New York: Henry Holt, 2006.

Gough, Deborah Mathias. *Christ Church, Philadelphia: The Nation's Church in a Changing City*. Philadelphia: University of Pennsylvania Press, 1995.

Greene, Jack P. *Landon Carter: An Inquiry into the Personal Values and Social Imperatives of the Eighteenth-Century Virginia Gentry*. Charlottesville: University Press of Virginia, 1967.

Gross, Robert A. *The Minutemen and Their World*. New York: Hill and Wang, 1976.

Hoffman, Ronald. *Princes of Ireland, Planters of Maryland: A Carroll Saga, 1500–1782.* Chapel Hill: University of North Carolina Press, 2000.

Hornsby, Stephen J. *British Atlantic, American Frontier: Spaces of Power in Early Modern British America.* Hanover: University Press of New England, 2005.

Hutson, James H. *Religion and the Founding of the American Republic.* Washington, DC: Library of Congress, 1998.

————, ed. *Religion and the New Republic: Faith in the Founding of America.* Lanham, MD: Rowman & Littlefield, 2000.

Isaac, Rhys. *Landon Carter's Uneasy Kingdom: Revolution and Rebellion on a Virginia Plantation.* Oxford: Oxford University Press, 2004.

————. *The Transformation of Virginia, 1740–1790.* New York: Norton, 1982.

Isaacson, Walter. *Benjamin Franklin: An American Life.* New York: Simon and Schuster, 2003.

Jardine, Lisa. *On a Grander Scale: The Outstanding Life and Tumultuous Times of Sir Christopher Wren.* New York: Harper Collins, 2003.

Jones, H.G. *North Carolina Illustrated, 1524–1984.* Chapel Hill: University of North Carolina Press, 1983.

Junger, Sebastian. *The Perfect Storm: A True Story of Men Against the Sea.* New York: Harper, 1997.

Kerber, Linda K. *Women of the Republic: Intellect and Ideology in Revolutionary America.* Chapel Hill: University of North Carolina Press, 1980.

Ketcham, Ralph L. *Benjamin Franklin.* New York: Washington Square Press, 1966.

Ketchum, Richard M. *Decisive Day: The Battle for Bunker Hill.* New York: Henry Holt, 1962.

————. *Divided Loyalties: How the American Revolution came to New York.* New York: Henry Holt, 2002.

————. *Victory at Yorktown: The Campaign that Won the Revolution.* New York: Henry Holt, 2006.

Kirk, Russell. *Edmund Burke: A Genius Reconsidered.* Wilmington, DE: Intercollegiate Studies Institute, 1967.

Kulikoff, Allan. *Tobacco and Slaves: The Development of Southern Cultures in the*

Chesapeake, 1680–1800. Chapel Hill: University of North Carolina Press, 1986.

Kurlansky, Mark. *Cod: A Biography of the Fish That Changed the World*. New York: Penguin, 1997.

Lambert, Frank. *The Founding Fathers and the Place of Religion in America*. Princeton: Princeton University Press, 2003.

Larson, Erik. *Isaac's Storm: A Man, A Time, and the Deadliest Hurricane in History*. New York: Vintage, 1999.

Lengel, Edward G. *General George Washington: A Military Life*. New York: Random House, 2005.

Lindberg, David C., and Ronald L. Numbers, eds. *God and Nature: Historical Essays on the Encounter between Christianity and Science*. Berkeley: University of California Press, 1986.

_____. *When Science and Christianity Meet*. Chicago: University of Chicago Press, 2003.

Longmore, Paul. *The Invention of George Washington*. Charlottesville: University Press of Virginia, 1999.

Longshore, David. *Encyclopedia of Hurricanes, Typhoons, and Cyclones*. New York: Facts on File, 1998.

Ludlum, David. *Early American Hurricanes, 1492–1870*. Boston: American Meteorological Society, 1963.

Maier, Pauline. *From Resistance to Revolution: Colonial Radicals and the Development of American Opposition to Britain, 1765–1776*. New York: Norton, 1972.

Mapp, Alf J., Jr. *The Faiths of Our Fathers: What America's Founders Really Believed*. Lanham, MD: Rowman & Littlefield, 2003.

Mayer, Henry. *Son of Thunder: Patrick Henry and the American Republic*. New York: Grove Press, 1991.

McCullough, David. *1776*. New York: Simon and Schuster, 2005.

_____. *John Adams*. New York: Simon and Schuster, 2001.

McDonald, Forrest. *Alexander Hamilton: A Biography*. New York: Norton, 1979.

_____. *E Pluribus Unum: The Formation of the American Republic*. Indianapolis: Liberty Fund, 1965.

McGaughy, J. Kent. *Richard Henry Lee of Virginia: A Portrait of an American Revolutionary.* Lanham, MD: Rowman & Littlefield, 2004.

McNeill, Ernest, ed. *Chesapeake Bay in the American Revolution.* Centreville, MD: Tidewater Publishers, 1981.

Meade, Robert Douthat. *Patrick Henry: Patriot in the Making.* Philadelphia: Lippincott, 1957.

Middlekauf, Robert. *The Glorious Cause: The American Revolution, 1763-1789.* New York: Oxford University Press, 1982.

Miller, Perry. *The New England Mind: From Colony to Province.* Cambridge: Harvard University Press, 1953.

Mobley, Joe A., ed. *The Way We Lived in North Carolina.* Chapel Hill: University of North Carolina Press, 2003.

Morgan, Edmund S. *Benjamin Franklin.* New Haven: Yale University Press, 2002.

————. *The Gentle Puritan: A Life of Ezra Stiles, 1727–1795.* New Haven: Yale University Press, 1962.

Morgan, Edmund S. and Helen M. Morgan. *The Stamp Act Crisis: Prologue to Revolution.* Chapel Hill: University of North Carolina Press, 1953.

Morrison, Jeffry H. *John Witherspoon and the Founding of the American Republic.* South Bend: University of Notre Dame Press, 2005.

Nash, Gary B. *The Urban Crucible: The Northern Seaports and the Origins of the American Revolution.* Cambridge: Harvard University Press, 1979.

Norton, Mary Beth. *Liberty's Daughters: The Revolutionary Experience of American Women, 1750–1800.* Boston: Little, Brown and Company 1980.

Novak, Michael. *On Two Wings: Humble Faith and Common Sense at the American Founding.* San Francisco: Encounter Books, 2002.

Novak, Michael, and Jana Novak. *Washington's God: Religion, Liberty, and the Father of Our Country.* New York: Basic Books, 2006.

Palm, Daniel C., ed. *On Faith and Free Government.* Lanham, MD: Rowman & Littlefield, 1997.

Paramore, Thomas C. *Norfolk: The First Four Centuries.* Charlottesville: University Press of Virginia, 1994.

Pope, Peter E. *Fish into Wine: The Newfoundland Plantation in the Seventeenth Century.* Chapel Hill: University of North Carolina Press, 2004.

Powell, William S. *North Carolina through Four Centuries.* Chapel Hill: University of North Carolina Press, 1989.

Puls, Mark. *Henry Knox: Visionary General of the American Revolution.* New York: Palgrave Macmillan, 2008.

_____. *Samuel Adams: Father of the American Revolution.* New York: Palgrave Macmillan, 2006.

Quarles, Benjamin. *The Negro in the American Revolution.* New York: Norton, 1961.

Ragsdale, Bruce A. *A Planters' Republic: The Search for Economic Independence in Revolutionary Virginia.* Madison: Madison House, 1996.

Rahe, Paul A. *Inventions of Prudence: Constituting the American Regime.* (*Republics Ancient and Modern*, vol. III) Chapel Hill: University of North Carolina Press, 1994.

Rakove, Jack. *The Beginnings of National Politics: An Interpretive History of the Continental Congress.* New York: Knopf, 1979.

Ready, Milton. *The Tarheel State: A History of North Carolina.* Chapel Hill: University of North Carolina Press, 2005.

Rediker, Marcus. *Between the Devil and the Deep Blue Sea: Merchant Seamen, Pirates, and the Anglo-American Maritime World, 1700–1750.* Cambridge: Cambridge University Press, 1987.

Richard, Carl J. *The Founders and the Classics: Greece, Rome, and the American Enlightenment.* Cambridge: Harvard University Press, 1994.

Royster, Charles. *A Revolutionary People at War: The Continental Army and American Character, 1775–1783.* Chapel Hill: University of North Carolina Press, 1979.

Rybczynski, Witold. *City Life: Urban Expectations in a New World.* New York: Scribner, 1995.

Schama, Simon. *Rough Crossings: Britain, The Slaves, and the American Revolution.* New York: Harper Collins, 2006.

Scott, Phil. *Hemingway's Hurricane: The Great Florida Keys Storm of 1935.* New York: McGraw-Hill, 2006.

Scotti, R. A. *Sudden Sea: The Great Hurricane of 1938.* New York: Back Bay, 2003.

Selby, John E. *The Revolution in Virginia, 1775-1783.* Williamsburg: Colonial Williamsburg Foundation, 1988.

Sobel, Dava. *Longitude: The True Story of a Lone Genius Who Solved the Greatest Scientific Problem of His Time.* New York: Penguin, 1995.

Stahr, Walter. *John Jay: Founding Father.* New York: Hambledon and London, 2005.

Van Doren, Carl. *Benjamin Franklin.* New York: Penguin, 1938.

Waldman, Steven. *Founding Faith: Providence, Politics, and the Birth of Religious Freedom in America.* New York: Random House, 2008.

Walmsley, Andrew Stephen. *Thomas Hutchinson and the Origins of the American Revolution.* New York: New York University Press, 1999.

Weintraub, Stanley. *General Washington's Christmas Farewell: A Mount Vernon Homecoming, 1783.* New York: Free Press, 2003.

_____. *Iron Tears: Rebellion in America, 1775-1783.* New York: Simon and Schuster, 2005.

Wiencek, Henry. *An Imperfect God: George Washington, His Slaves, and the Creation of America.* New York: Farrar, Straus, and Giroux, 2003.

Wills, Garry. *Cincinnatus: George Washington and the Enlightenment: Images of power in Early America.* New York: Doubleday, 1984.

Witham, Larry. *A City Upon A Hill: How Sermons Changed the Course of American History.* New York: Harper Collins, 2007.

Wood, Gordon S. *The Americanization of Benjamin Franklin.* New York: Penguin, 2004.

_____. *The American Revolution: A History.* New York: Modern Library, 2002.

_____. *The Radicalism of the American Revolution.* New York: Vintage, 1991.

_____. *Revolutionary Characters: What Made the Founders Different.* New York: Penguin, 2006.

Wright, Esmond. *Franklin of Philadelphia.* Cambridge: Harvard University Press, 1986.

ABBREVIATIONS

AA: Abigail Adams

AH: Alexander Hamilton

BF: Benjamin Franklin

CCA: Charles Carroll of Annapolis

CCC: Charles Carroll of Carrollton

GW: George Washington

JA: John Adams

PAH: *Papers of Alexander Hamilton*

PBF: *Papers of Benjamin Franklin*

PGW: *Papers of George Washington*

PJA: *Papers of John Adams*

INDEX

V

violent behavior in colonies, 13,
    147–148, 149–150, 151–152, 154
Virginia
    blockade of, 55
    capitals of, 54
    Convention, 36–37, 57–59
    delegation to First Continental
        Congress, 107, 108–109
    General Assembly, 120–121
Virginia Almanack, 51–52, 88–89

W

Wallace, Charles, 79, 85
Ward, Artemas, 184
Warren, James, 196–197
Warren, Joseph, 176–177
Washington, George
    agricultural practices of, 30, 68
    on beginning of Revolutionary
        War, 180–181
    on Canadian support of
        American cause, 200
    on challenges of achieving
        independence, 298
    on challenges of forming effective
        Continental Army, 191–193
    on civil vs. military supremacy,
        189–190
    as commander of Continental
        Army, 124–127
    crossing of Delaware River by, 134,
        193
    descriptions of, 78, 116, 124, 126,
        190, 202
    diary of, 193, 194, 195
    farewell to troops of, 99–102,
        239–240
    First Continental Congress and,
        108–109
    First Inaugural Address, 240
    on independence, 109, 241
    military experience of, 123, 124
    preparations for war by, 122
    on Providence of God, x, 240
    on public service, 125–126
    recovery of artillery from Fort
        Ticonderoga and, 202–203

on religious freedoms, 82
retirement ceremony of, 101–102
on rights of Englishmen, xvi
Second Continental Congress and,
    122–125
on slavery, 42
weather interests of, 193–194
weather
    eighteenth century ideas regarding,
        94–95
    forecasts in almanacs, 88–89
    inventions for measuring and
        predicting, 75, 91–92
    lore and prediction, 88–89,
        215–216
    role in battles of, 134, 193, 204,
        238
wheat planters compared to tobacco
    planters, 68
Whig ideas, 67
Whitefield, George, 197
William and Mary, College of, 53, 54
William and Mary, King and Queen, 77
Williamsburg, Virginia, 51, 53,
    54–55, 59
Winthrop, John, 91–92, 173
Witherspoon, John, xi, 5–6, 33, 68, 104
women, roles in cause of liberty of,
    14–15
Wren, Christopher, 75–77
Wythe, George, 129

Y

Yorktown, Battle of, 193

AUTHOR INTERVIEW
WITH TONY WILLIAMS

What drew you to tell the story of this dramatic hurricane?
I heard someone mention it very briefly years ago—I think on
C-SPAN'S "BOOK TV"—and thought it was very interesting. I
grabbed a 3 x 5 card and jotted it down. I was a teacher at the time
and hadn't started writing yet. I kept seeing it in my files and years
later finally went to the public library to investigate. All I could find
about the hurricane was a few entries of a couple of sentences each in
hurricane encyclopedias. All they said was the dates it hit and the
tragic loss of four thousand British seamen in Canadian waters. I did
not even know at the time whether they were sailors in the Royal
Navy or fishermen. It turns out they were unlucky young men who
happened to be in Newfoundland during the summer fishing for cod.

As I completed research into newspapers, government documents, weather almanacs, and diaries from the time, I discovered
that there was an entire cast of figures associated with the storm,
from George Washington and Benjamin Franklin to the common
soldier and slave. The hurricane struck the colonies just as the
American Revolution was beginning in the late summer of 1775. It

was a very dramatic year with Patrick Henry's rousing "Give Me Liberty or Death" speech, Paul Revere's Ride, the Battle of Bunker Hill, and George Washington's assuming command of the army, just to name a few events. The confluence of the appropriately-named Hurricane of Independence and the upheaval of the Revolution proved an irresistible story to tell to readers. No one with whom I have spoken about the book had ever heard of the hurricane. I wanted to rectify that as an educator and writer.

Did the Hurricane of Independence materially affect the outcome of the American Revolution?

Not directly, no. Other weather events such as George Washington crossing the Delaware during a Christmas night nor'easter had a much more obvious impact on the war. However, the story of the hurricane in my book is in many ways the story of the American Revolution. It is the story of wealthy planters who raised tobacco denouncing British taxes and tyranny. It is the story of slaves who desired freedom and escaped to the British side, some tragically caught during the storm and returned to their masters. It is the story of the delegates who were heading to the Continental Congress to debate how the American colonies would respond to oppressive British measures. It is the story of how General George Washington's men suffered terribly for their country's liberty and how he made military decisions based upon the weather.

Where did the Hurricane of Independence strike and what damage did it do?

The storm hit the Outer Banks of North Carolina—with no warning, mind you—and killed almost 200 people. It then took the lives of dozens more in Norfolk, Virginia. It proceeded up the Atlantic seaboard, menacing the important capitals of Revolutionary activity: Williamsburg, Annapolis, Philadelphia, New York, and Boston. Seamen were the ones who suffered the most loss of life by far. Farmers in many places lost their tobacco and corn crops. Soldiers were wet, cold, and hungry in their muddy tents.

The storm was losing steam over land and affected the northern colonies less than the southern ones. However, it was still powerful enough to raise a massive storm surge and claim four thousand lives in the waters surrounding Newfoundland. However, some have speculated that there was a second hurricane that never hit land. Others thought there might have been a tsunami triggered by an underwater earthquake. This controversy provided another fascinating twist to the story to write about and for readers. It took a lot of detective work to piece all the evidence together and make some firm conclusions.

Are there any differences with hurricanes during the American Revolution and today?

Yes, quite a few actually. First of all, there simply was no warning because television, wireless communication, and satellites did not exist. The death toll would have been perhaps a few instead of several thousands. Second, I was impressed by the self-reliance of the people. In an age before widespread insurance, people cleaned up, mourned their dead, and started over again. Third, on a related note, the media coverage was much different. The papers mentioned the hurricane briefly for an edition or two and then all reporting on the hurricane ended. Recriminations and the blame game did not last for months or even years as with Hurricane Katrina. Finally, most of the people of the eighteenth century understood hurricanes to be a sign of divine disfavor for their transgressions. Although some people persist in that belief today, the modern world generally assumes a scientific understanding of hurricanes.

Why is the general reading public so interested in the Founding Fathers and the American Revolution?

Although many different historical periods enjoy spells of faddishness and popularity, it seems to me that there is something more fundamental going on with what has been labeled (I think unfairly) "Founders' Chic." As a former educator, I celebrate the fact that the reading public is interested in learning more about the founding of America. I think most Americans look back on this dramatic era and find much that is admirable about the principles they held dear and the struggles they endured for their liberty. It is a great, heroic epic and one that very nearly tells itself. To paraphrase George Washington, who said on many occasions, future historians might not actually believe that the Americans were able to defeat the British and become free and independent with all the obstacles they overcame. We still hold the same principles true today, even if we freely debate their application just as much as the people at the time did. To me, that is the story of America.

QUESTIONS FOR DISCUSSION

What principles were the American revolutionaries fighting for against Great Britain? Are these principles still relevant today?

Who is the most important and interesting man or woman of the American Revolution?

In what ways did the Americans resist British policies?

How did the Hurricane of Independence affect various groups in different ways?

Why is there a different outlook in understanding hurricanes between 1775 and today?

Was there a conflict between religious and scientific views of hurricanes? Why?

What was the critical event of 1775 that contributed the most to the success of the American Revolution?

ABOUT
THE AUTHOR

Tony Williams taught history and literature for ten years, and has a Master's in American History from Ohio State University. He is currently a full-time author who lives in Williamsburg, Virginia, with his wife and children.